A NEW STUDY GUIDE TO STEINBECK'S MAJOR WORKS, WITH CRITICAL EXPLICATIONS

Edited by
Tetsumaro Hayashi

THE SCARECROW PRESS, INC.
METUCHEN, N.J., & LONDON
1993

British Library Cataloguing-in-Publication data available

Library of Congress Cataloging-in-Publication Data

A New study guide to Steinbeck's major works with critical
  explications / edited by Tetsumaro Hayashi.
      p.   cm.
  Includes bibliographical references and index.
  ISBN 0-8108-2611-9 (acid-free paper)
  1. Steinbeck, John, 1902-1968—Criticism and
interpretation.
  2. Steinbeck, John, 1902-1968—Outlines, syllabi, etc.   I.
Hayashi, Tetsumaro.
PS3537.T3234Z776   1993
813'.52—dc20   92-37198

Dedicated

to

Akiko,

Richard,

Gaby,

and

my first grandchild,

Sophie

SPECIAL ACKNOWLEDGMENTS

The quotations from the works of John Steinbeck used to illustrate the text in this book are made by permission of McIntosh and Otis, Inc., on behalf of the Steinbeck Literary Estate and Viking Penguin, Inc., a division of Penguin U.S.A., Inc.

As editor of this book I should like to express my profound gratitude first to Mr. Eugene H. Winick, President of McIntosh and Otis, Inc., and the Steinbeck Literary Estate for granting us permission to quote Steinbeck in this book and then to Ms. Florence Eichin, Viking Penguin, Inc., for waiving the permission fees for us.

Tetsumaro Hayashi, Editor

CONTENTS

PREFACE

A New Study Guide to Steinbeck's Major Works attempts to update my two previously published *Study Guides—A Study Guide to Steinbeck: A Handbook to His Major Works* (1974) and *A Study Guide to Steinbeck (Part II)* (1979), hopefully in a handier but still selective volume. For this book I recruited a new generation of active Steinbeck teacher-scholars in the 1990s and asked them to explicate Steinbeck's books not only for the benefit of college students interested in Steinbeck, but also for other teachers as well. The selected works of Steinbeck represent those books most frequently taught in English, humanities, and American studies throughout the United States and elsewhere.

The book reflects some of the latest reputable Steinbeck criticism, biographical studies, and published and unpublished letters of Steinbeck, made available or discovered by leading senior scholars since the earlier *Guides*. Here we strove to make more workable suggestions and to offer more pertinent advice to college students to encourage further research and spark classroom discussion.

In these attempts, as editor and project director, I have asked contributors to use their most elucidating and vivid style, to assume a readership consisting of a "live classroom audience" interested in Steinbeck studies and research papers, and to assist that classroom to understand, to appreciate, and to assess Steinbeck's literature through clear and pertinent discussion and analyses. Fortunately, my contributors are all experienced, dedicated classroom teachers who are simultaneously active, publishing scholars in a variety of fields, including Steinbeck studies. Professor Louis Owens, one of America's premiere teacher-scholars, for instance, happens to be an accomplished creative writer as well as a much admired expert in American Indian literature. Professor Reloy Garcia is an outstanding teacher-scholar as well as a distinguished

Steinbeck-D. H. Lawrence scholar. Professor Patrick Shaw has extensively and reputably published numerous essays on a variety of subjects in literature. I am indeed proud to have such contributors explicate Steinbeck's major teachable literary works afresh, sharing with the readers their expertise in literary analyses and scholarly publications.

As editor, I adopted a structure, format, and sequence in the book similar to that of the two previously published *Study Guides*. However, I reformulated the section "Apparatus for Research Papers" (which had consisted of questions for discussion, topics for research papers, and a bibliography) into a section entitled "Topics for Research and Discussion" with a separate "Selected Bibliography" section to make them simpler and more workable. I also endorsed a unique treatment in dealing with two major prose works— *America and Americans* and *Travels with Charley in Search of America,* as in Professor Barbara Heavilin's provocative essays.

In order to avoid awkward sentence style and to minimize rewording the contributors' writing, I have not changed masculine terms (e.g., man, mankind) to their gender-neutral alternatives (e.g., person, humankind). I apologize if this editorial decision offends anyone.

I sincerely hope that this book, the third *Study Guide,* will serve as a dynamic stepping stone for further quests into Steinbeck's literature, its magic and its fictional truth. May this book encourage our English majors, minors, and other students in the 1990s and beyond to engage in further, daring explorations into Steinbeck's literature, language, themes, and messages.

I am exceedingly grateful to my contributors for their exceptionally refreshing, provocative, up-to-date explications. I am delighted and gratified with Dr. Reloy Garcia's "Introduction," with which he enthusiastically endorses the book and introduces it to Steinbeck students here and abroad. I am also indebted to my loyal student secretaries—especially Miss Michelle L. Hunt and Miss Stephanie Ponder—for their first-rate cooperation and capable assistance in the preparation of the manuscript; to Mrs. Cathy D. Stewart and Ms. Tera L. Miles for their meticulous proofreading and critical reviews; and to Dr. Charles L. Houck, Mr. Thomas E. Spangler,

Dr. Donald E. Van Meter, and Dr. C. Warren Vander Hill for their staunch support during the preparation of this book.

TETSUMARO HAYASHI, EDITOR
Muncie, Indiana
March 22, 1992

INTRODUCTION

Lately I have been so preoccupied with the art of pedagogy, a phrase which, even as I write it, rings flat. When you get right down to it, "art" of any kind is mostly craft that sweats. What I really mean is the *teaching* aspect of teaching. In all my years of being a student and then a teacher, I can't recall a single teacher, including all the so-called "bad" ones, who didn't know his subject. But I can count on my left fingers those I consider exceptional classroom teachers.

How can we translate or exploit the knowledge gained over a long academic career to shape a class that sparkles with active and loud students tugging at the rope-idea, a common phenomenon in classes taught by teaching fellows? All the time we envy, as young teaching fellows excitedly exchange with their students. Often—although not yet in our Prufrockian senectitude—we tell ourselves that young people simply connect more readily with younger people. But is there not, too often, some missing element between all that one knows and how one *conveys* what one knows to electrify a classroom?

Even that last sentence misstates my thesis. A good teacher who doesn't really *convey* anything is not a conveyor belt. Wouldn't teaching be easy and pointless if all we had to do was to copy what we know, wrap it in recycled paper, and hand it through a window to our students?

To teach well we must create what someone called "a community of inquiry." To do that we must first marshal the strategies to make students, younger and less savvy, join our community to exchange, to challenge, to pull and tug, to talk. If we succeed, we find that a good teacher, like a flexible actor, plays many roles. That's an apt metaphor, perhaps frayed: the teacher as actor. Sometimes the teacher is— although less and less—a lecturer, a leader, a tour guide, and, when he can pull it off, one of the gang. He's a wise man, a stern disciplinarian, a friendly ear, a confessor.

Sometimes the teacher is at the front of the class, behind the lectern, sometimes along the side of the room, walking up the middle, moving. The smart teacher better be on the move or students get the "fix," with the inevitable "you-versus-them" opposition.

And the classroom, the stage, changes, too. Usually, now, the seats are arranged row on row, like grave markers, in our inflexible rectangular classrooms. Sometimes, with difficulty, we break the class into small groups. I see a twenty-first century classroom that adapts to meet changing needs and purposes, a circular class, perhaps, with desks on wheels or tracks, that sets up in different configurations. The classroom of the future will be dynamic, kinetic, rearrangeable. I see communities of inquiry in their private pursuits, with instant access to libraries, with mini-blackboards or computer screens to write their deliberations upon, with networking capabilities to other groups. I see small groups everywhere, now merging, now drifting apart as the task changes, regrouping. I see people moving everywhere, changing, debating. I don't see a desk up front for the teacher of the twenty-first century. I don't see a "front" at all. I still see a teacher, but he lectures less. No more vending machine with gumball answers. We live in a world of changing definitions and we had better adapt or risk extinction.

Comes a book, this one, with a smart pedagogy. One of the definitions that dances in front of us is the "classroom," as Tetsumaro Hayashi clearly acknowledges in his "Preface." He means to enlarge the classroom, to disassemble the artificial walls that separate one classroom from another, as we see done on television all the time, although seldom for such a good purpose. These Steinbeck scholars mean to unite a mass audience in a common pursuit of one elusive prey: John Steinbeck.

The sense of "community"—and of sharp inquiry, too— is the spine of this book. Here everyone is invited to join, for the book explodes the traditional, restrictive notion of "classroom." If "all the world's a stage," as that other fellow said, why can't it be a classroom, too?

Here a group of scholars approaches the most-taught Steinbeck works to shape new approaches, to provide fresh perspectives on the genesis of those works, to yield new interpretations, and to provide the bibliographical aid that insures that yet more interpretations are built on solid ground. Each essay contains its own apparatus section, with ideas for further study, as well as its own bibliography.

Two things. First, how the book relates to the reader, its temporary "student" or, better, "colleague." This is a supportive book, offering numerous nuggets of information, mined in years of classroom and library digging. It does not preach but rather invites us to join the community. Second, it does not so much give "answers" but charts paths of inquiry.

If something's not simple, I tell my students, watch out. Here the format is simple, logical, and clear. Each article is a perspective on Steinbeck at work. He's a crank, a storyteller, a critic, an anti-critic, an "American" (see Heavilin's essay on *Travels with Charley*), an internationalist, a sage, a prophet. He's up, he's down. Even, on occasion, he's pathetic, sad, washing the soiled bed-sheets of his terminally-ill, incontinent mother (see Shaw's essay on *The Red Pony*).

He's marvelously irascible. On the first draft of *The Grapes of Wrath,* which he burned (why do writers do rash things like that?), he wrote, ". . . it is a bad book and I must get rid of it. It can't be printed. It is bad because it isn't honest" (Owens on *The Grapes*). He is terrified by the witch Popularity, whom he calls rather terrible. "I'm scared to death of popularity," he writes (Hadella on *Of Mice and Men*). *The Winter of Our Discontent* "grew out of two aborted attempts at transforming and modernizing older texts," one of them "a modern western" (Meyer on *The Winter of Our Discontent*). We watch the works gestate, watch Steinbeck think, reconnoiter, plan, attack.

The thread I see through much here, perhaps culminating in *The Winter of Our Discontent,* is Steinbeck worried at the dissolution of American values, shoring up the bricks of art against "the terrors of greed," a flood (Shaw on *The Pearl*).

After background, we study plots, craft. These are not simple plot synopses, but careful block reconstructions of the main architecture. Each essay offers the latest critical explications, some so new they still shine. We study the language and discourse strategies of the various works. Then the writers turn the chore over to the reader, with topics for further work, and followed by selected bibliographies to help us.

I find myself, more and more, "talking" to papers I grade, books I read. I wonder if this talking is a mark of impending senility or experience. I fell naturally into that when reading the essays in this book. "Nice idea," I said a number of times. "I didn't know that," I said too often. "I have to try that." "So *that's* why he does such and such." Hayashi's experiment works. The book bridges the space-time differences.

This book is "student" talking *to*—not at—student. It borrows from the "talkiness" of Steinbeck. Too, it is teacher talking with teacher, sharing tips and ideas, each with the smooth feel of practice and experience. It does not preempt the reader. It falls easily into a supportive role. It is an eminently useable and useful book.

The "return" is one of my favorite teaching strategies. Often, I come back to a point discussed earlier. The lapse of time, the intervening discussion, invariably shapes a more experienced perspective. This book is such a "return." Having discussed the major works years ago, we come back to the nest to see what's hatched in the meantime. Hayashi always provides a new twist. Here, a scholar does two essays and we see the changing perspective of the author as he or she fits the tool to the task. Nice idea.

This book is a good friend in the sense that Wayne Booth uses the term in his book *The Company We Keep,* which explores the notion of a literary text as a friend. And why shouldn't it be? Isn't it always there, encouraging us, inviting us, challenging us, loyal, rigorous, testing and sharing our values, warm and unpredictable? We grow to love even the villains. We return to a work, years later, smile, find it still the same, or richer. We marvel at the complexity it gained in the years since our last visit. How much it learns from us! A friend confirms our humanity. We are not conveyor belts!

I recommend this book wholeheartedly to anyone who esteems capacious-hearted Steinbeck, who hates walls and loves books.

RELOY GARCIA
Professor of English
Creighton University

A NEW STUDY GUIDE
TO STEINBECK'S MAJOR WORKS
WITH CRITICAL EXPLICATIONS

1. STEINBECK'S *AMERICA AND AMERICANS* (1966)

BARBARA HEAVILIN

I. BACKGROUND

The two best sources for the background of *America and Americans* are *Steinbeck: A Life in Letters,* edited by Elaine Steinbeck and Robert Wallsten, and *The True Adventures of John Steinbeck, Writer* by Jackson J. Benson. These works provide Steinbeck's own comments about the book together with the circumstances surrounding its production. In August 1964 Thomas H. Guinzburg, his publisher at the Viking Press, asked John to write an introduction and captions for "a collection of photographs that he had commissioned to be taken all over the country, . . . designed to distill the spirit of America and its people."[1] Bringing to this task his memories of his journey recorded in *Travels with Charley,* Steinbeck does more than write an introduction and captions. He writes a series of related and connected essays based on his observations of America, carefully integrated with the photographs so that text and pictures complement one another. Working on *America and Americans* at the same time he was helping President Lyndon B. Johnson "with his acceptance speech for the nomination by the Democratic Convention," Steinbeck brings to the task "his accumulated frustrations" from a book he is trying to write in the Arthurian tradition (Benson, 955). In the process of composition, on February 17, 1965, he writes to John Huston and Gladys Hill:

> I went to work on my book of pictures of all of the fifty states and my essay on our people. It is called America and

3

Americans. I may have to run for my life when it comes out. I am taking "the American" apart like a watch to see what makes him tick and some very curious things are emerging.[2]

On March 14, 1965, he writes to Joseph Bryan III, telling of his fascination with this work:

> I am writing a book about "The Americans." We are a very curious people—and as far as I know no one has inspected us as we would inspect some other sub-species. It's most fascinating work—to me—and I hope to have it finished by summer.[3]

According to Benson, he writes to his agent in April 1965, giving his reactions to the first draft, which is nearing completion:

> I know there is lots of work to be done on it, but I think it is good. I know I have been fascinated with it as it went down and I shall be sorry to finish it. . . . Once it is down [I] will inspect it and add and subtract but the meat will be there. I should have it ready well before we move out here for the summer.[4]

On August 5, 1965, however, he writes Carlton A. Sheffield that he has had many interruptions from "persons from Porlock," perhaps because he simply does not want to write.[5] Later in this letter he continues, "I've beat around bushes and at last must face the last chapter about The Americans—a most difficult one."[6] He further outlines his problems in thinking through his conclusion to the book:

> This morning I awakened early, full of continued thinking out of sleep. You know that slow and sometimes excellent thinking. You will understand my reluctance to start when I tell you, this section is to deal with morals—not goody-goody morals—but pragmatic morals. I have floundered about with it because it has been such a fragmented subject and I want to put the pieces together. But who am I talking to—Americans? Europeans? or myself. My shadow-of-a-dream thinking said— "Why don't you write it to Dook and keep a copy? His skepticism will put a bridle on you and the direction will force

you to be clear." Most dream thinking will not stand daylight scrutiny, but this one does. So I will shift pencils so I can keep a carbon and fling my chapter at you. And maybe you will help me with it if I should get out of line.[7]

The final chapter, "Americans and the Future," stays very much "in line"—expounding on the loss of "rules," on the atrophy of a sense of responsibility, on an obsession with "things"; finding hope because Americans are not contented to stay as they are; and concluding optimistically that Americans will formulate "new rules," that they are endowed "for the change that is coming."[8] Robert S. Hughes, Jr. finds *America and Americans* "a Steinbeck pastiche" because of "his borrowings from journalistic pieces, as well as from previous narratives,"[9] but Benson finds it a "moral" statement essential to an understanding of the Steinbeck canon.[10] This book, then, goes beyond a mere rehashing of old viewpoints and opinions. It is both a worthwhile work in its own right, and an aid to understanding the canon of a complex writer.

II. PLOT SYNOPSIS

America and Americans is a series of nine related essays, prefaced by a "Foreword," followed by an "Afterword," and complemented by some 108 pages of photographs. The foreword provides the overall theme governing the entire book: "I believe that out of the whole body of our past, out of our differences, our quarrels, our many interests and directions, something has emerged that is itself unique in the world: America—complicated, paradoxical, bullheaded, shy, cruel, boisterous, unspeakably dear, and very beautiful" (7). Both the text and the accompanying pictures are opinionated, giving an individual's view of America.

Chapter 1, *"E Pluribus Unum,"* discusses the uniqueness of the land and the people which "are of every kind" and yet make up "one nation" (13). Although speakers at high-school graduations "refer to America as a 'precious inheritance,' early Americans had to work, fight, and die for it. At first these diverse peoples seemed an 'ethnic anarchy,' but soon became more alike than different, the many united into one nation" (13). These people now share an "American look," which foreigners can recognize even though they cannot describe it. Two racial groups "did not follow the pattern of arrival, prejudice, acceptance, and absorption: the American Indian, who was already here, and the Negro, who did not come under his own volition" (17).

Chapter 2, "Paradox and Dream," gathers generalities and examples which show the paradoxical nature of the American people. They cannot stand failure, but they are dissatisfied with success. They search for security but are not satisfied when they attain it. They are alert, sensitive, and hopeful, but they have one of the most serious drug problems in the world. Steinbeck finds such paradoxes everywhere—in American myths, in contradictory attitudes towards law, sex, and home, as well as in a contradictory self-image.

"The strong and imperishable" American dream puzzles foreign observers (30). The Americans' love of home is curious because they are a restless people who move about frequently (31). The mobile home, therefore, is one of their new dreams (31). Americans also hold the illusory dream of being "great hunters and inventors." Their folk tales of the Wild West may derive from tales such as the Arthurian legend. Even though this "national dream" cannot be clearly defined, it does have a name: "the American Way of Life" (34).

Chapter 3, "Government of the People," covers the uniqueness of the American system of government, including the people's fear of "perpetuation of power," their inherent distrust of politicians, and the customary festiveness of nominating conventions. The fact that such a system works, Americans owe to its founders who had the foresight to design a system which has the capacity to renew itself and to meet the needs of new generations (45-46). Foreigners are further amazed by Americans' relationship to the president— a curious mixture of pride and blame "for things he did not do" (46). The president's power is primarily moral, dependent upon "persuasion and discussion" (47). Some of the problems inherent in the American system of government are "civil rights and universal suffrage," which "are specifically mentioned in three constitutional amendments" (47). Steinbeck, an advocate for change, suggests that the country needs "a federal law making any crime committed for the purpose of denying or inhibiting a civil right a federal offense, subject to federal judges and federal juries, with the option of change of venue if the local authorities flout the law" (48).

Asserting that "today we believe that slavery is a crime and a sin, as well as being economically unsound under our system," Chapter 4, "Created Equal," continues with a historical overview of slavery, leading up to a discussion of the Civil War, its causes and consequences. The causes are primarily economic. A part of the consequences involve "a withdrawn separateness" between the races (59).

Chapter 5, *"Genus Americanus,"* discusses how "members of a classless society . . . work out changes in status levels without violating their belief that there are no such levels" (67). Status in America depends on ability, land-holding, and power. The source of power resides now in corporations rather than in individuals. But power has limitations, for it cannot satisfy a human being's creative needs or the "yearning toward greatness" (67-86). The latter yearnings Americans satisfy by organizations, such as the Elks and Masons (87). At the bottom of the American hierarchy are "the attackers" and the "screwballs" (90-91). The attackers are those who spy, denounce, threaten, and punish (88). While these people are not typically American, there are a large number of them. The "screwballs" fall into two categories of eccentrics: "showoffs" and "hiders" (90-91).

Chapter 6, "The Pursuit of Happiness," introduces those areas in which Americans seek happiness: in their children and in their use of leisure time. In both of these areas they have problems. For Americans have become obsessed by their children to the extent that it has become a sickness, and they have not yet discovered how to use leisure time creatively so that it is an asset rather than a liability. A youth-oriented people, Americans do not properly value the increasing numbers of old people who are living longer because of the benefits of modern medicine. The result is that "the young dread to grow up, the grown dread growing old, and the old are in a panic about sickness and uselessness" (105).

Giving a historical overview of the American's relationship to the land, Chapter 7, "Americans and the Land," states that the early settlers, the colonists, the traders, and the immigrants all exploited the land and points out that the desire for conservation has come about slowly and too late for some species, such as the passenger pigeon. While Americans now are interested in conserving the land and its animals, they continue to ravage and pollute, primarily for pragmatic reasons, chief among them to maintain power sources.

Chapter 8, "Americans and the World," focuses on the American attitude toward the rest of the world, an attitude strongly affected by the distance from Europe and Asia and a history of foreign exploitation. Some states, provinces, and cities were under foreign dominion more than once—New Orleans, for example, three times. Policies of isolation, therefore, are based on fear and also on the attitudes of some Europeans, who consider Americans uncouth and ignorant. American literature follows a typical pattern—first imitating English writers and then developing its uniquely American characteristics, some of which stem from the journalistic influence of newspaper writing. Such writers as Mark Twain, Artemus Ward, and Thomas Wolfe, for instance, worked as newspaper journalists. Although social historians try to discover the causes of events, people tend to see in history what they want to see even though it deals with facts. Dealing with philosophy and human emotions, literature sometimes gives a better sense of the past than history. Therefore, for a fuller understanding, people should read both. From our literature and our films the world has derived impressions of America, some of our films enticing immigrants to this country to fulfill dreams that prove illusory. Now advertising plays a similar role, dealing with illusory dreams and promises of happiness.

Chapter 9, "Americans and the Future," inspects human beings, finding that they are predators, that they are omnivorous, and that they are "aggressively individual" but still "swarm" and go "to hive in the noise and discomfort of his tenements and close-packed cities" (137). It seems that in Americans these human tendencies are increasing as a result of a loss of rules, an atrophy of responsibility, and the poison of an obsession with and desire for things. Not having had time to adjust to vast technological and medical advances, Americans lack a sense of perspective. Because they are not self-satisfied, however, they adjust to these changes, and they will search for and find new guidelines to live by. Endowed by their history and experience, Americans will adapt.

The "Afterword" states again that Americans are a unique people living in a unique land. They are the result of something that happened to them in the process of living in this place and molding a nation. Facing future dangers of success and overabundance, they will continue to adapt to change. They will make mistakes, but they will continue— they will go on.

III. CRITICAL EXPLICATION

Along with *The Winter of Our Discontent* and *Travels with Charley in Search of America,* Benson classifies *America and Americans* as part of Steinbeck's "moral trilogy," and he stipulates that this work is essential reading for "those who would understand the Steinbeck canon."[11] Roy S. Simmonds states that "it is not a portrait in words of the physical landscape of the country, but rather a genealogical and psychological portrait of the American people as filtered through the eyes and mind of a very opinionated writer who was never afraid to utter the verities as he saw them."[12] Hughes calls the book "a series of nine topical essays inspecting the whole nation and its people," which, like *Travels with Charley,* has an "autobiographical and patriotic impetus."[13] Richard F. Peterson finds it "a picture book commentary on American life which has its own individuality and purpose in Steinbeck's special understanding of America and the graphic illustrations which enrich these insights."[14] Steinbeck has written a series of nine related essays with a "Foreword" and an "Afterword," complementary to 108 pages of photographs. Both the text and the accompanying pictures are dogmatic, giving an individual's view of America. The expository prose of the text is organically unified by a control-

ling thesis in the "Foreword," nine related subtheses in the
essays, and a summation and conclusion in the "Afterword."

MODE OF DISCOURSE

America and Americans combines exposition, vignettes, and
portraits in prose to complement accompanying photographs
of monuments, landscape, events, and people. Giving a sense
of the majesty and grandeur of America, for example, on the
page following the "Foreword" is a brooding, symbolic church
steeple against a winter sky in Vermont at approaching dusk,
followed by a double spread of the rock spires in Monument
Valley, Arizona, and then by the cloud-covered peaks of
Mount Rainier in Washington. These pictures follow from
the declaration in the "Foreword" that America is "something
unique in the world" and lead to the beginning of the first
essay, *"E Pluribus Unum"*: "Our land is of every kind
geologically and climactically, and our people are of every
kind also" (9-13).

Steinbeck's purpose is to expound on his "opinions,
unashamed and individual," a purpose which he shares with
the book's photographers "whose ancestral origins cover the
whole world" (7). Thoughtful and carefully considered, these
opinions are "informed by America" and based on the
journey recorded in *Travels with Charley* as well as on a
lifetime of careful observation, "conjecture," and "specula-
tion" (7). They are inspired by "curiosity, impatience, some
anger, and a passionate love of America and the Americans"
(7). Beyond this stated purpose, as Roy S. Simmonds points
out, Steinbeck always "wanted to communicate and, in
communicating, give pleasure and promote understanding
between peoples," aims which he achieved "with resounding
success and perhaps never more fully than in his last book."[15]

ETHOS

The ethos, or character and personality of the writer, that
pervades *America and Americans* is that of "a gentle, genial

sage, given to outbursts of irascibility now and then, and at times salting his deliberations with extended asides of searching condemnation, uttered more in sorrow than in anger."[16] This "genial sage" speaks in three authentic voices. The first voice is that of the careful, thoughtful observer of events and people both contemporary and historical. Asking why Americans are close to "moral and . . . nervous collapse," he replies, "One can only have an opinion based on observation plus a reading of history" (140). This combination of Steinbeck's observations of immediate circumstances and events against a historical backdrop gives *America and Americans* an illuminating perspective, a way of looking at ourselves in relationship to those who have gone before. To illustrate, Steinbeck discusses America as "one nation" whose "people are Americans" against the background of an encapsuled overview of early American history (13). Similarly, in the chapter titled "Created Equal," the opening discussion of slavery moves from Greece to "great empires," to North and South America, thus giving a historic panorama for his discussion of slavery in the United States and current struggles for equality (57).

The second voice is that of the storyteller. Interspersed throughout the book are anecdotes based on Steinbeck's personal experience, his reading of history, or his family history. Among these are the stories of the young Indian man named Jimmy who cures his stomach trouble by taking a trout to the mermaid in Half Moon Lake as an atonement for wasting venison and of Mr. Kirk, Steinbeck's regretful reminiscence of the mentally ill recluse whom he and his friends tormented when they were small boys (19, 91-92). Steinbeck also tells fascinating stories about the etymology of words:

> Until very recently home was a real word, and in the English tongue it is a magic word. The ancient root word *ham*, from which our word "home" came, meant the triangle where two rivers meet, which with a short wall, can be defended. At first the word "home" meant safety, then gradually comfort. In the immediate American past, the home meant just these two things; the log houses, even the sod houses, were havens of safety, of defense, warmth, food, and comfort. (33)

And in discussing America's "screwballs," he explains that this term comes "from the kind of pitch in baseball which twists and turns in the air so that the batter can't figure how it will come over the plate, and it is a very apt description. While some of our screwballs are charming, original, and theatrical, others are malign and vicious, and a few are downright dangerous" (89). This storyteller's voice is a charming aspect of *America and Americans*—reminiscent of bards in ancient times, the Appalachian or Southern tradition of storytelling, and days before the advent of television when talking was itself a form of family entertainment.

The third voice is that of the prophet. This voice occurs primarily in the last chapter entitled "Americans and the Future," but it occurs early in the book as well and is implicit in the overall tone of optimism about the future—a viewpoint and tone placing Steinbeck squarely in the camp of the Romantics rather than of the Naturalists and Realists, who typically have a more pessimistic view of human beings. Although he objectively sees the dark side of the United States—bemoaning "the youthful gangs in our cities" and portraying our general national character as a people who "fight our way in, and try to buy our way out" and as "a nation of public puritans and private profligates"—he characteristically looks beyond the immediate into a future of possibilities, believing in the human powers of transcendence (29-34). In Chapter 2, "Paradox and Dream," he concludes:

> For Americans too the wide and general dream has a name. It is called "the American Way of Life." No one can define it or point to any one person or group who lives it, but it is very real nevertheless, perhaps more real than that equally remote dream the Russians call Communism. These dreams describe our vague yearnings toward what we wish [we] were and hope we may be: wise, just, compassionate, and noble. The fact that we have this dream at all is perhaps an indication of its possibility. (34)

This vocabulary and tone of optimism, the refusal to believe that the darker side may eventually triumph and destroy even the dream itself, pervades the entire book, culminating in the final chapter, "Americans and the Future," in which he looks into the future of his "people, a young people" with "some fear, more hope, and great confidence" (142). He is confident in the future of the American people because they are not complacent, not satisfied with themselves or with the world as it is. Their restless dissatisfaction Steinbeck sees as preparation for a "long journey—perhaps the longest, darkest journey of all, with the greatest light at the end of it" (143). He sees before them "a world or a universe unknown, even unconceived of, and perhaps at last open for exploration: the great and mysterious mind and soul of man, a land full of marvels" (143). With "places to go and new things to find," surrounded by "the fascinating unknown," Americans, Steinbeck believes, have the capacity to formulate "new rules" for new circumstances, to adapt to "the change that is coming" (143). The "Afterword" ends on a similar note: "We have failed sometimes, taken wrong paths, paused for renewal, filled our bellies and licked our wounds; but we have never slipped back—never" (205). And the implication here is that "we *shall* never slip back—never." Based on a study of history, observations, personal experience, and a faith that is never shaken, the voice of the prophet thus speaks with great optimism about the future of America and of the Americans.

THESIS, TONE, AND ORGANIZATION

The overall thesis governing the organization of *America and Americans* occurs in the "Foreword": "I believe that out of the whole body of our past, out of our differences, our quarrels, our many interests and directions, something has emerged that is itself unique in the world: America—complicated, paradoxical, bullheaded, shy, cruel, boisterous, unspeakably dear, and very beautiful" (7). Steinbeck's primary point here is that America is "unique." And the tone he establishes from the beginning is sincere—he will tell the bad as well as the good, objectively providing the paradoxical view of a national character which is both shy and boisterous, cruel and beautiful at the same time. In spite of this recognition of its negative aspects, however, the tone is affectionate—America is "un-

speakably dear"—as well as appreciative and admiring—
America is "very beautiful."

This emphasis on America as something "unique in the
world" continues in "*E Pluribus Unum*": "Our land is of every
kind geologically and climatically, and our people are of every
kind also—of every race, of every ethnic category—and yet
our land is one nation, and our people are Americans" (13).
Following an encapsuled overview of early American history,
Steinbeck tells how this uniquely American characteristic of
unity in diversity came about:

> America did not exist. Four centuries of work, of bloodshed,
> of loneliness and fear created this land. We built America and
> the process made us Americans—a new breed, rooted in all
> races, stained and tinted with all colors, a seeming ethnic
> anarchy. Then in a little, little time, we became more alike
> than we were different—a new society; not great, but fitted by
> our very faults for greatness, *E Pluribus Unum*. (13)

Contemplating the results of this unity in diversity, Steinbeck observes further that "from being a polyglot nation,
Americans became the worst linguists in the world" and that
"somewhere there is an American look," which "is not limited
to people of Caucasian ancestry" (16-17). Fittingly, Steinbeck's
discussion of the American people who are "of every race, of
every ethnic category" is followed by a series of pictures of
American faces: a Sioux Indian from South Dakota; New
England ladies gathered around a round table in a formal,
ornately decorated room, probably a literary gathering, for one
of them is reading from a book as the rest listen intently; the
statue of a Roman Catholic saint on a pedestal, bedecked with
dollar bills and carried through a milling crowd at an Italian
street festival in Boston; a double spread of the honest, open
faces of Amish farmers in Lancaster County, Pennsylvania; and
a double spread of tired, pensive faces with closed expressions
in the subway in New York City (21-27).

The picture of two drummers with the University of
Michigan band in action at a football stadium on the facing
page of Chapter 2, "Paradox and Dream," complements the
opening statement, which describes Americans as "a restless,

a dissatisfied, a searching people," and the discussion of the unique American paradox which follows (28-29). One of the drummers, tousled haired and angry looking, seems, from the expression on his face, to be shouting an invective while the other stares at the game worriedly. In the background three of the band members appear to be playing with abandon rather than in concert. At an event largely designed for entertainment and as the way many Americans fill their leisure time, the occasion hardly seems joyous.

The first three paragraphs of this chapter discuss the American paradox. Half humorously, Steinbeck generalizes that "we speak of the American Way of Life as though it involved the ground rules for the governance of heaven," and illustrates the paradoxes inherent in that way of life in a further series of generalities, each of which, he concedes, cancels out the other:

> We are alert, curious, hopeful, and we take more drugs designed to make us unaware than any other people. We are self-reliant and at the same time completely dependent. We are aggressive, and defenseless. Americans overindulge their children and do not like them; the children in turn are overly dependent and full of hate for their parents. We are complacent in our possessions, in our houses, in our education; but it is hard to find a man or woman who does not want something better for the next generation. Americans are remarkably kind and hospitable and open with both guests and strangers; and yet they will make a wide circle around the man dying on the pavement. Fortunes are spent getting cats out of trees and dogs out of sewer pipes; but a girl screaming for help in the street draws only slammed doors, closed windows, and silence. (29-30)

The three opening paragraphs are thus inductive, a gathering of "generalities" and examples showing the paradoxical nature of the American people and leading up to the chapter's thesis: "Americans seem to live and breathe and function by paradox; but in nothing are we so paradoxical as in our passionate belief in our own myths" (30). Viewing themselves as "natural-born mechanics," as self-sufficient, close to nature, and law abiding, proudly insisting that they base their political positions "on the issues," Americans create their own myths, believing in them ardently, paradoxically ignoring the fact that they rarely live up to them.

The American dream is itself a part of the paradox. The "hunger for home" combines with a spirit of "pure restlessness, pure nervousness" (30-31). "The mobile home" itself becomes a permanent dwelling place for some. The "dream that we are great hunters, trackers, woodsmen, deadshots with a rifle or a shotgun . . . is deeply held by Americans who have never fired a gun or hunted anything larger or more dangerous than a cockroach" (33). Perhaps, Steinbeck muses, "the inventiveness once necessary for survival may also be a part of the national dream," and our cowboy folk tales may descend from ancient tales of chivalry in which "virtue does not arise out of reason or orderly process of law—it is imposed and maintained by violence" (34). Without the necessity of being "clear-cut and exact," this "general dream" has a name. It is called "the American Way of Life" and describes a vague yearning "toward what we wish we were and hope we may be: wise, just, compassionate, and noble" (34). In their paradoxes and in their dreams, the Americans are thus a people "unique in the world."

Chapter 3, "Government of the People," covers the uniqueness of the American system of government, including the people's fear of "perpetuation of power," their inherent distrust of politicians, and the customary festiveness of nominating conventions. The opening sentence is the thesis: "Our means of governing ourselves, while it doubtless derives from European and Asiatic sources, nevertheless is not only unique and a mystery to non-Americans but a matter of wonder to Americans themselves. That it works at all is astonishing, and that it works well is a matter for complete amazement" (35). Steinbeck finds that Americans fear "any perpetuation of power"; view politics as "a dirty, tricky, and dishonest pursuit"; consider all politicians as crooks; and at the same time "demand second-rate candidates and first-rate Presidents" (35, 46). Despite the craziness and venality of American politics, however, "our nation was designed by a group of men ahead of their time and in some ways ahead of ours. They conceived a system capable of renewing itself to meet changing conditions, an instrument at once flexible and firm" (45-46). Steinbeck, an advocate for change, suggests that the country needs "a federal law making any crime committed for the purpose of denying or inhibiting a civil right a federal offense, subject to federal judges and federal juries, with the option of change of venue if the local authorities flout the law" (48). Underscoring the uniqueness of this "government of the people" and highlighting its historical background, seven pictures appear in the middle of this essay—ranging from the Liberty Bell in Philadelphia; to the Mayflower II, off Plymouth; to the scene of Lee's surrender at Appomattox Court House, Virginia; to two school girls gazing up at the statue of Lincoln in the Rotunda of the Capitol in Washington, D.C. Following the essay are pictures symbolic and representative of American government: a floodlit Washington Monument and the Capitol in the background, two scenes from a New England town meeting, John F. Kennedy with Lyndon B. Johnson and Hubert Humphrey during the 1960 presidential campaign, and Pope Paul VI addressing the United Nations.

On the left facing page of Chapter 4, "Created Equal," is Gordon Parks's photograph of the profile of a somber young African-American male looking out on Harlem through a broken window, a cigarette hanging from his mouth, his face highlighted, showing despair. Three pictures appear in the middle of the essay, themselves telling a part of the story of the struggle for equality in America: a little African-American boy and a little white girl sitting side by side in a classroom in Kentucky, a double spread of a civil rights demonstration in Alabama, and a small African-American girl holding an American flag. The essay opens with the thesis: "Today we believe that slavery is a crime and a sin, as well as being economically unsound under our system" (57). First providing a brief historical overview of slavery in Greece, "the great empires," and North and South America, Steinbeck discusses the history of slavery in the United States, leading up to a discussion of the Civil War, its causes and consequences. The causes are primarily economic. A part of the consequences involve "a withdrawn separateness" between the races (59). Just now are American Negroes "surging" towards that equality, a surge "started by four things": "religion," "art," "learning," and "economic importance and impact" (66). Slavery, however, has left behind a state of "trauma," which we will not overcome "until we cannot remember whether the man we just spoke to in the street was Negro or white" (66).

Chapter 5, *"Genus Americanus,"* opens with the thesis, showing again the uniqueness and the paradox of America: "Members of a classless society must work out changes in status levels without violating their belief that there are no such levels" (67). In a classless society, on what are status levels based? First, status is dependent upon ability, which Americans early discover has "nothing to do with birth" (67). "Land-holding" and "money" are further criteria, culminating in power. "Power fails, however, in fields of individual creativeness . . . the writing of good books and plays, the painting of great pictures, the composing of exquisite music" (67-86). Nor can it fulfill the human "yearning toward greatness," a yearning which some Americans satisfy through organizations, such as the Elks and Masons (86-87). Steinbeck also discusses the negative aspects of *"Genus Americanus"* in the search for power or "greatness": those with "the desire and will to spy on, to denounce, to threaten, and to punish" (88). Following the discussion of these "attackers" and completing his description of *"Genus Americanus"* is Steinbeck's depiction of the nation's "screwballs" and "eccentrics," the latter divided into two types: the "show-offs" and the "hiders" (89-92).

At the beginning of Chapter 6, "The Pursuit of Happiness," are eight pictures, each serving to emphasize a youth-oriented society. Among these are a wide-eyed baby; a young girl at a junior cotillion class; schoolboys walking a fence in Nantucket, Massachusetts; and a double spread of milling, bathing suit clad teenagers on the beach near Miami, Florida (95-102). This chapter emphasizes those things which cause unhappiness despite the American's ardent "pursuit of happiness." Americans, for example, tend to seek happiness in their children, a pursuit so intense that it has turned into "a national sickness which might be called paedosis," resulting in an extension of "adolescence far into the future, so that very many Americans have never and can never become adults"

(93, 103). People must often retire when "mental powers are at their peak," often replaced by inferiors who happen "to be younger," resulting in "a great burden of unhappy, unused, unfulfilled people" (104). Steinbeck further discusses the problems of "a great over-supply of widows" and "immaturity in American men," who are excited by "child-women" (104-05). He thus inductively leads up to the thesis that "The young dread to grow up, the grown dread growing old, and the old are in a panic about sickness and uselessness" (105). In such a state of "dread," "sickness," and "uselessness," even leisure, lacking "valuable direction," may cause "destructive and unsatisfactory trouble" and may prove to be "our new disease, dangerous and incurable" (105-06).

The pictures following this chapter portray young, adult, and old Americans in their pursuit of happiness. On the facing page is the photograph of an ancient dowager in vintage clothing, stepping out of an antique car. Among the pictures on the following pages are children in the gallery of the Philadelphia Museum of Art; a double spread of the stock car races in Darlington, South Carolina; a double spread of the Kentucky Derby at Churchill Downs; a baseball pitcher; football players in a scrimmage; an outdoor movie showing *The Ten Commandments*, with the mountains of South Dakota against the sunset in the background; newsstand literature; and a double spread of a scene from the musical *Hello, Dolly!* (107-25).

In the picture on the facing page of Chapter 7, "Americans and the Land," a bison grazes in Grand Teton National Park, Wyoming. Providing a historical perspective of Americans and their relationship to the land, Steinbeck describes the "early settlers," who "pillaged the country as though they hated it, as though they held it temporarily and might be driven off at any time"; the "colonists" who "farmed meager lands close to their communities and to safety"; the "explorer-traders" who "soon dressed, ate, and generally acted like the indigenous people around them"; and the "immigrants" who "went land-mad, because there was so much of it" (127-28). He thus leads up to the thesis:

> No longer do we Americans want to destroy wantonly, but our new-found sources of power—to take the burden of work

from our shoulders, to warm us, and cool us, and give us light, to transport us quickly, and to make the things we use and wear and eat—these power sources spew pollution on our country, so that the rivers and streams are becoming poisonous and lifeless. The birds die for the lack of food; a noxious cloud hangs over our cities that burns our lungs and reddens our eyes. (130)

Despite his optimistic thesis that Americans no longer "want to destroy wantonly," Steinbeck concludes that "we are an exuberant people, careless and destructive as active children" and ends on an ominous note, reminding us of "the atom bomb" and its potential for devastation, a potential which we have already proved in Hiroshima and Nagasaki (130).

Chapter 8, "Americans and the World," focuses on the American attitude towards the rest of the world, an attitude strongly affected by the distance from Europe and Asia and a history of foreign exploitation: "The American attitude toward foreign nations, foreign people, and foreign things is closely tied historically to our geographical position and our early history on this continent" (131). Here Steinbeck's historical perspective leads to insight and understanding. Separated from Europe and Asia by an ocean, "until recently, the chance that the average native-born American would ever see a foreign country was remote," making it unnecessary "to learn other languages than our own" (131). Since some states, provinces, and cities were under foreign dominion more than once—New Orleans, for example, three times—colonists viewed foreign ships as potential enemies, "bent on conquest and settlement" (131). Policies of isolation, therefore, are based on fear and also on the attitudes of some Europeans, who consider Americans uncouth and ignorant. For foreign visitors "from the upper levels of a sharply classed society" often viewed Americans contemptuously, disdaining "our clumsy attempts at equality and democracy" (131). This insularity, however, has passed, with Americans traveling "more than any other people today" (133).

American literature developed typically, first as an imitation of the English writers and then as a development unique to this country: writers who wrote about America for Americans, whose outlet was at first "in obscure and local journals" (133). Such writers as Mark Twain, Artemus Ward, and Thomas Wolfe, for instance, worked as newspaper journalists. The world's view of America, Steinbeck maintains, derives largely from these novels, short stories, and "particularly from our moving pictures" (136). Although Americans also hoped for the illusory dream life of the early films, they fully realized the commonplace reality, boredom, and hardships to which they would emerge afterwards. "But poor immigrants were drawn to our golden dreams and the promise of happiness" (136). Now advertising "has taken over where the dream film stopped," also dealing in illusion and holding forth an "exploding dream" of happiness (136).

Chapter 9, "Americans and the Future," inspects human beings, finding that they are predators, that they are omnivorous, and that they are "aggressively individual" but still "swarm" and go "to hive in the noise and discomfort of his tenements and close-packed cities" (137). These problems, have led to the "verge of moral and hence nervous collapse": a loss of principles of "rules," an atrophy of responsibility, and the "poison" of an "obsession with things" (140, 138-39). This inductive discussion leads to the thesis: "The roads of the past have come to an end and we have not yet discovered a path to the future" (142). With great confidence Steinbeck has inserted the word "yet," assured that these unique Americans, endowed with a rich history and experience, will meet "the change that is coming," that they will discover the path for the continuing journey (143). Because they have not had time to adjust to vast technological and medical advances, Americans lack a sense of perspective. Because they are not self-satisfied, they will adjust to change, will search for and find new guidelines to live by. Endowed by their history and experience, Americans will adapt. Pages 145 through 204 following this final chapter provide a wealth of pictures of America's grandeur and rich potential, its unique beauty— among them a Vermont farm in winter; fireworks over the White House in Washington, D.C.; a paddleboat on the Mississippi River; and the Grain Market in Chicago.

The "Afterword" states again that Americans are a unique people living in a unique land. They are the result of something that happened to them in the process of living in this place and molding a nation: "Something happened in America to create Americans" (205). Facing future dangers of success and overabundance, they will continue to adapt to change. They will make mistakes, but they will continue—they will go on. On the facing page of the "Afterword" is a photograph of a young couple watching an eruption of Old Faithful in Yellowstone National Park—a fitting concluding symbol of stability and of continuation, a phenomenon uniquely American. Thus organized so that each chapter and the "Afterword" follow from and contribute to the overall thesis that America is unique, *America and Americans* is a unified whole, with text and pictures blended and complementary, each enhancing the other.

WRITING STRATEGIES

In *America and Americans* Steinbeck has had time to mull over, to meditate on, and to codify "the small diagnostic truths" discovered on the journey recorded in *Travels with Charley in Search of America.* Written in objective, third-person narration, which frequently shifts into first person, Steinbeck's style is informal and often colloquial, designed for a general audience. The viewpoint is subjective in the sense that it is based on "opinions, unashamed and individual" but objective to the extent that it is based on the cool scrutiny of past experience and observation. His primary writing strategies are juxtapositions of events which provide a perspective, examples, anecdotes, and rhetorical questions.

Steinbeck juxtaposes the immediate against the backdrop of the past in order to provide a perspective—a way of looking at the present—sometimes by a historical comparison, sometimes by philosophically attempting to show why and how things have evolved, how they have come to be as they are. In a historical allusion in Chapter 1, *"E Pluribus Unum,"* for instance, he states that "the unit America has come into being in slightly over four hundred years—almost exactly the same amount of time as that during which England was occupied by the Roman legions" (13). In Chapter 3,

"Government of the People," he suggests that "the American fascination with the folktales of cowboys, gunslinging sheriffs, and Indian fighters . . . no doubt descended from the brave mailed knight of chivalry who battled and overcame evil with lance and sword" (34). And in Chapter 5, *"Genus America-nus,"* he points out that "the American Revolution was different from the French Revolution and the later Russian Revolution in that the revolting American colonists did not want a new kind of government; they wanted the same kind, only run by themselves" and shows how this view evolved into "the theory of the government by the common man" (67). This juxtaposition of the present against the backdrop of the past also provides a perspective by which Steinbeck can look into the future of America and Americans and proclaim that he believes that "our history, our experience in America, has endowed us for the change that is coming" (143).

Steinbeck amply uses examples to substantiate and illustrate general observations:

> This land was no gift. The firstlings worked for it, fought for it, and died for it. They stole and cheated and double-crossed for it, and when they had taken a little piece, the way a fierce-hearted man ropes a wild mustang, they had then to gentle it and smooth it and make it habitable at all. Once they had a foothold, they had to defend their holdings against new waves of the restless and ferocious and hungry. (13)

Pointing out that "how all these fragments of the peoples of the world who settled America became one people is not only a mystery but quite contrary to their original wishes and intentions," Steinbeck illustrates with examples: "the Pilgrim Fathers who . . . turned their guns on anyone, English or otherwise, who was not exactly like themselves"; "the Virginia and Carolina planters" who "wanted slaves and indentured servants, not free and dangerous elements"; "the poor Irish"; "the Jews"; the "Chinese"; "the newcomers" (14). To portray America's "pleasant, benign, and interesting screwballs," he again cites examples:

> Of such was the gentle Emperor Norton, who lived in San Francisco and called himself "Emperor of the United States

and Protector of Mexico." Of such is the man who runs for the
Presidency on a vegetarian ticket, and of such was One Eye
Connelly the gate crasher, and Leaping Lena Levinsky the lady
prizefight promoter; of such was Canvasback Cohen, the
prizefighter who was maintained by the Marx Brothers
because he lost all contests. (90)

Such uses of examples provide a sense of Steinbeck's acute-
ness of observation and his knowledge of American history
and events.

Most of Steinbeck's anecdotes are based on personal
experience or family history. Typically, they are colloquial
and informal, told in the storyteller's voice. To illustrate how
"the home dream can be acted out almost anywhere," for
example, he tells the following story of "a stout and benign-
looking lady" whom he had observed when he "lived on East
51st Street in New York City":

> She set out a canvas deck chair, and over it mounted a beach
> umbrella—one of the kind which has a little cocktail table
> around it—and then, smiling happily, this benign and robust
> woman rolled out a little lawn made of green raffia in front of
> her chair, set out two pots of red geraniums and an artificial
> palm, brought a little cabinet with cold drinks—Coca-Cola,
> Pepsi-Cola—in a small icebox; she laid her folded copy of the
> *Daily News* on the table, arranged her equipment, and sank
> back into the chair—and she was in the country. (32)

Sometimes these anecdotal reminiscences are humorous— the one, for instance, about Adlai E. Stevenson and
Sam Rayburn's discussion of "an open or uncontrolled
convention," which concludes with Rayburn's declaration:
"Look, son—look, Governor—I'm an old man, and I've been
through this for many years, and tell you I don't *mind* an open
convention—as long as it's rigged" (45). Among the anecdotes based on his own family history are the ones about his
Great-Grandfather Dickson who sailed with his large family
to the Holy Land, intending first "to teach the Jews agriculture" and then "gradually move Christianity in on them"; his
Great-Aunt Carrie whose school for Negro children the Ku

Klux Klan burned down; and his Uncle Charlie who told him the story about the hospitality of "a little old woman" who lived in a sod house furnished with packing crate furniture and an upright piano (59, 65). For anyone who has ever loved storytelling and storytellers, these anecdotes add a personable warmth and charm. They are friendly little stories interspersed generously throughout, revealing the personal side of Steinbeck.

Steinbeck uses the rhetorical question as he speculates on cause and effect, on how things have come to be the way they are. Wondering "whether our deep connection with firearms is not indeed a national potential" since "not long ago we had to be good hunters or we starved, good shots or our lives were in danger," he asks, "Can this have carried over?" (33). He then cites an Englishman's observation that perhaps Americans "are just born with the knack" for firearms (33). Similarly, in dealing with the topic of the American's child centeredness, which is a "child sickness" or "paedosis," he asks whether it is "a disease of the children or of the parents," followed by a speculative and insightful discussion of the extension of "adolescence far into the future, so that very many Americans have never and can never become adults" (93). In response to the rhetorical question which follows— "What has caused this?"—he finds that the cause may indeed be "the result of the parent's dissatisfaction with his own life, of his passionate desire to give his children something better or at least different" (103). Sometimes these rhetorical questions have the effect of conclusions as well as of speculations. For example, Steinbeck's questioning why Americans are "on this verge of moral and hence nervous collapse" is both a statement of fact and a search for a cause, calling for a response by the philosopher-observer (140). The question "How will the Americans act and react to a new set of circumstances for which new rules must be made?" functions similarly. While Steinbeck's views in *America and Americans* are unabashedly "opinionated," at the same time this frequent use of rhetorical questions adds a tentative, searching tone as he seeks for "the diagnostic truths" about the country and the people whom he loves.

WRITING STYLE

Roy S. Simmonds has enumerated some of the characteristics of Steinbeck's style in *America and Americans:*

> It is written in a style redolent with the easy rhythms and vocabulary of everyday speech.[17]
> Steinbeck does not blur his statements and arguments with impressive pseudo-academic phraseology.[18]

This informal, colloquial, unpretentious style decorously fits Steinbeck's purpose and audience: to expound on his "opinions, unashamed and individual" and to communicate, at the same time giving pleasure and promoting "understanding between peoples."[19] He writes about those things in which he passionately and wholeheartedly believes, and he wants people to understand him, a goal which he achieves admirably well, for "any reasonably-educated twelve-year-old can understand what he writes, or at least that part of what he writes which is within such child's range of experience."[20]

An informal, colloquial, and unpretentious style, however, does not of necessity preclude sophistication, for great elegance can reside in simplicity. Such is the case with Steinbeck. Drawing on such ancient, time-honored stylistic devices as metaphorical language, epigram, allusion, catalog or listing, and a wide variety of syntactical structures, he creates in *America and Americans* a work of art in his own authentic voice, with a tone of great sincerity, appealing to a wide audience.

Some of Steinbeck's uses of metaphorical language are the commonplace, the accepted cliches with which people ordinarily communicate: "the architecture of our government" (46); the "jagged holes in our system" (47); the warning that "no good society can grow if its roots are in sterile soil" (48); the loggers who "went through the great groves like a barrage, toppling trees" (130); "these exploding dreams" which have contributed to "a kind of sullen despair and growing anger and cynicism" (136); "young Americans" who "are rebellious, angry, searching like terriers near a rat's nest" (143); and "the long journey—perhaps the longest

darkest journey of all, with the greatest light at the end of it"
(143).

Other uses of metaphorical language are fresh, crystal
clear, and insightful: the American "reputation for gallantry"
which "is blotted out by the dust cloud of self-pity" (139);
"the quality of responsibility" which "has atrophied" (139);
"the huge reservoir of the anger of frustration" which "is full
to bursting" (139); the "pep pills" which open "access to a
false personality, a biochemical costume in which to strut"
(139); "vision" that "dims like the house lights in a theatre"
(143); "explosions of will and direction" (205); and "the
anaesthetic of satisfaction" (205).

Sometimes he uses extended metaphors. In looking into
America's future, he discovers a "cancerous growth" which
must be inspected "as a whole because if we cannot root it out
we have little chance of survival" (137):

> First, let us try to find something to call this subtle and deadly
> illness. Immorality does not describe it, nor does lack of
> integrity, nor does dishonesty. We might coin the word
> "an-ethics," but that would be too scholarly an approach to a
> subject that is far more dangerous than anything that has
> happened to us. It is a creeping, evil thing that is invading
> every cranny of our political, our economic, our spiritual, and
> our psychic life. I begin to think that the evil is one thing, not
> many. (137)

In another of these extended metaphors, he compares "our
national nervousness" to a kennel of bird dogs (139):

> Have you ever seen a kennel of beautiful, highly bred and
> trained and specialized bird dogs? And have you seen those
> same dogs when they are no longer used? In a short time their
> skills and certainties and usefulness are gone. They become
> quarrelsome, fat, lazy, cowardly, dirty, and utterly disreputa-
> ble and worthless, and all because their purpose is gone and
> with it the rules and disciplines that made them beautiful and
> good.
>
> Is that what we are becoming, a national kennel of animals
> with no purpose and no direction? For a million years we had
> a purpose—simple survival—the finding, planting, gathering,
> or killing of food to keep us alive, of shelter to prevent our

freezing. This was a strong incentive. Add to it defense against
all kinds of enemies and you have our species' history. But
now we have food and shelter and transportation and the
more terrible hazard of leisure. I strongly suspect that our
moral and spiritual disintegration grows out of our lack of
experience with plenty. (139)

Far more than poetic adornments, such metaphors reinforce,
enrich, extend, and clarify meaning, providing a perspective
and enhancing understanding.

Like his use of metaphorical language, Steinbeck's pithy,
epigrammatic statements serve both as poetical adornments
and as a practical, effective, and memorable means of communication. Taken from their context, they can stand alone as
insightful observations about things uniquely American or
about the human condition:

> It takes a special kind of man to run for public office, a man
> with armored skin and a practical knowledge of gutter
> fighting. (36)
> Nothing there is in nature is as thoughtlessly cruel as a small
> boy, unless it be a small girl. (92)
> For the most part, history is what we wish it to have been.
> (135)
> Perhaps the urge toward happiness has taken the place of
> the urge toward food and warmth and shelter. (136)

In effect these epigrammatic statements contribute to the
tone of sincerity and to the voice of the thoughtful, wise
observer—the seer who can divine the nature of things.

In like manner, Steinbeck's use of literary, contemporary, and historical allusions shows him to be a reliable,
experienced, well-read observer whose opinions are valuable.
For example, in discussing the plight of numerous aging
widows in the United States, he refers to Dorothy Parker's
"heartbreaking," "wonderful play about these women" (105).
He later tells of America's good fortune in the early development of "some mature writers of eye, ear, and enthusiasm":

> Washington Irving, for instance, looked with joy on our
> people, our speech, stories, and patterns of thought; Cooper
> made up a fund of misinformation about the American Indian;

> while Longfellow searched for Hellenic meter and meaning in the life and history of Americans. Meanwhile, the true seedlings of our literature were sprouting in the tall tales, the jests, the boasting, and the humor of the storytellers in the forests and on the plains. . . . Even Edgar Allan Poe, who surely wrote more like a European than an American, had to be acclaimed in France before he was acceptable to upper-brow Americans. (133)

He enumerates in alphabetical order some of those American writers "who took their basic training and found their first outlet in newspapers": "George Ade, Maxwell Anderson, Benchley, Bierce, Crane, Dreiser, Faulkner, Hammett, Hearn, Lardner, London, Norris, Mark Twain, Artemus Ward, Thomas Wolfe, are only a few" (133-34). Among the historical and contemporary allusions are references to John F. Kennedy, Adlai E. Stevenson, Lyndon B. Johnson, and World War II.

His use of catalog or listing serves for emphasis or reinforcement. To show the extent to which Americans have "from the first . . . treated our minorities abominably, the way the old boys do the new kids in school," he catalogs his evidence:

> The Pilgrim Fathers took out after the Catholics, and both clobbered the Jews. The Irish had their turn running the gauntlet, and after them the Germans, the Poles, the Slovaks, the Italians, the Hindus, the Chinese, the Japanese, the Filipinos, the Mexicans. (15)

Like a barrage the listing continues with the "disparaging names" Americans give these people: "Micks, Sheenies, Krauts, Dagos, Wops, Ragheads, Yellowbellies, and so forth" (15).

In the discussion of the American's "yearning toward greatness," a catalog of organizations reinforces his statement that Americans have "a need for grandeur against a background of commonness": "Elks, Masons, Knight Templars, Woodmen of the World, Redmen, Eagles, Eastern Star, Foresters, Concatenated Order of Who's Who International—the *World Almanac* lists hundreds of such societies and associations, military and religious, philosophic, scholarly, charitable, mystic, political, and some just plain nuts" (87).

Informal and colloquial, Steinbeck's sentence style has the deceptive simplicity of the master writer. For example, consider a typical passage (numbered in brackets for purposes of discussion):

> [1] In the beginning, we crept, scuttled, escaped, were driven out of the safe and settled corners of the earth to the fringes of a strange and hostile wilderness, a nameless and hostile continent. [2] Some rulers granted large sections of unmapped territory, in places they did not own or even know, as cheap gifts to favorites or to potential enemies for the purpose of getting rid of them. [3] Many others were sent here as a punishment for penal offenses. [4] Far from welcoming us, this continent resisted us. [5] The Indigenes fought to the best of their ability to hold on to a land they thought was theirs. [6] The rocky soils fought back, and the bewildering forests, and the deserts. [7] Diseases, unknown and therefore incurable, decimated the early comers, and in their energy of restlessness they fought one another. [8] This land was no gift. (13)

Sentences 1, 2, 3, 4, 5, and 8 are all simple sentences, but note the variety. Sentence 1 begins with a prepositional phrase, has a series of compound verbs, and ends with an appositive. Sentence 2 is a simple sentence with a series of prepositional phrases, one with a modifying adjective clause. Sentences 3 and 4 have prepositional phrases, one at the beginning and the other at the end of the main clause. Sentence 5 is intricately woven, with modifying clauses, and in Sentence 8 the main clause stands alone. Sentences 6 and 7 are compound, but Sentence 6 has three main clauses, the last two with understood verbs. Close inspection thus reveals Steinbeck's informal, colloquial, unpretentious style to be one of grand simplicity, sophisticated grace, and the apparently careless ease of what the Renaissance calls *sprezzatura,* or a seemingly effortless elegance.

The entire book is similarly a combination of simplicity and elegance, of well-considered opinions and hypotheses. As a wise observer, storyteller, and prophet, Steinbeck's tone is sometimes affectionate, sometimes angry, but always sincere. Although he realizes that critics will label him sentimental, he reveals his love for his country and its people, his distress over its problems, and his optimistic hope for its future in a style decorously suited to his topic and audience, he creates in *America and Americans* a unified, organically conceived work of art—an American view of the uniqueness of this land and its people.

NOTES

1. Jackson J. Benson, *The True Adventures of John Steinbeck, Writer* (New York: Viking Press, 1984), p. 955.
2. John Steinbeck, *Steinbeck: A Life in Letters,* eds. Elaine Steinbeck and Robert Wallsten (New York: Viking Press, 1975), p. 807. Hereafter cited as *SLL*.
3. *Ibid.,* p. 816.
4. Benson, pp. 964-65.
5. *SLL,* p. 829.
6. *Ibid.,* p. 829.
7. *Ibid.,* pp. 829-30.
8. John Steinbeck, *America and Americans* (New York: Viking Press, 1966), pp. 137-43—hereafter cited parenthetically in the body of the text.
9. Robert S. Hughes, Jr., "Steinbeck's *Travels with Charley* and *America and Americans,*" *Steinbeck Quarterly,* 20 (Summer-Fall 1987), p. 81.
10. Benson, p. 968.
11. *Ibid.,* p. 968.
12. Roy S. Simmonds, "'Our land . . . incredibly dear and beautiful': Steinbeck's *America and Americans,*" in *Steinbeck's Travel Literature: Essays in Criticism,* edited by Tetsumaro Hayashi (*Steinbeck Monograph Series,* No. 10) (Muncie, Indiana: Steinbeck Society of America, Ball State University, 1980), pp. 23-24.
13. Hughes, pp. 77, 80.
14. Richard F. Peterson, "The Mythology of American Life: *America and Americans* (1966)," in *Steinbeck's Travel Literature,* ed. Hayashi, p. 11.
15. Simmonds, p. 25.

16. *Ibid.*
17. *Ibid.*, p. 24.
18. *Ibid.*, p. 25.
19. *Ibid.*
20. *Ibid.*

IV. TOPICS FOR RESEARCH AND DISCUSSION

(1) *America and Americans* was first published in 1966. In this book Steinbeck optimistically believes that Americans will formulate "new rules" that, by experience and past history, they are endowed for any future changes. Survey several current newspapers and magazines. Using these materials as evidence, write a paper in which you refute or support Steinbeck's optimistic assertion. What are the "new rules," if any, which Americans have formulated? What "new rules," if any, should they formulate?

(2) Read newspapers and magazines published between July 1 and October 3, 1965, the time when Steinbeck was writing the final chapter, "Americans and the Future," and write a paper in which you discuss events of the time in comparison with and contrast to Steinbeck's moral viewpoints.

(3) Write a paper in which you discuss one of Steinbeck's fictional works in relationship to *America and Americans,* showing the extent to which *America and Americans* enhances your understanding of his fiction.

(4) Discuss Steinbeck's views of "the American Way of Life" in the light of current depictions of this way of life in current newspapers and magazines. Is there still a recognizable "American Way of Life"? Do Americans still have illusory dreams? If so, what are they? How do they contribute to the overall dream?

(5) After studying the photographs in *America and Americans* along with the text, write a paper in which you discuss the relationship between photographs and text. In what ways are they complementary? Are there any ways in which they are not complementary?

V. SELECTED BIBLIOGRAPHY

1. Jackson J. Benson, *The True Adventures of John Steinbeck, Writer* (New York: Viking Press, 1984). Benson has provided not

only a definitive biography of Steinbeck but also the definitive eye and voice of the critic who knows his canon thoroughly. Therefore, he provides not only background material but insightful viewpoints and interpretations as well.

2. Tetsumaro Hayashi, editor, *Steinbeck's Travel Literature (Steinbeck Monograph Series,* No. 10) (Muncie, Indiana: Steinbeck Society of America, 1980). This collection is very valuable because it brings under one cover some of the best studies on this body of literature.

3. Robert S. Hughes, Jr., "Steinbeck's *Travels with Charley* and *America and Americans,*" *Steinbeck Quarterly,* 20 (Summer-Fall 1987), 76-88. This essay provides an excellent overview and discussion of Steinbeck's form and technique in both *Travels with Charley* and *America and Americans.*

4. John Steinbeck, *Steinbeck: A Life in Letters,* eds. Elaine Steinbeck and Robert Wallsten (New York: Viking Press, 1975). Steinbeck's own letters, together with commentaries, are the best source for background and for ascertaining Steinbeck's struggles with writing and his views on his own work.

2. STEINBECK'S *CANNERY ROW* (1945)

I. BACKGROUND

According to two of Steinbeck's letters, *Cannery Row* (1945) is described as a "silly book that is fun anyway" and "a funny little book that is fun and pretty nice."[1] Several critics have suggested that it grew out of Steinbeck's disgust for the battlefield during his assignment as a war correspondent in Germany and his desire to escape to something light and cheerful. This motive is affirmed in a letter to Carlton A. Sheffield where Steinbeck states that he has had "too much of a look at [war]" and emphasizes the pleasure of his return to "a comfortable relaxed house . . . where people like each other."[2] In a subsequent letter, also to Sheffield, Steinbeck again emphasizes that the book "never mentions war" but that it reiterates "things we talked about years ago [when] we were thinking more universally."[3]

Although there are some indications that Steinbeck's motives involved "amusing the home front and cheering up service men who had time to read," he also confesses that the book was "born out of homesickness."[4] This confession, when combined with the knowledge that Steinbeck had struggled with Tom Wolfe's theme, *You Can't Go Home Again,* suggests yet another motive for the work, recreating a nostalgic and sentimental past, where life was simple and easy and the dissatisfaction and malaise brought about by success and fame were not factors in the artist's life.

Jackson J. Benson notes that "since he [Steinbeck] had returned from the war, his letters were full of nostalgia for Monterey, the fog and the smell of the fish."[5] He had strong emotions that were no doubt a major factor that led him to write *Cannery Row,* and he talked frequently of moving back to the area. Perhaps part of the nostalgia was based on what Benson calls contradictions in his personality. While trying to adjust to his new status as a celebrity and to fit into a new social milieu, Steinbeck had found it difficult, "as if he didn't know quite what to do with it [success] or how to take it." According to Benson, he "questioned whether he should embrace fame and its privileges wholeheartedly or reject it all and withdraw from society as he had tried to do at various times in the past." He seemed to sense something corrupting about such pleasures and felt they might ruin him as a writer.[6]

Certainly another motive for the book was to celebrate his friendship with Ed Ricketts with whom he had collaborated on *The Log from the Sea of Cortez.* Ricketts, owner of the Pacific Biological Laboratory in Monterey, was a philosophical soul-mate for Steinbeck and their interaction sparked many new ideas in Steinbeck's work while at the same time exposing him to a great deal of reading, including Whitman, Goethe, and Lao Tze, as well as ecological theorist W. C. Allee, whose *Animal Aggregations* stressed mutual interdependence and cooperation as a fundamental trait of living organisms. Thus social behavior was not a matter of conscious decision but was an innate quality of living beings. Steinbeck, ever the perceptive listener, incorporated much of this new material into *Cannery Row.*

Benson further suggests that, as a close friend, Ricketts was a living example of the theorem Steinbeck tried so often to demonstrate in his fiction: that the people condemned or looked down upon by society are often the best people. Certainly, *Cannery Row* stresses this insight as readers observe Dora and the whorehouse, Mack and the boys, and other down-and-outers who permeate its pages.

However, it seems obvious that Ricketts and Steinbeck's collaboration on *The Log,* a careful record of their expedition to the lower shores of California to collect biological specimens, was most influential in the formation of *Cannery Row.* According to Steinbeck, *The Log* was carefully planned and designed with four levels of statement in it just like the novel. In addition, Steinbeck saw *The Log* as a tricky book—full of

intellectual traps as well as jokes, suggesting parallels to the
poison cream puff theory about *Cannery Row* posed by critic
Malcolm Cowley. Steinbeck even wrote to his friend and
publisher Pascal Covici that when *The Log* was published, he
would have finished a cycle of work that had been biting at
him for years. The book, he said, "is simply the careful
statement of the thesis of work to be done in the future."[7]

In fact, Steinbeck biographer Benson goes so far as to
suggest that *Cannery Row* is a summation of all Steinbeck's
conflicts and contradictions and all he had learned from the
voyage with Ricketts. It is another presentation of the
Steinbeck/Ricketts philosophy of nonteleological "is" thinking. Since *The Log,* which did not sell very well, had not
proved a satisfactory forum for the ideas, largely because the
philosophy was lost in details of the trip and because the
presentation was expository rather than poetic, Steinbeck
decided to present the ideas in a different context. Benson
goes on to label the book as a fictional, poetic version of *The
Log* and Doc a metaphor for the spirit of Ed as Steinbeck
perceived him.

Perhaps another factor in the structural composition of
the book was Ricketts' and Steinbeck's mutual infatuation
with classical music. Bach's *Art of Fugue* seems to have
influenced the patterning of many of Steinbeck's novels with
parallels of the original melody/story line being picked up by
other voices/characters. Steinbeck had even begun a work
entitled *Dissonant Symphony* in the early 1930s—a psychological exploration and experimentation of the way personalities
are formed and altered by interaction with other personalities. The work, though never published, was to stress the fact
that the smallest circumstance can lead to profound changes
in a person's action. As a result, personalities are never fixed
or stable but are subject to and influenced by the interpretations of the observer, almost as if the two were chemicals
interacting with each other. Thus the structure of *Cannery
Row* features intercalary chapters similar to those used in *The
Grapes of Wrath* and utilizes a contrapuntal technique similar
to the structure of a fugue, with notes and melody lines
reoccurring, at times harmonizing and at times clashing,
offering pleasing dissonance to the main thematic emphasis.

John H. Timmerman agrees with Benson's assessment, saying that the book's purpose is "to bring to light a set of characters and their natural environment on a life stage where the tragic and the comic intermingle and offset one another," as if in concert with the nonteleological thinking in *The Log*.[8] In addition, Peter Lisca calls the reader's attention to the fact that openness and the freedom of structure in the novel are "a formal expression of those same qualities in the Cannery Row community, upon which no convention or authority imposes conformity or direction. It has instead the natural order of a biological organism, manifesting its own inner dynamics."[9] The central image of the swirls and eddies of a tide pool also seems to reflect a musical ebb and flow.

A final influence on *Cannery Row* is the *Tao Teh Ching* of Lao Tze, which Lisca labels the novel's informing spirit. According to the preface to a 1942 edition of the *Tao,* this book "teaches the wisdom of appearing foolish, the success of appearing to fail, the strength of weakness." Taoism rejects the desire for material goods, fame, power, and even the holding of fixed or strong opinions, all of which lead to violence. Instead, man is to cultivate simple physical enjoyments and the inner life. Given the fact that these general principles inform both texts, Lisca goes on to suggest that even specific passages in the *Tao* are mirrored in *Cannery Row*. Doc as the Taoist sage becomes a "wordless" teacher, at one with his "total environment," deeply in touch with his inner being.[10]

The Eastern philosophy suggests a need to escape from Western values or concepts of success while at the same time escaping from Western activism, the necessity to impose order and direction. Instead, there is a need to realize that freedom exists in recognizing the many perspectives through which life can be seen. It exists in indulging variety without fear of contradiction and in accepting the paradoxes that real life presents to us. Taoism's benevolent chaos, a concept both feared and respected by Steinbeck, offers a mixture of good/evil just as complex and incomprehensible as life itself.

In conclusion, the varied substance of the background material suggests a *Cannery Row* which cannot be easily labeled or categorized but which will continue to intrigue readers by its very complexity and diversity, traits which will constantly place it among books that incite criticism and praise, controversy and consensus.

II. PLOT SYNOPSIS

Steinbeck's *Cannery Row* begins with a prose-poem that describes the ambiguous nature of the environs of Monterey. The Row is described as "a poem, a stink, a grating noise . . . as well as a nostalgia, a dream." Similarly, its inhabitants are called "whores, pimps, gamblers, and sons of bitches," but Steinbeck stresses that through another peephole these residents could be "saints, angels, martyrs and holy men."[11]

The brief prologue then laments how to adequately transfer, or set down alive, the message of *Cannery Row*. Using an image of flatworms from marine biology, Steinbeck decides just "to open the page and let the stories crawl in by themselves" (12).

CHAPTER 1

Chapter 1 introduces several of the major characters on the Row. Lee Chong, the Chinese grocery owner, is the first introduced and is described as generous, trusting, full, benevolent, rich, and warm while at the same time business and money oriented. Chong has just accepted the Palace Flophouse and Grill from Horace Abbeville as payment of accumulated debts in his grocery, an event which later causes Abbeville's suicide. As new owner of the property, Chong must decide how to use it. Eventually he decides to let Mack and the boys—Eddie, Hazel, Hughie, and Jones—occupy the structure in return for watching out for the place. Money is mentioned, but it is understood that quoting the rent is a formality. Payment will not be through money but through assistance when needed and through restrained theft. As the chapter ends with Mack and the boys ensconced in a home of their own, the major plot line is introduced when the group appreciates the music from Western Biological Lab and decides to do something for Doc, the fine fellow who owns this biological supply company.

CHAPTER 2

Chapter 2 begins a pattern of intercalary chapters. These randomly placed stories seldom extend the major plot line about the Row which demonstrates appreciation for Doc and his friendship. Rather they provide parallels, contrasts, or extensions of the thematic emphases. Here Steinbeck examines the ambiguity in all men's natures. Lee Chong is described as "evil balanced by good" while Mack and the boys are "the Beauties, Virtues and Graces" rather than "no-goods, thieves, rascals and bums" (15).

CHAPTER 3

Chapter 3 introduces more major characters on Cannery Row including Dora Flood, the madam of The Bear Flag Restaurant, the local whorehouse, and Alfred, the watchman of the brothel. Once more the book examines how "evil" is turned to "good" by Dora's generous donations to charity and by Alfred's careful handling of her customers. Unfortunately, Alfred's predecessor William is not nearly so well adjusted. Rejected by Mack and the boys, he allows his dark and lonesome nature to be twisted with brooding. Unlike the friendly group introduced earlier, William is an isolated man and threatens suicide since he believes that no one loves or cares about him. Seemingly of use to no one, William eventually sees no choice but to drive an ice pick into his own heart. Thus the glowing picture of brotherhood initially shown on the Row is seen as inconsistent and varying.

CHAPTER 4

This fluctuating picture returns in Chapter 4 with an old Chinaman who walks through the area daily. To some he is

God while others believe him to be Death. Mockery, however, rather than respect, greets the old man. When a townsboy named Andy continues the harassment, a cosmic transformation takes place as the Chinaman momentarily becomes a huge eye, again suggesting that human life has several dimensions and serious ambiguity. Loneliness—the disparate cold aloneness of the landscape—again envelopes a character (this time Andy) and reiterates Steinbeck's opinion that pleasure may be easily transformed into fear.

CHAPTER 5

Chapter 5 describes Doc's Western Biological Lab and paints a picture of a microcosm of animals and sea life that once more suggests the complexity of human existence. Doc's own complex personality is also depicted by the variety of his interests in science, music, and art, while the variety and ambiguity of the cosmos is stressed as Doc is described as half Christ/half satyr, a fountain of philosophy, fine arts, and scientific inventions. The versatility of his taste influences the Row, changing nonsense to wisdom and motivating a desire among the residents to return the favor. The party, something nice for Doc, returns as the major focus of the novel.

CHAPTER 6

The tide pool of Chapter 6 parallels Doc's personal complexity in Chapter 5. The initial reaction of beauty is superseded by a perception of violence, and it becomes difficult to distinguish whether the tide pool is the source of life or death, good or evil. Doc is pictured working, gathering specimens with Hazel, one of Mack's boys. The introduction of Hazel offers Steinbeck another opportunity to explore the "bums" of the Row: Hazel himself and, through his eyes, Gay. Gay is revealed as a victim and instigator of wife abuse, one who only feels comfortable in jail or in the Palace Flophouse. Acceptance and belonging are stressed as the conversation continues and draws in Henri, the painter, another down-and-outer.

Henri is portrayed as weird, painting in chicken feathers and nutshells and constantly working on a boat which he will never sail. However, according to Doc, he is no more crazy than the other residents of Cannery Row. Like them, he is composed of opposites and contradictions; he is as idiosyncratic as the stink bugs Hazel observes at the end of the chapter that inexplicably put their tails in the air and cause observers to question why.

CHAPTER 7

Chapter 7 records the establishment of the Palace Flophouse and the organization necessary for group interaction while at the same time preserving individualism. The bare interior eventually is transformed into a home as each member contributes furniture and pride. This mixture of diverse personalities into a group is symbolized by Eddie's gallon jug—a collection of leftover drinks from La Ida, a rival whorehouse. It is a mixture of all sorts of alcohol collected by the bartender and combined in a strange punch he offers to his friends.

While enjoying the punch, Mack and the boys return to their initial idea to do something more for Doc—like throwing a party. Their discussion ranges over what would please Doc and how they could raise the money to fund such an event. Eventually they decide on a frog hunt, collecting specimens for Western Biological at 5¢ per frog. The resulting earnings will be used to fund the gala.

CHAPTER 8

Chapter 8 is another intercalary chapter which presents a parallel story: the tale of Mr. and Mrs. Sam Malloy who live in an old boiler and transform it into an apartment. Using their own experience as an example, they later rent out large pipes as sleeping quarters and become entrepreneurs of a sort. Unfortunately, this wealth transforms their original happiness as Steinbeck records their upward mobility by purchasing material goods such as a rug, washtubs, and lamps for the boiler. Soon brotherhood/companionship has been super-seded by greed and success, and yet another marriage has been examined where spouses are at times unable to interact and interrelate.

CHAPTER 9

Chapter 9 returns to the plot of Mack and the boys as they prepare for the frog expedition and try to enlist Doc's participation in the plans for his own party while still keeping their intentions secret. They even request gas money so they can collect the frogs. After convincing Doc, Mack also cons Lee Chong into contributing the truck for the expedition. Trickery and conniving are ironically parts of the brother-hood's actions, even though each individual is intent on doing good for Doc.

CHAPTER 10

Chapter 10 shifts to another parallel story—an abandoned child named Frankie who is mentally retarded and somewhat physi-cally handicapped. Frankie's home and interrelationships with "uncles" are examined, again stressing a strong need to belong to someone, an individual or a group. Parties are Frankie's special love and helping Doc is his major interest. But unfortunately, his devotion backfires (prefiguring Chapter 28) and one special party is ruined by his good-natured intentions to help out; instead, he is isolated and rejected when his efforts to serve at the party result in spilled beer. Ambiguity has entered his life as "good" intentions have resulted in "bad" results. Consequently (like others before him) he retreats from brotherhood and unfortunately accepts the loneliness which is forced on single individuals.

CHAPTER 11

Chapter 11 records the beginning of the frog collecting episode as Steinbeck delineates the coincidences that led to

Lee Chong owning the dilapidated truck used by Mack and the boys for the expedition. As Gay works to revitalize the truck, he is compared to St. Francis, the mechanic of God. The determination of the group is praised since cooperation and interaction are essential to completing their goal. Luckily, they overcome difficulties because they have a single mind to honor Doc. Although the truck has to climb hills backward and blows a carburetor, Mack and the boys are persistent. Despite the fact that "the infinity of possibility" and the interconnectedness of life eventually land Gay in jail for disorderly conduct, the tiny group goes on without him, persevering in their intent to get money for Doc's party.

CHAPTER 12

Chapter 12 is a brief intercalary comment on the death of the American humorist Josh Billings and how his entrails had been discarded in a gulch near Alvarado Street. The chapter also relates to respect and caring as the town decides that degradation and dishonor will not come to this famous literary man. They will not allow his *tripas* to be used on a fishing expedition or to be eaten by dogs.

CHAPTER 13

Eddie, one of Mack's boys, returns with a "borrowed" carburetor, and the frog hunt resumes. The chapter stresses that some individuals, specifically the owner of the carburetor and the owner of a red rooster, contribute to the party unaware. Theft, with its many faces, is condoned since the "goal" or end is lofty. The group proceeds to a small pool in the valley and begins a party of its own, enjoying the relaxation and happiness without the worry associated with "success." The chicken stew made for supper is another picture of positive interaction of many items that individually would have been worthless. The suggestion by Jones that perhaps the strange alcoholic mixture in Eddie's jug would be better if separated into whiskey, beer, and wine is yet one more way in which the book examines the importance of intermingling and then summarily rejects separation and isolation.

Just as quickly, however, the conversation around dinner turns to McKinley Moran, an example of how money and marriage do not mix. Like Gay, Moran has lost the freedom in his lifestyle, and the boys discuss the dilemma that faces all men: how to be considerate and caring of others and at the same time satisfy their own self-serving natures.

The proposed party, at first spontaneous and thoughtful, is suddenly transformed into selfish and inconsiderate gratification of personal needs. Gifts and presents (mostly worthless) are mulled over when suddenly a landowner confronts the group and orders them off his property. At first the Captain is hostile and angry, but soon Mack convinces him to help them with the frog hunt. In return Mack will cure the Captain's dog. Mack's "sweet-talkin'" conversation is so convincing that Hazel observes he could have been president if he wanted. Jones, however, observes that there's "no fun in that"; the laid back, uninvolved life of the Flophouse is more appealing (84).

CHAPTER 14

Chapter 14, again intercalary, observes the Row in early morning—a time of magic. Four individuals, two soldiers and two prostitutes from La Ida, are seen tired but happy, enjoying the parklike property of the Hopkins's Marine Station. Once more relaxation and lack of worry are an integral part of the scene, and, when the watchman of the station tries to evict them, the four barely move, savoring the moment of slow motion and exerting no energy in their defiance. The parallel to Chapter 13 and the Captain is no doubt intentional.

CHAPTER 15

Chapter 15 returns to the frog hunt and initially relates how the Captain's marriage has affected him. Again government is criticized (she's in the State Assembly) as is spending all one's time in work and organization. The Captain's spirit is significantly changed by the interaction with Mack. Brotherhood flourishes with whiskey and the gift of a pup while regulation and rules are ignored. Two hours later the group remembers the hunt and resumes their quest. The confusion caused by five men running amok in the pool creates a great deal of laughter and fun. After awhile even the Captain feels easy, and the boys leave contentedly with whiskey, a pup now named Darling, and enough frogs to sell so that Doc's party will be a success.

CHAPTER 16

Chapter 16 shifts the focus to the Bear Flag Restaurant and its proprietor Madam Dora. Despite being short-handed and busy, Dora and her ladies work diligently when Doc asks them for help during an influenza epidemic. Unselfishly they mix their jobs—doing shifts of "evil" and then shifts of "good."

CHAPTER 17

The irony of Doc's double nature—isolated and lonely yet part of the community and popular—is the topic here. His diverse personality parallels the diversity of the tide pools where he collects specimens. He is perhaps just as isolated as the flagpole skater at the department store as he recognizes and copes with the fact that none of his friends can accompany him on his collecting tour. He begins lackadaisically as Steinbeck again stresses the "easy life" and the value of trying new things, such as a beer milkshake. While driving to the shore, Doc contemplates the prejudice he once experienced in the past. On a walking tour of America, stereotyped by his beard and his avid desire to learn, he had been rejected by the majority of people; these individuals didn't appreciate his search for truth. Sadly Doc was forced to change his motive; he said his goal was money instead of true things, and suddenly he was accepted. More people valued this motive, indicating they treasured lies over truth. The nostalgic chap-

ter ends with a return to the present and potential brotherhood with a hitchhiker. However the "deep lines beside his
[the hiker's] mouth and his dark brooding eyes" predeter-
mine a disastrous outcome as he and Doc argue over the
freedom to drink and drive (105). Eventually, the argument
turns violent and results in the hiker's ejection from the car
and the return of lies as Doc makes a medical excuse for
trying a beer milkshake.

CHAPTER 18

Surprisingly, Chapter 18 continues the tale of Doc's travel
and an intercalary chapter is skipped. The exploration of the
tidal flat at La Jolla dominates this section as life and death
intersect in one place. The flat is the source of life yet at the
same time is described as a "fantastic" cemetery. Unfortunately, while collecting, Doc also discovers a human corpse
on the flat—a young girl with dark hair, who in death seems
surprisingly comfortable, at rest, and beautiful. Dissonant
music echoes for Doc as he tries to comprehend the intermingling of great beauty and ecstasy with fear and disgust.
Money, a bounty for the discovery, is again rejected.

CHAPTER 19

The isolation of the flagpole skater is the central focus of
Chapter 19. Ironically his presence is used as a sales pitch,
and, when people worry about him, it is not about his safety
but rather about the trivial information of where he goes to
the toilet. As in several other episodes on the Row, human
curiosity seldom reflects caring and concern but rather an
insensitive and selfish need for information which causes
dissension and problems rather than concord and peace.

CHAPTER 20

The return from the frog hunt occupies Chapter 20, and plans
for the party begin. The boys barter with Lee for groceries

based on the money the frogs will bring. Although Lee is indebted to Doc, he loses no chance to make a buck at the same time. In fact, "frog" prices rise as Lee ignores brotherhood and prefers money. Evil is also chosen over good as Mack and the boys spoil and bribe Darling, offering her no discipline and almost complete freedom. Here the negative side of the easy life is stressed.

The end of the chapter involves the surprise party. This time Lee Chong's store becomes symbolic of the variety of the universe, stocked as it is with the leftovers of decades. The confused planning includes "decorations," a cake, and the frogs, and the celebration begins and ironically ends without Doc ever arriving. Unfortunately, the celebrants create chaos, and instead of pleasing Doc, they leave a messy trail of glasses, frogs, and broken records that indicate the failure of their goal!

CHAPTER 21

Chapter 21 depicts the calm and tranquility of Cannery Row and then follows a fatigued Doc as he discovers the results of the party. Anger surges within him, and, as he tries to control his rage, Mack apologetically returns. Doc begins a fight, but it is unsuccessful since Mack refuses to retaliate. Doc, his anger cooling, makes connections of sadness with music and literature and eventually tries to smooth over the argument with a beer. Mack's explanation for the failed party indicates his own lack of self-worth. "If I done a good thing, it got poisoned up some way," he says as the duality of life theme returns (131). Unfortunately, the chapter suggests that Mack has not learned from his mistake. Men will continue to have "good times" and be happy when in fact they are causing wreckage and destruction. The chapter ends as Doc begins to clean up the mess.

CHAPTER 22

The life of Henri the painter is closely examined here. Again the reader is shown confusion in his name, nationality, and occupation. His boat, never finished and never designed to sail, indicates Henri's isolation as well as his freedom to be a nonconformist like others on the Row. Other details Steinbeck provides about Henri reinforce these observations. Henri's vision of evil (the murder of a child by a dark and handsome young man) parallels the Chinaman episode in Chapter 4 and reiterates the idea that even when a person looks nice they may be evil and "not give a damn." The answer to the fear of such ghosts is companionship, even if it is only transitory or sometimes illusory. It is all man has.

CHAPTER 23

Chapter 23 returns to Mack and his guilt after the failed party. His sadness and depression seem to get the best of him and unfortunately influence the boys negatively as well! Rumor exaggerates and distorts their "evil" motives, and they become social outcasts like several other characters in the book. No one seems to understand how such a positive motive could backfire, and many residents of the Row want to punish the group. Consequently, Mack and the boys try to balance the scales of good and evil. Doc observes that they are true philosophers "knowing everything that has ever happened in the world and possibly everything that will happen" (141). He then praises them for being relaxed in a world of ambition, nervousness, and covetousness. They are healthy and they do what they want—ignoring money and greed which will ruin their lives. After discussing their lack of need and using the Fourth of July parade as an example, Doc proceeds to verbalize what he has observed in Mack and the boys.

> "It has always seemed strange to me," said Doc. "The things we admire in men, kindness and generosity, openness, honesty, understanding and feeling are the concomitants of failure in our system. And those traits we detest, sharpness, greed, acquisitiveness, meanness, egotism and self-interest are the traits of success. And while men admire the quality of the first, they love the product of the second." (143)

Despite this realization, Doc is unable to relieve the pain and self-destructive criticism of Mack. Instead, more evil is bred in the Row as other citizens are affected by the "node of trouble." Steinbeck lists a plethora of problems that all seem to spring from the bad time. The Malloys fight; Dora is harassed by high-minded ladies and forced to close the Bear Flag for two weeks; several boats are wrecked; and Darling, the puppy acquired on the frog hunt, gets sick. Doc is consulted for advice on the last crisis, and by following his prescription, Darling recovers, and a crack develops in the wall of evil. Just as quickly there is a reversal of attitudes as things seem to gravitate toward good. Love, companionship, and fellowship return, and plans for a second party—one that Doc will attend—are initiated.

CHAPTER 24

The next intercalary chapter stresses the value of parties by examining another resident of the Row, Mary Talbot. The gaiety and happiness of Mary are infectious and serve as weapons against despondency and darkness. Mary uses her talent as a partygiver to buoy the spirits of her husband by hosting tea parties for local cats. Though the concept seems insane, it does work to relieve her husband's tensions and worries and diverts his attention to fantasies and dreams of success. The chapter affirms the contagious quality of both depression and excitement and suggests that caring and a sense of brotherhood are essential to maintain a positive attitude.

Such a positive attitude returns for Mack once he decides to throw a second party. Mack's joy multiplies and begins to influence the rest of the community just as Mary has influenced Tom. Again a list of those influenced has a wide range including the Malloys, the girls at the Bear Flag, and even the sea lions on the offshore rocks. Plans for the party proceed, now including a potential birthday celebration. Mack is designated to find out Doc's birthdate.

CHAPTER 25

Mack thinks that he cleverly "finds out" from Doc that his birthdate is October 27, but Doc fools Mack, whose technique and method the doctor knows too well. The real birthdate is December 18!

CHAPTER 26

Chapter 26 again offers an intercalary, contrasting and negative view as two boys from the Row, Willard and Joey, argue with each other. They are portrayed as covetous and argumentative, and it seems as if Willard especially takes delight in evil. He teases Joey about his father's suicide and jokes that his pa died because he felt he was an animal, a rat. Joey, laughing outwardly but inwardly hurt by the harsh words, tries to explain his father's dilemma, but Willard persists in his cruelty, and the chapter closes with his wish that Joey like his father might take rat poison.

CHAPTER 27

Plans for the party progress as the Row plans appropriate presents for Doc. It is a community effort, a symbol of brotherhood and love. Doc's discovery of the town's plan and his decision to help the citizens of the Row celebrate close the chapter. Steinbeck portrays this as a lucky occurrence since none of the other planners has thought of supplying food and drink.

CHAPTER 28

Frankie, the rejected orphan of Chapter 10, returns in the next intercalary Chapter 28, as he looks for an appropriate gift for Doc's birthday. After seeing a black onyx clock with a bronze figure of St. George and the Dragon, he is determined to have it as his present. He associates the figure with Doc (a deliverer from evil), but ironically he must commit evil (theft) in order to obtain it. Sadly, Frankie's good intentions are again destroyed, and the bond of brotherhood is broken by the laws of society. Frankie, caught stealing and known to have a mental defect, is institutionalized; the reason for the theft— the love of Doc—isn't even considered as a deciding or a contributing factor in the crime. Heartsick and compassionate for the child but unable to help, Doc retreats to collecting, hoping to block the incident from his mind.

CHAPTER 29

This chapter brings the reader to the day of the party and Doc's preparation for his "surprise." Each of the Row's residents prepares differently, but the bulk of the chapter centers on Dora and her girls and how cooperation is necessary to allow each member of the group to attend the party. Again sadness and resentment are overcome through generosity and caring. Ironically, despite the high spirits of the Row, Doc is sentimental and sad as indicated by the music he plays in the laboratory. The tension mounts for the beginning of the celebration.

CHAPTER 30

The chapter continues with the party which initially is quiet and subdued unlike the first celebration, which was wild and got out of hand. The presents are offered—each a gift from the heart, rather than being motivated by selfishness. Propriety seems to be a key word as Doc serves the food and sets out the whiskey and wine. Steinbeck describes the mood as "rich digestive sadness" and "golden pleasant sadness" as Doc plays Monteverdi and reads "Black Marigolds," a poem from the Sanskrit (184, 185). The poem combines love and loss of love in paradoxical tension and moves the partygoers to tears. But this world sadness does not last long as a full-scale fight breaks out when the crew of a tuna boat mistakenly crashes the party looking for prostitutes. The destruction characteristic of the first party returns as the residents of the Row evict the strangers and proceed to restore the party to a more riotous scale— complete with more drinking, dancing, noise, and Lee Chong's gift of a 25-foot string of firecrackers.

CHAPTER 31

A strange intercalary chapter follows about a gopher who sets up his hole by a vacant lot on Cannery Row. The text emphasizes his perfection as well as the perfection of the home site, but soon the gopher discovers the emptiness of his home because he cannot find a mate. Interaction with others of his kind is essential for happiness even if he must suffer on account of it. Eventually in order to experience companionship he undergoes a savage fight and a move to a dahlia garden where there are traps which might cause the gopher's death. Again, Steinbeck seems to stress that life without pain is not really life at all. A mixture, a tension of opposites, is necessary for all species of animals.

CHAPTER 32

This chapter returns us to the view of Chapter 21 and the mess of the first party. This time, however, the celebration has caused no anger, no guilt, no hard feelings. The wreckage is similar, but Doc's attitude has changed. He is not bitter or resentful, for he recognizes and accepts the intermingling of good with evil, love with loss, joy with sadness. The book closes with glimpses of the microcosm of the sea and Doc's quotation from the Sanskrit—"I know that I have savored the hot taste of life . . . just for a small and forgotten time . . . the whitest pouring of eternal light" (196). As Doc wipes the tears from his eyes, the reader views his lab animals, active yet complacent, confused yet understanding; Steinbeck's design is the recognition that the human animal has the same dilemma as these specimens—accepting life with all its paradoxes and contradictions.

III. CRITICAL EXPLICATION

Cannery Row has been called Steinbeck's most perfectly realized novel based on the concept of non-teleological "is" thinking. This philosophy, developed by Steinbeck and Ed Ricketts during their 1940 collecting voyage on their boat, *The Western Flyer,* involves the acceptance of whatever exists in the natural world. Questions of why or how events occur are of no importance. Rather, individuals using "is" thinking are careful to avoid imposing any prior values or systems in evaluating the world around them. Pure in heart, they strive for objectivity: to understand that whatever "is" is right. Such objectivity, of course, is not simple or easy to achieve. It requires a spontaneous planlessness that is often contrary to human nature.

The Log offers philosophical statements which are fictionally illustrated in *Cannery Row.* For example, Steinbeck states that "Man is the only animal whose interest and whose drive are outside himself."[12] Consequently, he ruins the earth by trying to acquire external things—property, houses, money, and power. *The Log* then asserts that by projecting himself into these external complexities, man becomes them. Since such ornamentation and complication precede extinction according to paleontologists, it is no wonder that Steinbeck's concern is so intense.

Still another borrowing from *The Log* is Steinbeck's belief that although individuals love abstract good qualities and detest the abstract bad, they will nevertheless envy and admire the person who, though possessing bad qualities, has succeeded economically and socially and will hold in contempt that person whose good qualities have caused failure (98). In fact, this concept is repeated almost verbatim by Doc in Chapter 23 of *Cannery Row,* a fact which confirms the intended parallelism of nonfiction with fiction.

Therefore, like *The Log, Cannery Row* is the record of Steinbeck's search for the truth, for the principle which can key man to the pattern of all life and the relation of one man to another. In *The Log* Steinbeck even speculates that among primitive peoples human sacrifice alone creates such a sense of wholeness of sense and emotion—the good, bad, beautiful, ugly, and cruel all welded into one thing. In *Cannery Row,* of course, the drowned girl found during Doc's exploration of the tidal flat exemplifies this unity. After the find, Doc hears cosmic music, the music of the spheres. The vision implies great beauty and even ecstasy, although it is simultaneously appalling and fearful. In this vision of death the purposiveness of events is shown to be irrelevant; there can be no answers, only pictures which become larger and more significant as one's horizon increases. Steinbeck seems to imply that although everyone continually searches for absolutes, realities are only a glimpse—or a challenge—to envision the whole picture. Absolutes must be avoided, for they result in closed minds which deny opposites, and thus resist the struggle which may lead to a potential rebirth.

Steinbeck also asserts in *The Log* that the "truest reason for anything's being so is that it is" (151). As a result, the underlying pattern of life goes everywhere and is everything and cannot be encompassed by the finite mind, for the mind runs into the impossibility of perfection while at the same time insisting on the validity of perfection. In short, the anomalies evident in the Row encompass this "is" pattern, a structure which suggests the deep ultimate reality of truth and "being."

Finally, one passage from *The Log* relates to *Cannery Row* because it indicates just why Steinbeck valued the gift of laziness (62). Since he found most busyness a nervous tic, only in laziness could one achieve a state of contemplation which offers an opportunity for the balancing of values, a weighing of oneself against the world and the world against itself. Thus the lazy contemplative residents of *Cannery Row* are admirable, for by using this hopeful trait, each resident can work toward understanding how to accept what "is" without questioning how or why. This understanding or wholeness of vision, described by Steinbeck as "breaking through," is most evident in *Cannery Row*'s protagonist, Doc, who struggles to understand life and its paradoxes but finds that the price for such understanding is isolation, being set apart from the fullness of experience and forced to accept disengagement and loneliness. In fact, the novel has often been labeled an "essay in loneliness" and "a poisoned cream-puff," which suggests pain rather than pleasure. The text reveals that the opinion of the world without is often too simplistic, and the novel counters with the world within, the internal resources which mirror life's complexity.

The outside world imposes societal values on individuals. Respectability, progress, possessions, and responsibility all imply some sort of regulation that controls men and women, and Steinbeck acknowledges that those who withdraw from such control of their lives are labeled as eccentric or weird like Mack and the boys. Their "good" life is anarchical as opposed to the structured goals and aims of the civilized world. They live in benevolent chaos and seem to opt out of the eternal intellectual struggle of most men to make their lives worthwhile. Instead, these nonconformists enjoy life for what it "is." Nevertheless, Peter Lisca points out that Mack and the boys are hardly paragons of virtue.[13] They are merely individuals who have retreated from the society and who have championed individual freedom and personal integrity against the forces of regimentation. They, too, have their problems, problems largely created by their unconventional philosophy of life. Although it might appear as if Steinbeck is advocating the virtues of poverty, hard luck, and laziness and that he lauds the sense of community which is not evident in the rest of society, there is also a recognition that there is a price to pay for such an independent existence. Individuals must cope with personal guilt for not following the lead of the majority. They must endure isolation and derision for their failure to accept "normal" patterns. They must sacrifice their physical security to satisfy psychic needs. *Cannery Row,* therefore, is not a simple book which advocates a Bohemian, laid-back lifestyle. Its complexity reveals the positives and the negatives caused by the duality of human beings, and it is designed to help readers recognize that life itself is many faceted. One has to be open to new worlds in order to replace the world which is continually in the process of self-destruction.

At times it appears as if *Cannery Row*'s "is" thinking seems to lead logically to such a simple lifestyle, and that the novel is merely Steinbeck's homesick and nostalgic attempt to recreate the Monterey peninsula and the Row he knew so well. Several critics, including John H. Timmerman, view the novel as a

condemnation of the technological, materialistic society that
Steinbeck felt destroyed a sense of unity (*comitatus*).[14] Although there is no doubt that Steinbeck recognized that too
many Americans were on the outside looking in, yet the Row
also demonstrates that the darker side of man is lurking
beneath the surface and that it is difficult to cultivate simple
physical enjoyment and the inner life when one is constantly
confronted with laws, rules, and expectations of the majority.

One of Steinbeck's aims certainly seems to be urging
intellectual beings to come away from the rush and the
demands of the city and discover true peace. Finding value in
isolation and passivity, mankind will then reject the materialistic desire to add to possessions and property.

Maintaining this simple life, however, is not easy. Even
members of the Row are unable to consistently persevere in
their rejection of societal values. For example, Mack and the
boys are compelled to dress up the Palace Flophouse, the
Malloys seek curtains for a boiler that has no windows, and
Frankie thinks an expensive gift is necessary in order to
express his love. Consequently, any simplistic reading of the
novel as advocating one lifestyle over another must be
dismissed as wholly inadequate.

Rather a close reading reveals that the Row contains the
poison of despair and rejection, in addition to the easy laid-back
lifestyle. Often Steinbeck portrays the pain as overwhelming,
resulting in self-destruction. In fact, suicides are recurrent
events on the Row: Horace Abbeville shoots himself when he
loses his property over a grocery debt; William, the bouncer at
Dora's, stabs himself with an ice pick; the drowned girl on the
reef seems to have ended her own life; and the young boy
Joey's father has eaten rat poison in despair when he loses his
job. None can escape depression so easily.

Nonetheless, there are certain indications that the inflexibility of absolutes is being condemned. For example, the
orderliness of the Captain's wife in Chapter 15 has created a
world of hell for her husband. In addition, the rigid moral
codes of Monterey citizens have condemned the Bear Flag
brothel without realizing what Dora and her girls have done
for the community. Ultimately, the reader is forced to
conclude that the only solution is to strive to be the best

imperfect man in an imperfect universe. At times, puritanic viewpoints create inhumanity, and at times the "good" life seems to equal the pure in heart and those who are caring and loving, but "is" thinking prevents this generalization from being absolute. Often human love founders helplessly in the face of animal drives that conflict with civilization. The failure of the first party indicates that even admirable goals can backfire and create evil. Heroic men often totter on feet of clay. Mack and the boys mean good, but their kind-hearted intentions do not obliterate the fact that they are the flotsam and jetsam of the American dream, individuals who at times hide from commitment and refuse to accept their own failures.

Aside from non-teleological thinking and the simple lifestyle, most critics suggest that *Cannery Row* can best be seen as an allegory, displaying the universal tendencies of man in the words that the setting microcosmically represents. The waves and the tide pools seem to function symbolically, echoing natural rhythms of life and at the same time suggesting the chaotic swirl of existence with its eddies, vortexes, and still waters. "Is" thinking is also evident in the apparent anarchy of Steinbeck's style which is designed to parallel the supposed anarchy of life. The stories are allowed to crawl in randomly and the less than obvious structuring of intercalary chapters reflects the confusion presented in the tide pool. Like society, the pool is complex; it can neither be condemned nor oversentimentalized. Rather, it is jumbled and spontaneous, like the Flophouse and the Row itself. The pool reflects the interrelation of opposites, especially the opposites of life and death.

The pool also demonstrates parasitic as well as commensal relationships, mirroring the fact that humans occasionally prey on other humans and at other times long to live in mutual benevolence, understanding, and acceptance. Moreover, the pool is evidence of a stable ecological balance, and it demonstrates the importance of a biological organism that follows its own inner dynamics. The free flux demonstrated by the pool also prefigures the patchwork of time that Steinbeck utilizes throughout his work. This sense of timelessness is suggested first by the frequent insertion of anachronisms and also by lack of chronological pattern in the text.

Besides the tide pool imagery, Steinbeck's repetitious use

of parties in the novels is also deserving of attention. Charles Metzger discussed this in his critical explication of *Cannery Row* in Hayashi's first edition of *A Study Guide to Steinbeck* (1974).[15]

Metzger points out that although most critics center on two parties given for Doc, there are far more celebrations in the novel. First of all, his essay points out Mack and the boys' informal cookout before the frog hunt complete with the impromptu stew and wining jug. The unusual mixture demonstrated by the stew and Eddie's jug suggests the strange combinations sometimes necessary in order to survive in a world of paradoxes. The next party given by the Captain in Chapter 14 also is quite spontaneous and congenial. The party begins with Mack's offer to help remove the tick from the Captain's dog; in return, the Captain offers his frog pond and a sharing of his corn whiskey stored away during the Prohibition. The whiskey and the puppy given to Mack after the second party are generous gifts from the heart, again indicating the value of the camaraderie and interrelationships that such celebrations symbolize.

This is in contrast to the first party thrown for Doc that turns into a riotous debacle. This party is forced and results in narrow-minded self-indulgence instead of caring and sharing. Doc does not even arrive at the first party before Mack and the boys have selfishly consumed all the food and caused $300 worth of damage to his lab. Despite the apparent happiness and good time for those who attended, this party is a disaster and results in a time of gloom and despair on the Row.

Metzger speculates that a good party is a cross between a natural organism and a work of art and that it needs to be both planned and spontaneous the way organisms and art forms are.[16] The party of the two soldiers and their prostitutes and those parties given by Mary Talbot for the stray cats and her husband Tom are examples of such successful uninhibited expressions of joy and celebration. The soldiers' party begins during the hour of the pearl and as a result is very casual; wrinkled clothes, unbuttoned tunics, and childlike actions all produce a tired, peaceful, and wonderful secret that cannot be spoiled even by the angry caretaker.

Similarly, Mary's parties in Chapter 24 bring excitement and a special glow to herself and others. Birthday parties, costume parties, holiday parties, and tea parties for the neighborhood cats all bring enjoyment into her life. As Steinbeck notes, the parties "covered and concealed the fact that she didn't have very nice clothes and [that] the Talbots didn't have any money" (152). Mary's parties occur when the Talbots are really scraped and when they lack hope, but they infect the whole house with gaiety. Metzger sees the gift of parties as a weapon against despondency and an evidence of Mary's positive attitude, her hopefulness in the middle of despair. Any excuse for a party will do, and even pretended parties have a positive effect. Parties even have the potential to remove the lines of worry and concern and revitalize human beings.

The final party which ends the novel is again a cooperative event with Doc finding out about the secret and preparing for the celebration by supplying food and drink, items forgotten by the planners. The gifts brought by the partygoers for Doc also reflect cooperation, the necessary joining of opposites which is needed to succeed in life. For example, the quilt made by Dora and the girls of the Bear Flag and the combination of different genres of music indicate the importance of collaboration. The party, although planned for months, is not a "dismal slave party, an act or demonstration whipped and controlled and dominated" (182). Rather it is informal and even has a fight or two. This time, however, the riotous ending is positive as more individuals are drawn into the celebration. Lonely human beings, sometimes despondent and set apart, find salvation in the festivity provided by such infectious merrymaking.

Finally, the *Tao Teh Ching* of Lao Tze, a Chinese philosopher of the sixth century B.C., is also a significant source for some of the philosophy advocated in *Cannery Row*. Developed in detail by Peter Lisca in his book *John Steinbeck: Nature and Myth,* the parallels between the *Tao* and *Cannery Row* are striking.[17] Both were written during a time of brutal war and presented a system of values that was opposed to the qualities which had caused the war. For example, Taoism rejects holding fixed and strong opinions because they usually lead to violence. In this faith the moral life is one of inaction, and there *can* be success in failure. Believers hold to the right of individuals to cultivate simple physical enjoyments and the inner life.

Lisca cites several places where specific passages of the *Tao* are echoed by Steinbeck and notes that there is even a similarity of linguistic expression. Doc becomes the symbolic Taoist sage, free of ambition and serving as a teacher and role model to the Cannery Row citizenry. He also adheres to the following Taoist principles: (1) by not believing people, you turn them into liars, (2) by analyzing all life, you can assure that there is no useless person, and (3) by looking at nature, you can come to know yourself.[18] In contrast to the tenets of the *Tao* is the evil that men bring upon themselves through greed, acquisitiveness, meanness, egotism, and self- interest. These are the elements which impede the Taoist faith. Like "is" thinking, Taoism does not desire to impose one standard on others or a single standard for all. Lisca notes that even Steinbeck's description of the stories oozing into the book by themselves becomes a moral statement since the *Tao Teh Ching* has no formal order either. Lisca concludes that *Cannery Row* has twin themes: an escape from both Western materialism and Western activism. Material success and rigid order and direction are rejected as the ultimate evidence of personal achievement. The passivity of Eastern philosophy, also stressed in *East of Eden,* is revealed as more valuable than the Western emphasis on acquisitiveness and aggression.[19]

Taoism is shown as valuing pastoral existence and praising primitive but comfortable marginal existence. Lao Tze's personal emphasis on contemplation in search of unity is also evident in *Cannery Row* through Doc's attempt to understand the beauty and horror of the drowned girl. The contention that there is order in great disorder and stability in irregular orbits is also reflected in the Lao Tze's text. This also brings to mind yet a more contemporary literary connection by suggesting Steinbeck's reliance on his American heritage: the independence and self-reliance valued by Ralph Waldo Emerson and the isolation and contemplation practiced by Henry David Thoreau.

In conclusion, accommodation and transformation seem to be goals of *Cannery Row.* Although love is portrayed as fragile and risky, there is no better way to become completely human and to see wholeness momentarily. Doc, the detached lonely observer of the good life, is pulled into the human commune by Mack and the boys, but as the insightful sage, he recognizes that pleasure is fleeting and that life is consistently a mixture of good and evil. The book's conclusion with Doc's paradoxical joy/sorrow is therefore appropriate to the reality of *Weltschmerz* (world sorrow). The individual who is truly in tune with his inner self acknowledges his own duality and the inevitability of a life intermixed with positives and negatives.

NOTES

1. John Steinbeck, *Steinbeck: A Life in Letters,* eds. Elaine Steinbeck and Robert Wallsten (New York: Viking Press, 1975), pp. 269-75.
2. *Ibid.,* pp. 268-69.
3. *Ibid.,* p. 273.
4. Jackson J. Benson, *The True Adventures of John Steinbeck, Writer* (New York: Viking Press, 1984), p. 553.
5. *Ibid.,* p. 543.
6. *Ibid.,* pp. 545-46.
7. *Ibid.,* p. 480.
8. John H. Timmerman, *John Steinbeck's Fiction: The Aesthetics of the Road Taken* (Norman: University of Oklahoma Press, 1986), p. 143.
9. Peter Lisca, *John Steinbeck: Nature and Myth* (New York: Thomas Y. Crowell, 1978), p. 115.
10. *Ibid.,* pp. 116-23.
11. John Steinbeck, *Cannery Row* (New York: Viking Penguin, 1986), p. 1. All further references will be inserted parenthetically in the text.
12. John Steinbeck, *The Log from the Sea of Cortez* (New York: Viking Press, 1951), p. 89. All further references will be inserted parenthetically in the text.
13. Peter Lisca, *The Wide World of John Steinbeck* (New Brunswick, New Jersey: Rutgers University Press, 1958), Chapter 11.
14. Timmerman, pp. 167-68.
15. See Charles Metzger in *A Study Guide to Steinbeck,* ed. Tetsumaro Hayashi (Metuchen, New Jersey: Scarecrow Press, 1974), pp. 21-26.

16. *Ibid.*, p. 23.
17. See Lisca, *John Steinbeck: Nature and Myth,* Chapter 6.
18. *Ibid.*, p. 120.
19. *Ibid.*, p. 123.

IV. TOPICS FOR RESEARCH AND DISCUSSION

(1) Explore the two sides of Doc. How is he loving/loveless, isolated/companionable, half-Christ/half-satyr?

(2) In what way does the image of the tide pool control the novel? How does the philosophy of the tide pool established by Steinbeck and Ricketts in *The Log from the Sea of Cortez* also pervade the text?

(3) What are some of the evidences in the novel that Steinbeck's own fear of fame and fortune slipped into his characters and plot? Discuss different ways in which *Cannery Row* deplores success and accomplishment.

(4) In what way does the gopher episode in Chapter 31 (the most disparate of the intercalary chapters) fit into the thematic plot of *Cannery Row?*

(5) What are some indications in *Cannery Row* that Steinbeck believes that only individual perspective determines good from evil in life? Cite instances where good motivates evil and vice versa.

(6) In what way do the deaths and tragedies on *Cannery Row* have something in common?

(7) What is the difference between the two parties staged for Doc? Are both successful? Do both have the same result? Are other parties in the novel also significant?

(8) What types of wit and humor add to comic elements of *Cannery Row?* Examine understatement, hyperbole, slapstick, verbal jibes, jokes, sarcastic remarks, and unexpected interjections.

(9) Examine the plight of the artist in *Cannery Row.* What is the problem with "creating" which is illustrated by the painter Henri, the flagpole skater, Blaisdell the poet, Josh Billings, and Steinbeck himself. List any others you might also include in your definition of artist.

(10) What recurring concerns are dealt with in *Cannery Row* that can be seen in other Steinbeck fiction? Some suggestions include retarded or abnormal characters, oppressive marriages, animal imagery, and Chinese philosophy.

(11)   What is the significance of "Black Marigolds" and its double reading in *Cannery Row*? How does the "text" offer parallels or contrasts to the message of the novel?

V. SELECTED BIBLIOGRAPHY

1.   Stanley Alexander, *"Cannery Row:* Steinbeck's Pastoral Poem," in *Steinbeck: A Collection of Critical Essays,* ed. Robert Murray Davis (Englewood Cliffs, New Jersey: Prentice-Hall, Inc., 1972). Alexander's essay draws attention to Steinbeck's use in the novel of a conventional genre known as pastoral— stressing a oneness with humanity itself and a oneness with forces in nature. The pastoral brings together the low man or peasant (unsophisticated) with the learned man of civilized society (sophisticated). Doc attempts to bridge both worlds: to create a unity of these two opposites. The tide pool as an analogy to the city of men is also developed as is the mind as both a conscious and unconscious interpreter of how disparity and disunity can be overcome.

2.   Joseph Fontenrose, *John Steinbeck: An Introduction and Interpretation* (New York: Barnes and Noble, 1963). Chapter 8, "The Moralities," identifies *Cannery Row* as a criticism of American culture and explains the principal mythical theme of the novel, the Logos. It is the Word made flesh, consisting of both Christian and pagan doctrine and used to interpret myths. Fontenrose sees Steinbeck using words to impose order on chaos; meanwhile his characters—Doc, Lee Chong, Dora, Mack and the boys—do the same in their respective niches in society. The importance of group organisms and ecology is also stressed as is the fact that idleness, creative activity, and fun are the only escapes or remedies from the acquisitive society.

3.   Warren French, *John Steinbeck,* 2nd edition (Boston: Twayne, 1975). Chapter 8, *"Cannery Row* and Transcendent Man," compares the structure of the novel to the pattern of a wave that grows slowly, hits a reef or barrier, divides, and crashes at last with thunderous strength on a beach. French suggests a pattern for the interchapters, a pairing of associations and contrasts, and also reveals the subject matter of a deleted interchapter, 'How the Wolves Ate the Vice Principal." French ultimately sees the novel as a defense of art, poetry, and music, and as a method of coping with all of life, not just the challenge and horror of war.

4. Maxine Knox and Mary Rodriguez, *Steinbeck's Street: "Cannery Row"* (San Rafael, CA: Presidio Press, 1980). A pictorial commentary on the Row's beginning, past, and present, this book also provides a listing of places to see on a visit to Monterey and then identifies corresponding settings in the novel. The photographs will help students visualize the Row and recreate the mood Steinbeck tries to establish in words.

5. Howard Levant, *The Novels of John Steinbeck: A Critical Study* (Columbia, Missouri: University of Missouri Press, 1974). Chapter 6, "Is Thinking," presents the most thorough cultural explanation of Steinbeck's non-teleological philosophy. Praising the enormous freedom in narration, Levant labels *Cannery Row* a delightful and entertaining novel whose panoramic structure combines with a specific theme to give the work drive and buoyancy. Levant also lauds the linguistic magic of Steinbeck and nominates love as the central image which controls the text. Basically a critic of Steinbeck's structural deficiencies, Levant sees *Cannery Row* as a success because the usual contrived plot is lost, leaving a relaxed narrative which evidences "the creative depth and force of Steinbeck's future power."

6. Peter Lisca, *John Steinbeck: Nature and Myth* (New York: Thomas Y. Crowell, 1978). Chapter 6, "Varieties of Adjustment," is most helpful in understanding *Cannery Row*'s relationship to the *Tao Teh Ching* of Lao Tze, a Chinese philosopher of the sixth century B. C. The parallels are informative as Lisca concludes that the twin themes of *Cannery Row* are the escape from Western material values—the necessity to "succeed" in the world—and the escape from Western activism—the necessity to impose order or direction.

7. Peter Lisca, *The Wide World of John Steinbeck* (New Brunswick, New Jersey: Rutgers University Press, 1958). Chapter 11, *"Cannery Row,"* denies that *Cannery Row* is in any way a mere repetition of *Tortilla Flat,* although both advocate individual freedom and personal integrity. Lisca discusses the biological parallels of the tide pool, delineating the difference between parasitic and commensal relationships and explaining the analogy to business and nature. The structure, complete with the digressions of the intercalary chapters, is shown as a pattern of comparisons and contrasts, parallels and allegories. Lisca concludes that even in the face of mutability, time, and death, *Cannery Row* demonstrates a reverence for life complete with its loneliness.

8. Stoddard Martin, *California Writers* (New York: St. Martin's

Press, 1983). Chapter 3, "John Steinbeck," offers an analysis which takes into account Steinbeck's own history during the writing of *Cannery Row,* centering specifically on his mental distress based on his second wife's disapproval of his nonconformist friends and his work. Martin also draws parallels to earlier Steinbeck works such as *Tortilla Flat* and *In Dubious Battle,* but concludes that in *Cannery Row* Steinbeck is "sure of his art but no longer sure of his purpose" and that he just barely avoids turning into a posturing, insincere crowd-pleaser.

9. Paul McCarthy, *John Steinbeck* (New York: Frederick Ungar, 1980). In Chapter 5, "Wartime Heroes and Communities," McCarthy attempts to place *Cannery Row* in the historical tradition of Romantic and Western fiction. Thematic contrasts and organic development of the work are examined as elements of control in Steinbeck's loose-woven structure, and McCarthy also spends time analyzing the use of satire and irony in the work. The chapter closes by examining the importance of understanding and integrating opposites and by asserting the role of art in attaining peace and completeness.

10. Louis Owens, *John Steinbeck's Re-Vision of America* (Athens: University of Georgia Press, 1985). *"Cannery Row:* An Essay in Loneliness" appears in Owens's Section III dealing with books from Steinbeck's canon which rely on the sea. The emphasis here is on twin peepholes—different ways of seeing the aloneness so evident in the novel. The chapter also tries to relate the novel to Ed Ricketts, Steinbeck's friend and a model for Doc, and his collaboration with Steinbeck on *The Log from the Sea of Cortez.* Finally, Owens notes the ambivalence of receiving a wholeness of vision while at the same time under standing one's essential apartness and a sense of not belonging.

11. John H. Timmerman, *John Steinbeck's Fiction: The Aesthetics of the Road Taken* (Norman: University of Oklahoma Press, 1986). Chapter 6, "Angels in Midheaven: The *Cannery Row* Novels," offers a competent physical description of the area covered in the novels. Labeling the novel as modern tragic-comedy, Timmerman suggests the symbiosis of tears of laughter and tears of sorrow and speculates that the fear of loneliness dominates all three Row novels. The tone of *Cannery Row* is described as fun riddled with horror, a darker view of the heart of man and his agony. Man versus civilization is asserted on the thematic concern of *Cannery Row,* and Timmerman explores three separate levels on which it works.

3.   STEINBECK'S *EAST OF EDEN* (1952)

LOUIS OWENS

I. BACKGROUND

For John Steinbeck *East of Eden* was "the book," the one for which he had been practicing all of his life. "I have written each book as an exercise," he told his publisher-editor, Pat Covici, "as practice for the one to come. And this is the one to come. There is nothing beyond this book—nothing follows it. It must contain all in the world I know and it must have everything in it of which I am capable."[1] *East of Eden* is, in fact, Steinbeck's most ambitious and complex undertaking, a novel that had long been gestating. As early as 1944, Steinbeck had written from his home in New York to his close friend Carlton A. Sheffield to say, "Within a year or so I want to get to work on a very large book I've been thinking about for at least two years and a half. Everything else is kind of marking time."[2] Before he could get to work on this "very large book," however, Steinbeck's life would change dramatically, the most drastic alterations coming in the death of his closest friend, Edward F. Ricketts, on May 11, 1948, followed within three months by the disintegration of his second marriage.

The death of Ricketts, the model for "Doc" figures in *Cannery Row, Sweet Thursday, In Dubious Battle,* and "The Snake," shook Steinbeck deeply, causing him to write that "The death of Ed Ricketts changed many things. . . . I am having to do a reorganization job with myself."[3] The divorce from his second wife, Gwyn Conger, also came as a devastating blow. As a result, in September of 1948 Steinbeck found himself back in California in the tiny Pacific Grove cottage where, supported by a $25-a-month stipend from his father, he had begun his writing career long before. Within a few months, however, he would be ready to begin writing the book he thought of first as "The Salinas Valley," announcing to a friend that he is about to "start on my long novel for which I have been practicing so long. And in that time I'm going to put on the crown of my life and no one is going to take it off until that work is done."[4] To American novelist John O'Hara he wrote, "I've been practicing for a book for 35 years and this is it. I don't see how it can be popular because I am inventing method and form and tone and context."[5]

East of Eden, in combination with its companion volume, *Journal of a Novel: The "East of Eden" Letters,* represents the greatest challenge facing the critic who would come to terms with Steinbeck's achievement as an artist. Written daily as a warm-up to his work on his novel, the *East of Eden* letters were addressed to Covici but not to be read until, after the novel's completion, they were delivered to the editor in a talismanic box hand-carved by Steinbeck. The letters help to illuminate a crucial element in *East of Eden*—the thread of self-reflection, or self-consciousness, that unifies the sprawling work from first line to last—and they testify again and again to the intensity with which Steinbeck approached this novel. "This is my most complicated and at the same time, my most simple sounding book," Steinbeck wrote in the letters, claiming "you have to look closely to see the innovations even though there are many." Steinbeck anticipated unfavorable critical responses to his innovations, predicting: "But oh! Jesus am I going to catch critical hell for it. My carefully worked out method will be jumped on by the not too careful critic as slipshod. For it is not an easy form to come on quickly nor to understand immediately."[6]

To ensure accuracy in this epic-length novel set amidst what has come to be called "Steinbeck Country," Steinbeck undertook painstaking historical research, writing to Paul Caswell, editor of the *Salinas-Californian:*

> I am gathering material for a novel, the setting of which is to be the region between San Luis Obispo and Santa Cruz, particularly the Salinas Valley; the time, between 1900 and the present.

>An exceedingly important part of the research necessary will involve the files of the Salinas papers; will it be possible for me to consult these files?[7]

A month later, having moved briefly back to Monterey, California, Steinbeck wrote to Caswell again to request more background information:

>editorials on subjects of either momentary or permanent interest, advertising of foods, clothing at intervals of say every six months. Personals and back page country news. A sampling of this sort of thing would be very valuable to me. . . . It will not only make my work much easier but will greatly increase its accuracy and perhaps its sound of reality and verisimilitude.[8]

Soon, he was again writing to request "modern detail maps of the county—maps with place names as well as contours."[9]

As he labored to ensure verisimilitude in the details of his fiction, not only researching newspaper files but also calling upon relatives for family history, Steinbeck simultaneously worked consciously within two less concrete realms: those of allegory and self-consciousness. The allegorical framework of *East of Eden,* the novel's Trask narrative, owes much to another sprawling allegory of a struggle between good and evil: Herman Melville's *Moby-Dick.* "I remember a friend of my father's," Steinbeck writes in the *Journal* letters, ". . . a whaling master named Captain Trask. I have always loved the name. It meant great romance to me."[10] From a whaling captain named Trask, it is but a short leap of imagination to a Calvinistic captain named Ahab, and the *Journal* letters make it obvious that Steinbeck saw parallels between the two works. "I believe that Moby Dick," Steinbeck writes, "so much admired now, did not sell its first small edition in ten years. And it will be worse than that with this book."[11] The self-reflexive element in the novel is repeatedly underscored in the *Journal* letters' obsession with the tools, circumstances, and processes of writing fiction. Again and again, Steinbeck worries about the subject of invention, writing to Covici at one point: "I know you make fun of my inventions and my designs. But they are the same thing as writing. I come from a long line of inventors. This is in my blood. We are improvisors and will continue to be."[12]

Though he frequently despaired of readers' willingness or ability to penetrate the complexities of *East of Eden*, Steinbeck never wavered in his faith in this novel. "I stay fascinated with *East of Eden*," he declared to his agent, Elizabeth Otis.[13] Shortly before completing the first draft of the novel, he complained to Covici that "it has things in it which will probably never come out because readers do not inspect very closely. . . . The hell with it."[14] In the *Journal*, he wrote, "I know it is the best book I have ever done."[15] And finally, after completing the novel, he wrote to a friend: "I finished my book a week ago. . . . Much the longest and surely the most difficult work I have ever done. . . . I have put all the things I have wanted to write all my life. This is 'the book.' "[16]

Though he expected the book to be a failure, much to Steinbeck's surprise, *East of Eden* was soon heading best-seller lists in the United States. Less surprising to Steinbeck, perhaps, was the general attack upon the book by critics who promptly declared that while the novel might be a popular success, it was an artistic failure.

II. PLOT SYNOPSIS

PART ONE

East of Eden begins with a description of the Salinas Valley given through the memory of the narrator. In this crucial introductory description, the narrative voice lays out the symbolic terrain of the valley, with the Gabilan Mountains to the east identified in a childish imagination with life and sunrise, and the Santa Lucia Mountains to the west identified with death and the end of the day. The valley's place names are introduced, as well as the periodic droughts. The second chapter introduces the narrator's memories of his mother's family, the Hamiltons, and ends with a single-line introduction of Adam Trask. Next, the narrative focuses upon Adam's father, Cyrus, and the boyhood of Adam and Charles Trask. We learn that Cyrus has rejected Charles's birthday present

while embracing Adam's present, an allusion to the Cain-and-
Abel story and a foreshadowing of Adam's later rejection of
Cal's present and acceptance of Aron's. Charles beats Adam
brutally. Adam enters the military. The focus shifts from
Trask to Hamilton narratives, describing the thriving Hamilton dynasty in the bone-dry Gabilans and Samuel's inventiveness. After another narrative shift, we learn of Charles's
solitude, Adam's discharge and re-enlistment, and Adam's
visit to his father in Washington. Adam is discharged a second
time from the army, and as he travels through the South, he is
jailed for vagrancy. When he escapes and comes home, he
finds his father has died, leaving a large and perhaps tainted
inheritance to his sons. Cathy Ames is introduced with the
narrator's declaration, "I believe there are monsters born in
the world. . . ." Cathy murders her parents, becomes a
prostitute, and is beaten nearly to death by the "whore-
master," Edwards. Adam and Charles begin quarreling on the
little farm and Adam wanders off on random trips across the
country. When Adam returns, Cathy crawls to the Trask door
after her beating by Edwards and is taken in against Charles's
objections. Part One of the novel ends with Cathy in control
of the gullible Adam and sleeping with Charles.

PART TWO

The narrator begins this second book of the novel by
addressing the reader directly: "You can see how this book
has reached a great boundary that was called 1900." The
narrative voice quickly surveys the pulse of the country
before going on to introduce Adam Trask's new life with
Cathy in California, where Adam buys an idyllic farm and
contracts with Samuel Hamilton to have a well drilled. The
narrator describes Olive Hamilton, John Steinbeck's mother,
and the notorious airplane ride which Steinbeck predicted
would upset critics. Adam attempts to create his own version
of Eden on the Salinas Valley ranch, Cathy's pregnancy
advances, and Lee Chong meets Samuel Hamilton. Samuel is
disturbed by Cathy and recalls a childhood scene in which a
murderer was hanged in Ireland. A crucial moment in the

novel, Chapter 17 begins with the narrator's equivocation as to Cathy's true nature, reminding us to read the "small print" and "footnotes" of the text. The twins are born, "Each one born separate in his own sack," and Liza comes to take care of the babies for a week. The chapter ends with Cathy shooting Adam and abandoning both husband and infants. In the next chapter Horace Quinn, the deputy sheriff of King City, investigates the shooting, discovers that Cathy is working in Salinas as a prostitute, and determines, along with the sheriff in Salinas, to keep the fact a secret. The narrator provides a quick overview of prostitution in the area and introduces Cathy in her new role as Kate in Faye's brothel. Kate quickly gains control over Faye, murders Faye, and inherits the brothel. Another pivotal moment in the novel, the final chapter in Part Two shows Adam's disintegration following Cathy's departure and brings Samuel down from the hills to name the twins. At the core of the chapter is Lee Chong's interpretation of the Cain and Abel story, which lays out the allegorical pattern of dualistic thinking that the novel is designed to repudiate.

PART THREE

This third book begins with an overview of the Hamilton clan, including Una's death, and Samuel's "retirement" from the Gabilan homestead, a poignant moment that leaves Tom Hamilton alone at the ranch. Samuel comes to the Trask home for a final visit and provides Steinbeck the opportunity to introduce the Hebrew word *timshel,* which Lee interprets as "Thou mayest," an interpretation that nullifies predestination, a cornerstone of Calvinist thought, and thus the possibility of "bad blood" that torments Cal. Samuel's funeral takes place and Adam confronts Kate in her brothel. Lee announces his plans to open a bookstore in San Francisco. Cal and Aron meet Abra for the first time, and we see striking differences in the boys' personalities. Lee tells the horrifying story of his own birth. Comic relief occurs when Adam buys a new car. Adam learns of Charles's death and Cal prays to be good "like Aron." Adam informs Kate of her inheritance from Charles and then drops in for a visit with the Steinbeck family, including little Johnny Steinbeck peeking around his mother's skirts at Adam, the character whom he will later create in the novel we are reading. Dessie returns to the Hamilton ranch to live with her brother, Tom, and Chapter 33 includes both Dessie's death and Tom's suicide, the final notes in Part Three.

PART FOUR

Steinbeck begins this section of the novel with a first-person reflection upon the "one story in the world," then moves the Trask family to Salinas from the valley ranch. Lee leaves for San Francisco but soon returns because of "loneliness." Cal and Aron go to school, and Aron's romance with Abra grows. Adam attempts the experiment of shipping lettuce to the East and loses most of his fortune. Cal learns about Kate's house and questions Lee about his mother. Lee replies that "There is something that she lacks," and refuses to let Cal believe he has inherited his mother's badness. Cal begins to follow Kate and finally talks with her, saying "I was afraid I had you in me." Kate is blackmailed by Ethel and, beginning to panic, builds the gray lean-to as a retreat from the world. Cal invests in beans with Will Hamilton, and the U.S. enters World War I. Aron enters Stanford, and Abra becomes closer to Lee and Cal. Kate's arthritis and paranoia both worsen, and she sends Joe in pursuit of Ethel with the result that Joe decides to extort money from Kate. The narrator breaks into the flow of narrative to tell the reader about the general response to the war, including John Steinbeck's taunting of a neighbor of German ancestry. Adam suffers from his role on the draft board. Cal attempts to give Adam the money Cal has made with the bean crop, but Adam refuses the money angrily. Humiliated and rejected, Cal takes Aron to see Kate, with the result that Aron enlists and goes off to war. Kate commits suicide, and Joe is killed while resisting arrest. Aron is killed in the war, and Adam suffers a stroke upon receiving the news. At Lee's insistence, Adam forgives Cal, and on that note of resolution the novel ends.

III. CRITICAL EXPLICATION

CAIN AND ABEL—GOOD AND EVIL

It is difficult, if not impossible, for any reader to mistake the overarching allegory of light and dark, good and evil, that dominates the surface structure of *East of Eden*. Structurally, the novel forms a kind of dialectic, moving as it does between the paired narratives of Trask and Hamilton. Within the Trask narrative appears a sharper duality: the opposed "goodness" of Adam Trask and "badness" of Cathy/Kate. Surrounding this binary center are dual clusters of "C" and "A" characters, with "C" characters seemingly associated with the fallen state of Cathy Trask, and "A" characters partaking of Adam's goodness. Thus Cyrus and Charles Trask are convincingly "bad" in contrast to Adam, while Cal Trask also seems marked with that character tendency. Aron, on the other hand, and Abra are clearly associated with what is considered "good." Charles and Cathy are marked like Cain, and both mimic the crime of Cain by attacking and nearly killing Adam.

Steinbeck, who briefly considered the title "Canable" for this novel,[17] uses the Cain-and-Abel story to form a crude framework for *East of Eden*. At the core of this heavy allegory lies Lee Chong's definition of the Hebrew word *timshel:* thou mayest. The simple message is that while we may indeed all be children of Cain inhabiting a fallen world to the east of Eden, we all are given, like Cal Trask, the freedom of choosing to do good or evil. The Calvinistic sense of inherent depravity from which Cal suffers, and which the novel's dualism seems to reinforce, is overturned through Lee's definition, and we are all given responsibility for our own destinies.

Through Cathy and Adam, Steinbeck illustrates the belief that a refusal to accept responsibility for our complete self—that is, to recognize our potential for both good and evil—is dangerously delusive. Adam's absolute denial of evil, in Cathy or anywhere else, nearly destroys Adam as well as his twin sons. Cathy's refusal to see what is good is even more destructive. Steinbeck's uncomplicated message here is that we must all be like Ishmael in Herman Melville's *Moby-Dick,* the "balanced man" who perceives good as well as evil. He or she who accepts the fallen state—the Ishmael who embraces full knowledge—has the potential to survive in this world and, perhaps, to grow to greatness. Samuel Hamilton is such a man, and Cal Trask is becoming one. He or she who does not attain this fullness of vision will perish, literally and/or spiritually.

If this allegory in broad brush strokes, with its at-best unchallenging and heavily didactic message, were all that Steinbeck accomplished in this novel, *East of Eden* would be an eminently forgettable work. A great deal more, however, is at stake within this novel, and a closer scrutiny can illuminate beneath the surface of this simple-seeming allegory a sophisticated and fascinating text.

A way of profitably approaching *East of Eden* is to see the characters of Cathy Trask and Samuel Hamilton as two poles around which the novel revolves and takes form. Both Cathy and Samuel evolve within the course of the novel, and their paired evolutions may serve as indices to the evolving consciousness of the author who is both creator and participant in the dynamics of the text. The Russian critic Mikhail Bakhtin has written that the "form of a poetic work is determined . . . in many of its factors by how the author perceives its hero. . . ."[18] While neither Samuel nor Cathy exhibits the potential for meaningful change or loss usually reserved for the modern protagonist—even in naturalistic fiction—together they serve nonetheless as the bipartite "organizational centers" for their novel and thus play large roles in determining the dialectical form of the work as a whole.

Of his problematic villain in *East of Eden,* Steinbeck wrote in the early pages of *Journal of a Novel,* "And Cathy is going to worry a lot of children and a lot of parents about their children but I have been perfectly honest about her and I certainly have her prototype."[19] It may be that Cathy has worried more critics than she has parents or children. Joseph Fontenrose was one of the earliest critics to be troubled by Cathy, raising questions about her apparent lack of free will in a novel that argues "thou mayest."[20] To this concern for an apparent inconsistency in Steinbeck's conception of Cathy, we can add a second major anguish of critics, one including

Samuel and one Steinbeck himself clearly anticipated. Critics would complain about the book's two-part structure, he predicted, putting the words in the mouth of a hypothetical editor: "The book is out of balance," Steinbeck's invented editor complains. "The reader expects one thing and you give him something else. You have written two books and stuck them together."[21] Steinbeck was prophetic as usual. While a few perceptive critics have defended *East of Eden* and argued for a more careful reading, many more have despaired over Cathy's inconsistency of characterization and lamented the structural failure of the novel.

Much of Steinbeck's life and family history went into *East of Eden,* not merely in the Hamilton episodes taken from family stories but also in the intense effort to come to terms with the nature of good and evil, the painful investigation of fathers and sons, and the exploration of place. That *East of Eden* took form in part out of Steinbeck's attempts to deal with personal trauma—most especially the divorce from his second wife—was suggested by John Ditsky in his seminal study of the novel, *Essays on "East of Eden,"* in which Ditsky wrote that the novel might be "an act of exorcism of private poisons." Ditsky also leads us toward a much more crucial element in *East of Eden* when he says, "It takes no stretching of the point to conclude that for Steinbeck, this most planned of his novels is most genuinely his portrait of the artist as a mature man."[22] For, beyond Steinbeck's allegorical worrying of the Cain and Abel myth, beyond his lifelong fascination with the American myth, beyond his lengthy laying to rest of private ghosts is what I believe to be a much more intriguing dimension to this novel: that of self-consciousness and invention. More than anything else, *East of Eden* is a novel about its own creation, with the authorial consciousness peering at us through the text like the palimpsest on Sweetheart's bumper in *The Wayward Bus.*

It takes no stretching of the critical imagination to see that as he increasingly used the letters in the *East of Eden* journal as mirrors for the daily process of creation, Steinbeck became more and more interested not merely in the conventional process of plot and character generation but rather in the workings of the fiction-making consciousness reflected

back from the journal pages *facing* the novel. Reacting to a
troubling element many critics have felt in this novel, Steinbeck's biographer, Jackson J. Benson, suggests that when
Steinbeck tries "to use a strong plot, as in *East of Eden,* the
novel becomes very labored and one has the feeling constantly that he is following a plot reluctantly. . . ."[23] The
labored feeling that critics have reacted to may well arise from
the fact that, as he became immersed in the creation of what
he considered his greatest work, the plot of *East of Eden* came
to mean less and less to its author, becoming primarily a
device through which the fictionalizing impulse might be
explored and illuminated. Thus, the labored feeling may exist
only for those of us who insist on reading *East of Eden* as a
conventional novel, while ignoring the more exciting dimension of the author's involvement in the novel. The insistence
throughout the *East of Eden* letters that this would be his
"most complicated and at the same time . . . most simple
sounding book" and that "you have to look closely to see the
innovations even though there are many" and that it "took
three years of puzzled thinking to work out this plan for a
book"[24] all suggest that much more is at stake than a mere
allegorical rendering of a too-obvious moral laid out in a
ponderous plot. The "great covered thing" and the "carefully
worked out method" that Steinbeck predicted critics would
fail to see, that would not be "an easy form to come on quickly
nor to understand immediately," may well be this self-
reflexive element.

In the opening paragraphs of *East of Eden,* Steinbeck
carefully establishes both his setting and the novel's dialectic
as he describes the Salinas Valley and the opposing ranges of
the Gabilan and Santa Lucia Mountains:

> I remember that the Gabilan Mountains to the east of the
> valley were light gay mountains full of sun and loveliness and
> a kind of invitation, so that you wanted to climb into their
> warm foothills almost as you wanted to climb into the lap of a
> beloved mother. They were beckoning mountains with a
> brown grass love. The Santa Lucias stood up against the sky to
> the west and kept the valley from the open sea, and they were
> dark and brooding—unfriendly and dangerous. I always found
> in myself a dread of west and a love of east. Where I ever got

such an idea I cannot say, unless it could be that the morning
came over the peaks of the Gabilans and the night drifted
back from the ridges of the Santa Lucias. It may be that the
birth and death of the day had some part in my feeling about
the two ranges of mountains.[25]

A key to how we should read *East of Eden* is found in this
paragraph in which Steinbeck begins with his usual method of
carefully establishing setting before introducing characters,
but in which he also deftly moves from setting to symbol,
from nature to narrative consciousness. In describing the
metaphorical roles of these mountains of light and darkness in
his mind as a child, Steinbeck introduces the good-and-evil
duality upon which the more obvious element of the plot will
be constructed. At the same time, Steinbeck subtly introduces a self-conscious element as he shows us how this sense
of opposed absolutes arises from a sensitive imagination's
engagement with landscape.

From place, the microcosmic Salinas Valley, Steinbeck
moves rapidly in the opening pages to introduce his mother's
family, the Hamiltons, out of whom the creative source of the
novel—John Steinbeck—springs. Samuel, *East of Eden*'s epic-
sized hero, seems to have been modeled for the most part
upon Steinbeck's grandfather of the same name, a farmer,
storyteller, and ingenious inventor who had homesteaded a
ranch in the Gabilan Mountains an hour's drive south of
Salinas. Samuel, who drills wells and dreams of blasting
through the valley's hardpan to free the trapped waters, is the
novel's fisher king and artist, a Daedalian artificer who stands
at his anvil forging art from words as well as wood and metal.
In the course of "inventing method and form and tone" for
this novel, and in the process of re-imagining his fictional
grandfather, Steinbeck seems to have identified closely with
the inventive Samuel. Surely Samuel looms large in the
author's thoughts when Steinbeck writes to Covici to say, "I
know you make fun of my inventions and my designs. But
they are the same thing as writing. I come from a long line of
inventors."[26]

Once the dualism at the heart of the novel has been
deftly introduced in the opening chapter, Steinbeck brings in

the whole Hamilton clan in the second chapter with the autobiographical statement, "I must depend upon hearsay, old photographs . . ." (5). With the appearance of the Hamiltons, Steinbeck has introduced the soil from which the creative consciousness of the novel will grow. Following the introduction of the Hamiltons, Steinbeck must create the fictional superstructure that will make this the story of America, and out of this need the Trask narrative evolves.

Since Steinbeck knew with such certainty that his divided plot stream would be labeled a structural flaw, why did he create it? Why, since chapters focusing upon the Hamiltons constitute less than ten percent of the entire novel, did he insist upon including the Hamiltons? The contrast in pace and color offered by the Hamilton narrative is minimal and disappears entirely in the fourth book of the novel. Whatever contrast in pace and color exists in the final book comes only through Steinbeck's authorial participation as he tells us what he believes, what the collective "we" felt about the war, and how "we" responded to the war along with the Trasks.

It may be that Steinbeck took the risk he did with the Hamiltons out of a perceived need to keep the reader fully aware, throughout the novel, of the so-called "real" world out of which his fiction grows, and at the same time to illuminate the imaginative subsoil from which the novelist's creative impulse springs. "In fact," Steinbeck told Covici, "all of the Hamilton stories are true."[27] The one Hamilton who slips away from the "real," however, is Samuel. In Samuel, the Hamiltons produce their one figure of suspect reality, a larger-than-life patriarch with shining aura, a flawed man so good he tips the scale.

The reason for Samuel's growth toward Trasklike symbolhood is precisely Samuel's growing involvement in the Trask narrative in which Steinbeck is operating in the realm of allegory, with very little concern for making his symbol-people believable. What, in an earlier reference to his short fiction, Steinbeck called the "stream underneath" is all that counts in this portion of the novel, and with the Trasks—the story of the pre-lapsarian Adam and very fallen Eve—the stream flows rapidly above the surface of the story itself. When Samuel becomes involved with Adam Trask, Samuel

immediately begins to grow beyond the dimensions of Steinbeck's remembered grandfather to fill a vacuum in the larger
story—he grows into the heroic dimensions required to fill
the need for a non-teleological visionary and balanced man.
One could say that Samuel is shanghaied from the autobiographical Hamilton narrative and forced to ship out as a
fictional conscript aboard the allegorical Trask vehicle, a
modern Ishmael whose job it is to see both good and evil in
the "valley of the world," as Steinbeck called the Salinas
Valley. And Samuel's metamorphosis may well be neither
accidental nor meant to go unnoticed. Evidence in the novel
suggests that Steinbeck intends for his readers to note
Samuel's movement away from biography toward fiction. For
in Samuel's metamorphosis we are allowed to see the free
inventive play of the author's imagination.

Samuel's transformation from remembered grandfather
to fictional creation is highlighted for the reader in Steinbeck's treatment of Samuel's supposed long-lost love back in
Ireland. In the beginning pages of the novel, as he pretends to
be working in the non-fictional realm of remembrance,
Steinbeck tells us of his grandfather's past, saying, "There was
a whisper—not even a rumor but rather an unsaid feeling—in
my family that it was love that drove him out [of Ireland], and
not love of the wife he married. But whether it was too
successful love or whether he left in pique at unsuccessful
love, *I do not know*" (6, my italics). Steinbeck follows this with
the declaration, "I think there must have been some other girl
printed somewhere in his heart, for he was a man of love and
his wife was not a woman to show her feelings" (6). By
Chapter 24, Steinbeck has allowed that early conjecture, and
the character called Samuel, to evolve to the point that
Samuel is able to tell Adam of the vision of love that has come
to him "night after month after year, right to the very now,"
adding, "And I think I should have double-bolted my mind
and sealed off my heart against her, but I did not. All of these
years I've cheated Liza . . ." (263). Obviously, Samuel's
confession of a long-lost love has grown slowly and surely
from the author's words uttered three hundred pages earlier:
"I think there must have been some other girl printed
somewhere in his heart. . . ." Steinbeck is demonstrating his

freedom to re-imagine his grandfather, and we should note the fact that the other girl is "printed" in Samuel's heart, for that is precisely how the "girl" gets there—she is printed in Steinbeck's prose.

The contour maps Steinbeck consulted in his research for this novel show the "real" Salinas Valley, those geological features that precede human inhabitation and provide the foundation for the mind's imaginative encounter with landscape. Superimposed upon the undulating landscape lines of such maps, however, are evidences of humanity's own patterned reality found in such place names as Paraiso, or Corral de Tierra, or Salinas. Similarly, Steinbeck's maternal grandfather served as the ground for Steinbeck's imaginative invention called Samuel Hamilton. And in the character of Samuel, Steinbeck is demonstrating the way in which fiction grows out of the real. What happens to Samuel is that he is contaminated by the fictional Trask narrative and its demands in a way the other Hamiltons are not. And by repeatedly entering the text to remind us of the creative process, Steinbeck attempts to ensure that we are aware of this process taking place.

Just before he introduces Samuel to Adam Trask, Steinbeck begins his chapter with a sermon on the freedom essential to the creative mind: "And this I believe," he writes, "that the free, exploring mind of the individual human is the most valuable thing in the world. And this I would fight for: the freedom of the mind to take any direction it wishes, undirected" (114). Here, Steinbeck seems to be defending the unorthodox methods of his novel and anticipating the new direction the character of Samuel will take as the author's "free, exploring mind" learns more about this character while it simultaneously explores the conflict between good and evil, between self-imposed blindness and the human need to attain full knowledge. Samuel becomes the highly charged point of contact between autobiography and fiction, a role most appropriate to the eloquent artificer and teller of tales at his forge. In this role, Samuel becomes a proto-Daedalus, from whom John Steinbeck, the artificer of this amazing novel, will descend.

Throughout the novel, Steinbeck breaks into his narrative to remind us of his authorial presence, addressing his reader directly, as when he writes, "You can see how this book has reached a great boundary that was called 1900" (111); or ruminating upon those beliefs he holds most dear; or mimicking the collective voice of the nation; or analyzing his characters and then coming back to qualify and contradict himself. To introduce Horace Quinn's role in the Trask narrative, for example, Steinbeck enters the story, saying, "We could not imagine anyone else being sheriff," and later, as Cal prepares to take Abra on their important picnic, Steinbeck adds, "We knew—or at least we were confident—that on May Day, when all the Sunday School picnics took place in Alisal, the wild azaleas that grew in the skirts of the streams would be in bloom" (520). By this point, near the end of the novel, autobiography and fictional narrative have merged completely, with the authorial voice joining the authorial constructs as a participant—a character—within the fiction. Cal and Abra and Johnny Steinbeck have attained equal existence within the realm of the fictive.

Counterpointed against the re-imagined Samuel is the fully invented Cathy, who comes replete with difficulties. Is Cathy (C.A.T.) a genetically misshapen monster predetermined to be evil because of something she lacks? (Perhaps a product of Steinbeck's pondering upon what he believed to be the cruelty of his second wife.) Or is she more psychologically and aesthetically complex than this? Cathy's obsession with the Wonderland Alice, who can escape through the looking glass of her own reflection into an imagined world where words mean just what we want them to mean, suggests that Steinbeck, mirroring himself in the pages of his journal, as he re-imagined his own world in the novel, may have recognized something of himself in the character he was in the process of creating. Regardless of prototypes in Steinbeck's real life, Cathy Ames Trask could only spring ultimately from the mind of her author, and the authorial voice in *East of Eden* seems both aware of this and eager to make certain that his readers are aware of it.

When he introduces Cathy, Steinbeck tells us that she is a monster, a naturalistic accident. In this reading of his inherently depraved creation, Steinbeck declares, "I believe there are monsters born in the world . . ." (62). Later, the author qualifies this unequivocal position, writing: "It doesn't matter that Cathy was what I have called a monster . . ." (114). In the opening line of *The Log from the Sea of Cortez,* Steinbeck and Ricketts declare, "The design of a book is the pattern of a reality controlled and shaped by the mind of the writer." The patterned reality of *East of Eden* changes significantly when, in his final direct address to the reader upon the subject of Cathy, the author confesses: "When I said Cathy was a monster it seemed to me that it was so. Now I have bent close with a glass over the small print of her and reread the footnotes, and I wonder if it was true" (162). With this intratextual involvement, Steinbeck is bending closely over the pattern and print of his own evolving authorial conscious- ness within the novel. He is pointedly reminding us of what we often forget in our own interaction with fiction: that to write is to learn, that every work of fiction is not merely the writing of a story, but "the story of a writing." We write in order to make the world coherent and meaningful through the act of articulation. With this allusion to the "small print" and footnotes of his character, Steinbeck is reminding us that Cathy is made of words, that she has existence only on the page and within the consciousness of the author. Cathy is, to use a term from Bakhtin, a "character zone."[28]

In his introduction of Cathy, Steinbeck also rather subtly shows us the process through which a fictional creation takes form. At the beginning of Chapter 8, the authorial voice not only declares that there are "monsters born in the world" but provides the first description of Cathy:

> Her nose was delicate and thin, and her cheekbones high and wide, sweeping down to a small chin so that her face was heart-shaped. Her mouth was well shaped and well lipped but abnormally small. . . . Her ears were very little, without lobes, and they pressed so close to her head that even with her hair combed up they made no silhouette. They were thin flaps sealed against her head.

Cathy's resemblance to a serpent can't be missed in this description, and Steinbeck adds: "Her feet were small and round and stubby, with fat insteps almost like little hoofs"

(63-64). In this rather unsubtle description, Steinbeck is demonstrating the way in which a character's form grows quite clearly out of the author's conception of that character. The authorial voice has told us that it believes in monsters and that Cathy is a monster. Because at this point in the novel the author conceives of Cathy as predetermined to evil, she assumes a snakelike and Satanic form.

In the course of *East of Eden,* Cathy Trask evolves as her author's conception of her changes. From a flat, predetermined "monster," Cathy becomes a psychologically convincing character tortured by a paranoia that grows throughout her life, driving her farther and farther from humanity until she ends in the dark cave of her tortured consciousness. When we look back upon Cathy from the vantage point of the novel's end, we can see her not as a "misshapen monster" but as a terribly warped child and woman using what she perceives to be her only weapon—her sexuality—to defend herself, often viciously, from what she perceives to be a domineering and threatening masculine world. When Adam tries to imprison Cathy within the rigid perfection of his self-conceived Eden, Cathy recognizes Adam's trap: he would force her to play the reductive role of unfallen Eve within a garden constructed entirely out of Adam's masculine imagination. Throughout his fiction, most directly in the stories of *The Long Valley,* Steinbeck writes of women imprisoned within such gardens—women such as Elisa Allen in "The Chrysanthemums," the Hawkins sisters in "Johnny Bear," and Mary Teller in "The White Quail." Elisa sublimates her frustration—at least partially—with flowers, Amy Hawkins kills herself, and Mary Teller constructs her own garden (appropriating the masculine trope) and turns it against her husband; but Cathy Trask can think only of escape and empowerment. Once free of Adam, Cathy—a frightening psychopath—turns sexuality against men in horrifyingly effective fashion as proprietress of a brutal whorehouse (an anti-garden within the tropology of the Eden myth).

Steinbeck depicts Cathy's paranoia as accompanied by a growing sense of her inability to control her life and world, a loss of control symbolized by her increasingly deformed and useless hands (contrast them with the perfect, controlling hands of Slim, the "godlike" skinner in *Of Mice and Men*). Simultaneously, Cathy's psychological complexity is underscored in her unexpectedly maternal attraction to Aron as well as her final disappearance through suicide. In escaping at least partially from the rigid allegory of the Trask narrative, Cathy, in all her twisted hostility, moves closer to what we conceive of as "real."

"A writer," the British poet and essayist Matthew Arnold declared, "must begin with an Idea of the world in order not to be prevailed over by the world's multitudinousness."[29] Such a grand, predetermined idea, the critic J. Hillis Miller suggests, "not only composes and elevates the mind but also fences it off from the confused multitudinousness outside and the danger therefore of confused multitudinousness within."[30] In his fictions prior to *East of Eden*, Steinbeck had begun almost every work with such an idea, or thesis, that work would be designed to illustrate. In *In Dubious Battle*, for example, the controlling idea is that of the phalanx, or groupman, certainly not an idea of the world on the scale of which Arnold conceived, but just as certainly an effective method of defending the author and work against confusing multitudinousness. Toward that end, Steinbeck omitted the complexities of race and gender and first-person narrative from that all-white, all-male novel. While Steinbeck experimented relentlessly with form in his writing, it isn't until he arrives at the great experiment of *East of Eden* that he takes the enormous risk of allowing a work to assume as its final form the outlines of its own invention. While the novel begins with a Calvinistic pattern of good versus evil, ultimately no single, predetermined idea—not even *timshel* or the idea of free will—controls the forms of Cathy Trask and Samuel Hamilton, or the form of the novel itself. Both characters and novel evolve as their author imagines and re-imagines them, and as readers we are allowed to participate in this sometimes confusing process. When he intrudes to underscore his own scrupulous re-reading of the fine print and footnotes of his creation, rejecting the privileged authority of his own prior authorial voice, Steinbeck is assuming the role J. Hillis Miller has defined for the reader. "Nothing previous critics have said can be taken for granted," Miller writes, "however authoritative it may seem. Each reader must do again for himself the laborious task of a scrupulous slow reading, trying to find out what the texts actually say rather than imposing on them what she or he wants them to say or wishes they said."[31] Steinbeck's method also resembles that described by the novelist and critic Austin Wright as the creation of a "narrator-controlled world," one in which "the autonomy of the fictional world breaks down the inventive/narrative distinction: in effect, the inventor's manipulations have become the teller's, implicitly seeming to reflect the latter's creative, expressive, or rhetorical needs."[32]

In the *East of Eden* letters, Steinbeck lamented in frustration, "I don't know why writers are never given credit for knowing their craft."[33] Given the general failure of reviewers to comprehend the carefully worked out methods of so many of his works, Steinbeck's frustration is more than understandable. *East of Eden* may be the most misunderstood of all of Steinbeck's creations. It is a work that illustrates the author's desire and courage, at the apex of his career, to explore newer territory, to make his real subject the creative consciousness that had led him already through a stunningly successful career of fiction-making.

NOTES

1. John Steinbeck, *Journal of a Novel: The "East of Eden" Letters* (New York: Viking Press, 1969), p. 9.
2. Quoted in Jackson J. Benson, *The True Adventures of John Steinbeck, Writer* (New York: Viking Press, 1984), p. 552.
3. Steinbeck to Paul Caswell, May 16, 1948, John Steinbeck Research Center, San Jose State University, San Jose, California (hereafter JSRC).
4. Steinbeck to Wanda Van Brunt, February 22, 1949, JSRC.
5. Benson, p. 697.
6. Steinbeck, *Journal of a Novel*, pp. 14, 29, 31.
7. Steinbeck to Caswell, January 2, 1949, JSRC.
8. *Ibid.*, February 22, 1949, JSRC.
9. *Ibid.*, May 3, 1949, JSRC.
10. Steinbeck, *Journal of a Novel*, p. 7.
11. *Ibid.*, p. 29.
12. Quoted in Benson, p. 679.

13. *Ibid.,* p. 683.
14. *Ibid.,* p. 691.
15. Steinbeck, *Journal of a Novel,* p. 112.
16. Benson, p. 697.
17. *Ibid.,* p. 7.
18. Mikhail Bakhtin and V. N. Volosinov, "Discourse in Life and Discourse in Art (Concerning Sociological Poetics)," in *Contemporary Literary Criticism: Literary and Cultural Studies,* eds. Robert Con Davis and Ronald Schleifer (New York: Longman, 1989), p. 406.
19. Steinbeck, *Journal of a Novel,* p. 112.
20. Joseph Fontenrose, *John Steinbeck: An Introduction and Interpretation* (New York: Holt, Rinehart and Winston, 1963), p. 126.
21. Steinbeck, *Journal of a Novel,* pp. 180-81.
22. John Ditsky, *Essays on "East of Eden" (Steinbeck Monograph Series,* No. 7) (Muncie, Indiana: Steinbeck Society of America, Ball State University, 1977), pp. 9, 11.
23. Benson, p. 181.
24. Steinbeck, *Journal of a Novel,* pp. 14, 29, 31.
25. John Steinbeck, *East of Eden* (New York: Viking Press, 1952), p. 3. Herafter page references will be cited in parentheses following quotes.
26. Benson, p. 679.
27. Steinbeck, *Journal of a Novel,* p. 63.
28. Mikhail Bakhtin, "Discourse in the Novel," in *The Dialogic Imagination: Four Essays,* ed. Michael Holquist, trans. Caryl Emerson and Michael Holquist (Austin: University of Texas Press, 1981), p. 316.
29. Quoted in J. Hillis Miller, "The Search for Grounds in Literary Study," *Contemporary Literary Criticism,* eds. Davis and Schleifer, p. 570.
30. *Ibid.,* pp. 571-72.
31. *Ibid.,* p. 572.
32. Austin Wright, *The Formal Principle in the Novel* (Ithaca: Cornell University Press, 1982), pp. 70-71.
33. Steinbeck, *Journal of a Novel,* p. 14.

IV. TOPICS FOR RESEARCH AND DISCUSSION

(1) Gardens appear frequently in Steinbeck's fiction, most centrally in the stories collected in *The Long Valley.* In every case,

female characters are closely associated with these gardens. Compare and contrast one or more female "garden" character(s) from *The Long Valley* with Cathy Trask. What similarities and differences do you find between these characters, their situations, and responses to those situations, their attitudes toward and relationships with men?

(2) As Steinbeck predicted, *East of Eden* has been criticized for its lack of structural coherence, a common complaint being that the Hamilton and Trask narratives cause the novel to fall into two parts. Examine the novel carefully and explore the ways in which Steinbeck attempts to create a coherence between the two narratives.

(3) Adam Trask has an eye-catching first name. Using R. W. B. Lewis's *The American Adam,* discuss ways in which Steinbeck's protagonist resembles or differs from the paradigmatic "American Adam" as outlined in Lewis's study.

(4) A well-known feminist critique of women in literature is *The Mad Woman in the Attic,* by Sandra Gilbert and Susan Goobar. By the end of *East of Eden,* it would be accurate to label Cathy/Kate as "the mad woman in the lean-to." Incorporating critical principles or ideas from the Gilbert and Goobar study, or any other feminist criticism and theory, examine the character called Cathy/Kate.

(5) Lee Chong and Samuel Hamilton serve as primary points of contact between the Hamilton and Trask narratives in *East of Eden*. Both of these characters have significant influence upon Adam Trask. Compare the roles of Lee and Samuel. As literary devices, what purposes do the two characters serve?

V. SELECTED BIBLIOGRAPHY

1. Daniel Buerger, " 'History' and Fiction in *East of Eden* Criticism," *Steinbeck Quarterly,* 14 (Winter-Spring 1981), 6-14. In this essay, Buerger calls for a more ambitious criticism of the novel, with special attention to "the fictive narrative voice."

2. Robert DeMott, "The Interior Distances of John Steinbeck," *Steinbeck Quarterly,* 12 (Summer-Fall 1979), 86-99. This essay is most noteworthy for DeMott's emphasis upon "the shaping processes of the creative imagination" in *East of Eden,* a discussion that opens up the subject of self-consciousness in the novel.

3. Robert DeMott, "Creative Reading/Creative Writing: The

Presence of Dr. Gunn's *New Family Physician* in Steinbeck's *East of Eden*," in *Rediscovering Steinbeck: Revisionist Views of His Art, Politics, and Intellect,* eds. Cliff Lewis and Carroll Britch (Lewiston, New York: Edwin Mellen Press, 1989), pp. 35-57. DeMott examines the influence of Dr. Gunn's famous book in *East of Eden* and, more significantly, goes beyond such influence-hunting to suggest the complex territory of Steinbeck's moral roots in the Hamilton clan and the holistic vision Steinbeck brought not only to *East of Eden* but to his life's work.

4. John Ditsky, *Essays on "East of Eden"* (*Steinbeck Monograph Series,* No. 7) (Muncie, Indiana: Steinbeck Society of America, Ball State University, 1977). In this seminal study of the novel, Ditsky argues for a new evaluation of *East of Eden.* Ditsky illuminates connections between Steinbeck's personal life and the novel, and he points readers toward the important element of self-consciousness in the text.

5. Peter Lisca, *The Wide World of John Steinbeck* (New Brunswick, New Jersey: Rutgers University Press, 1958), pp. 261-75. Lisca's discussion of the novel is valuable as an example of early critics' almost universal dismissal of *East of Eden* as a failed work of art. Lisca's book provides often excellent background material on Steinbeck's work in general.

6. Louis Owens, *John Steinbeck's Re-Vision of America* (Athens: University of Georgia Press, 1985), pp. 140-55. In this discussion I focus on thematic elements in the novel, most particularly Steinbeck's creation of an ironic Eden and suggest that in *East of Eden* "all of the major themes that wind their way in an unbroken stream through Steinbeck's California fiction are brought together. . . ." However, like Lisca and others, here I ultimately dismiss the novel as a failed effort: "extraordinarily ambitious and . . . flawed."

7. Louis Owens, "The Story of a Writing: Narrative Structure in *East of Eden*" in *Rediscovering Steinbeck,* eds. Lewis and Britch, pp. 60-76. Contradicting my own earlier reading, as well as the readings of most critics of this novel, I examine narrative structure and suggest that Steinbeck consciously seeks to facilitate an exploration of authorial consciousness.

8. Louis Owens, "The Mirror and the Vamp: Invention, Reflection, and Bad, Bad, Cathy Trask in *East of Eden,*" in *Writing the American Classics,* eds. James Barbour and Tom Quirk (Chapel Hill, North Carolina: University of North Carolina Press, 1990), pp. 235-57. Relying on *Journal of a Novel: The "East of*

Eden" Letters as well as previously unpublished Steinbeck correspondence, I chart the process of Steinbeck's composition of *East of Eden* and argue again for the central importance of self-reflexivity in the text as well as the importance of Steinbeck's aesthetic achievement in this novel.

4. STEINBECK'S *THE GRAPES OF WRATH* (1939)

Louis Owens

I. BACKGROUND

The Grapes of Wrath, Steinbeck's greatest achievement and one of the great novels in American literature, was born out of a matrix of intense political conflict. During the first decades of the twentieth century, the western United States had become the setting for violent confrontations between labor and management in the mining towns of the Rocky Mountains, the logging camps of the Northwest, and the docks and urban centers of the entire region. The human cost of America's emergence as a preeminent industrial power in the world had begun to be documented in the late nineteenth century and would continue to attract the attentions of writers such as Stephen Crane, Frank Norris, Upton Sinclair, and many others into the 1920s and '30s. When, in the early 1930s, the ecological disaster of the Dust Bowl combined with a transition to large-scale mechanized agricultural methods to send between three and four hundred thousand displaced Americans in flight toward California, the stage was set for Steinbeck's masterpiece.

In 1934, John Steinbeck was living in Pacific Grove, California, as an unknown writer whose published works had thus far generated little attention and even less income for their author. "Still we have no money," Steinbeck complained in a letter. "I've sent off story after story and so far with no result."[1] Meanwhile, the flood of migrants pouring into California was creating a crisis situation. As the state's average population of farm laborers more than doubled, corporate agriculture began to take advantage of the desperate "Okies." Wages and working conditions plummeted. Efforts to organize farm labor were met with increasing violence, while thousands of families suffered from starvation and disease in roadside camps.

By 1936, Steinbeck had published *In Dubious Battle,* a novel that offers a brutally objective look at an agricultural strike in California. About this novel, Steinbeck had written, "I'm not interested in [the] strike as a means of raising men's wages, and I'm not interested in ranting about justice and oppression, mere outcroppings which indicate the conditions."[2] Within a few months of that novel's publication, however, Steinbeck was writing to a friend to say, "There are riots in Salinas and killings in the streets of that dear little town where I was born."[3] Steinbeck's interest in writing "about justice and oppression" was growing rapidly. That same year, Steinbeck traveled to the squalid migrant camps to research and write a series of articles for the *San Francisco News* offering first-hand descriptions of starving children, disease, filth, and despair in the camps. These grim essays, describing conditions more brutal than anything he would later show in *The Grapes of Wrath,* were collected and published in a pamphlet entitled *Their Blood Is Strong.*

In 1937, Steinbeck published *Of Mice and Men,* his popular play-novella focusing on the dreams of two migrant ranch hands. Meanwhile, conditions for the Dust Bowl refugees in California had plunged to such a nadir of despair that one observer wrote that "people are seeking shelter and subsistence in the fields and woods like wild animals, and . . . children [are] working in the cotton fields for 15 and 20 cents a day."[4] Steinbeck was becoming more and more emotionally involved in the enormous tragedy, writing to his agent, Elizabeth Otis, early in 1938 to say,

> I must go over to the interior valleys. There are about five thousand families starving to death over there, not just hungry but actually starving. The government is trying to feed them and get medical attention to them with the fascist group of utilities and banks and huge growers sabotaging the thing

all along the line. . . . I've tied into the thing from the first and
I must get down there and see it and see if I can't do
something to help knock these murderers on their heads. . . .
I'm pretty mad about it.[5]

What Steinbeck finally determined to do was what he knew
he did best: to write about the tragedy.

Perhaps because of the intensity of his anger, Steinbeck
initially got off to a false start, completing and burning a first
draft of his novel. He wrote to his publisher, Pascal Covici, to
say,

> You see this book is finished and it is a bad book and I must
> get rid of it. It can't be printed. It is bad because it isn't honest.
> . . . My whole work drive has been aimed at making people
> understand each other and then I deliberately write this book,
> the aim of which is to cause hatred through partial under-
> standing. . . . If I can't do better I have slipped badly. And that
> I won't admit—yet.[6]

Steinbeck started over and quickly completed the novel the
world knows as *The Grapes of Wrath*.

One of the most politically powerful and artistically
impressive works in American literature, *The Grapes of Wrath*
was also a stunning commercial success, selling as many as
10,000 copies a week and 400,000 total during the first year.
If the public loved the novel, however, all responses were not
so uniformly positive. Steinbeck had predicted that his novel
would be attacked "because it is revolutionary," and he was
correct. The novel was denounced by the Associated Farmers
of Kern County, California as "obscene sensationalism,"
while across the nation it was banned and even burned. One
editorial writer declared it to be "a morbid, filthily-worded
novel!" and another complained of the "bedraggled, bestial
characters." An Oklahoma congressman even denounced the
novel before Congress as a "dirty, lying, filthy manuscript"
and "a lie, a black, infernal creation of a distorted mind." A
writer for the *Los Angeles Examiner* found the novel "porno-
graphic" and the work of "a propaganda-fevered brain," and
Newsweek criticized it for its supposed encouragement of
"agricultural violence."[7] According to historian and California

agriculture expert Carey McWilliams, during federal hearings in San Francisco in 1939, "John Steinbeck was warmly denounced as the archenemy, defamer, and slanderer of migratory farm labor in California. . . ."[8]

Judging from the intensity of such reactions, it is clear that *The Grapes of Wrath* succeeded resoundingly in one of its goals: it cast a brilliant spotlight upon a sordid and painful moment in American history. As I shall argue in my "Critical Explication," Steinbeck's novel succeeds just as impressively on aesthetic as on political grounds.

II. PLOT SYNOPSIS

As Peter Lisca, Warren French, and Joseph Fontenrose have made abundantly clear, *The Grapes of Wrath* divides rather neatly into three parts: the Joads' time in Oklahoma, the journey to California, and the family's experiences once they have arrived in the Golden State. Within this tripartite structure Steinbeck created a much more complex and fascinating dialectic of two kinds of chapters: the "intercalary chapters," or interchapters, and the narrative chapters which tell the story of the Joads' exodus. In the interchapters, the novel's focus moves back to examine the Dust Bowl tragedy from epic distance, while in the narrative chapters the point of view is very close to the Joads, a representative family of sharecroppers caught up in the tragedy.

PART ONE—OKLAHOMA

The Grapes of Wrath begins with an intercalary chapter, one of those chapters Steinbeck himself called "repositories of all the external information" in the novel. In this chapter, Steinbeck describes the drought-stricken setting and introduces generically the sharecroppers who watch the encroaching dust clouds with growing despair. Chapter Two introduces Tom Joad, the novel's protagonist, who, fresh out of prison, manipulates a truck driver into giving him a ride home. Chapter Three describes a desiccated landscape surprisingly replete with the seeds of life and focuses in close detail upon a land turtle's struggle across a road, an unmistakable metaphor for the migrants' journey "across" Route 66 to California. Chapter Four brings about Tom's meeting with the preacher, Jim Casy. Casy discusses his own spiritual crisis and the two look down upon the abandoned Joad farm as Tom exclaims, "Somepin's happened." Chapter Five shows what has happened as a representative, faceless tenant voice argues unsuccessfully with an equally faceless "owner" voice for a chance to remain on the land; the chapter ends with tractors rumbling through dooryards, evicting the farmers. In Chapter Six, Casy and Tom discover that the Joad farm has suffered the fate illustrated in the preceding chapter and is now deserted. In this chapter Muley Graves provides a first-hand account of the experience of being "tractored out." Chapter Seven is another interchapter, this one allowing the reader to experience the confusion and cacophony of a used-car lot as the migrants prepare for their journey. In Chapter Eight, Tom and Casy arrive at Uncle John's home to find the Joad family. The reader recognizes that the car-lot experience of the preceding chapter has been the Joads' experience, and Casy preaches his holistic sermon about man's integration within the "one thing" that is "holy." Chapter Nine, an interchapter, again gives the reader a direct experience of the generic migrant trauma of selling off cherished possessions, while Chapter Ten focuses upon the Joads' final preparations for their personal journey. In this chapter, Casy is taken into the family "clan," the first step in a process that will eventually transform the nuclear family into "manself"—the family of humanity. A final interchapter in this initial part, Chapter Eleven, allows the narrative to shift back for an epic view of a deserted farmhouse being reclaimed by nature.

PART TWO—ON THE ROAD

Part two of the novel's structure begins with Chapter Twelve, an interchapter montage of migrant travel westward along Route 66, "the path of a people in flight." Chapter Thirteen follows the established pattern of the novel by providing a close-up of the Joads' experiences on this same highway, experiences that include a meeting with the Wilsons and the death of Grampa, two events that further erode the nuclear family and simultaneously open the Joads up to the larger unit of "manself." In Chapter Fourteen the narrative voice defines "manself"—and the transformation from "I" to "we" that is the beginning of collective action—and celebrates humanity's ability to overcome obstacles. Chapter Fifteen provides a vignette of generosity by the laboring class at a highway truck stop. Chapter Sixteen, a pivotal moment in the novel, introduces a major shift in the dynamics of power within the Joad family as Ma threatens Pa with a jack-handle to prevent the family from splitting up. Tom Joad is further likened to Christ as he teaches in parables to a junkyard attendant, and the family and reader hear grim tidings about reality in California from a man whose family has died there of starvation. Chapter Seventeen, another interchapter, illustrates the growth of a new communal identity and spirit among the migrants camped along the highway, foreshadowing the movement toward organization that will take place later in the novel. Finally, in Chapter Eighteen the Joads make it across Arizona and camp at the Colorado River, where Noah inexplicably elects to remain, further disintegrating the family. The Joads cross the Mojave Desert and arrive at Tehachapi Pass overlooking the Central Valley of California, the Promised Land. Granma has died during the night, and the chapter ends with the family peering down at the apparent cornucopia of the green and golden valley.

PART THREE—THE PROMISED LAND

In Chapter Nineteen, the beginning of part three of the novel, Steinbeck draws the reader quickly away from the pathos of Granma's death with an interchapter that summarizes the history of agriculture and land-conflict in California, making the point that those with the greatest hunger for land invariably triumph and thus hinting at the migrants' eventual success. Chapter Twenty brings the Joads down into the poisoned garden of the valley and into their first Hooverville, a shanty-town filled with starving children and desperate men and women. During a quarrel with a labor contractor, Tom strikes a deputy sheriff and Casy is arrested for the crime. Connie Rivers deserts Rose of Sharon to go off in search of the American Dream, and, along with the other squatters, the family flees from a mob intent on burning the camp. Chapter Twenty-One, an interchapter, briefly describes corporate agriculture's exploitation of the labor supply to lower wages and warns that "the companies, the banks worked at their own doom and they did not know it."

Chapter Twenty-Two introduces another tonal shift in the novel as the Joads take up residence in the Weedpatch government camp, a chapter that allows Steinbeck to demon-strate the migrants' talent for self-determination. Tom gets a job ditch-digging and is warned that a sheriff's mob plans to raid the camp during an upcoming dance. Chapter Twenty-Three shifts away from the Joads for a detached examination of the migrants' entertainment, including Steinbeck's dazzling prose imitation of a square-dance caller's cadence. Chapter Twenty-Four shows the migrants' ability to thwart the planned riot at the camp, while Chapter Twenty-Five, an interchapter, contains the author's brilliant jeremiad against the corruption and waste in California agriculture, a jeremiad concluding with the famous "grapes of wrath" warning.

In Chapter Twenty-Six, a lengthy pivotal chapter in the plot structure, the Joads leave the government camp to find work and end up at the Hooper Ranch where workers are on strike. Tom sneaks out of the camp and finds Casy leading the strike. Casy is murdered by strike-breakers, and Tom kills one of Casy's attackers. The chapter ends with the family smuggling Tom out of the camp inside the "cave" of a rolled mattress in the back of the truck. An interchapter, Chapter Twenty-seven, briefly depicts the experience of cotton-picking in preparation for Chapter Twenty-Eight, in which the Joad family finds work in the cotton fields. Al and Aggie announce their plans to marry, Ruthie boasts about Tom's crime, and Tom is forced to leave the cave of vines where he has been hiding. Before he leaves, Tom tells Ma about his determination to dedicate his life to the working people in imitation of Casy, saying "I'll be ever'where—wherever you look."

Chapter Twenty-Nine provides an impersonal description of the migrants' suffering during the rainy season, culminating with a hint of rebirth in the hills that are "pale green with the beginning year." Chapter Thirty, the final chapter in the novel, focuses upon flood waters lapping at the Joads' boxcar shelter. Rose of Sharon's baby is stillborn, and Uncle John sends the dead infant down the flood waters with the words "Go down an' tell 'em." Failing to stop the encroaching flood, the few remaining Joads struggle to a barn on high ground. There, the novel ends with a tableau of Rose of Sharon breast-feeding a starving stranger.

III. CRITICAL EXPLICATION

John Steinbeck was not fond of critics or criticism. "Literary criticism," he declared in "A Letter on Criticism," "is a kind of ill tempered parlor game in which nobody gets kissed." He went on to write, "I don't think the *Grapes of Wrath* is obscure in what it tries to say. As to its classification and pickling, I have neither opinion nor interest."[9] In spite of this disavowal, however, Steinbeck had very definite opinions about the complexity of his work and the task confronting the novel's readers and critics. Refusing to bow to requests that he change the novel's conclusion, he wrote to his editor:

> I know that books lead to a strong climax. This one doesn't except by implication and the reader must bring the implication to it. If he doesn't, it wasn't a book for him to read. Throughout I've tried to make the reader participate in the actuality, what he takes from it will be scaled entirely on his own depth or hollowness. There are five layers in this book; a reader will find as many as he can and he won't find more than he has in himself.[10]

To dissect this novel in search of an exact number of "layers" would be a mistake, an approach uncomfortably close to the "classification and pickling" process Steinbeck dreaded. However, careful reading can illuminate the extraordinary complexity of Steinbeck's achievement here, including the subtle methods by which the author attempts to "make the reader participate in the actuality" of the text.

THE BEGINNING

A good place to begin with any work is at the beginning, and *The Grapes of Wrath* (New York: Penguin Books, 1939) offers a great deal in its first paragraph:

> To the red country and part of the gray country of Oklahoma, the last rains came gently, and they did not cut the scarred earth. The plows crossed and recrossed the rivulet marks. The last rains lifted the corn quickly and scattered weed colonies and grass along the sides of the roads so that the gray country and the dark red country began to disappear under a green cover. In the last part of May the sky grew pale and the clouds that had hung in high puffs for so long in the spring were dissipated. The sun flared down on the growing corn day after day until a line of brown spread along the edge of each green bayonet. The clouds appeared, and went away, and in a while they did not try any more. The weeds grew darker green to protect themselves, and they did not spread any more. The surface of the earth crusted, a thin hard crust, and as the sky became pale, so the earth became pale, pink in the red country and white in the gray country. (3)

The pattern here will be familiar to anyone who has read Steinbeck's fiction, for almost invariably he begins with a carefully realized setting before introducing his characters. Environment has profound impact upon human inhabitants in Steinbeck's work, just as humanity leaves its mark upon the environment. In the first paragraph of *The Grapes of Wrath,* however, a great deal more is going on.

The opening line of the novel is broadly panoramic, describing "the red country and part of the gray country." At once, however, the narrative eye begins to close the distance to focus upon the plows that crossed the "rivulet marks." Finally, the narrative eye has zoomed in to focus closely upon not just "the growing corn" but the fine "line of brown" that marks the leaf edges. Once this close-up is accomplished, the narrative begins to pan back to register broader details of cloud and vague "weeds" until the paragraph ends where it began, with a panoramic image of the earth which "became pale, pink in the red country and white in the gray country." Steinbeck follows the same pattern of contracting and expanding focus in the second paragraph of the novel, zooming in for a detailed description of the "water-cut gullies" and panning back for a panorama of the pale earth and sky.

In these first paragraphs, Steinbeck is subtly, even subliminally, preparing the reader for the structural pattern of his novel. The shifting narrative eye, as it provides first a broad, epic panorama and then a detailed close-up of the region called the Dust Bowl, imitates the pattern of expansion and contraction that will be established in the dialectic of intercalary and narrative chapters throughout the novel. The interchapters will provide a broad, documentary perspective of human crisis on an enormous, epic scale; the narrative chapters will bring the narrative eye into intimate focus upon a representative family, the Joads. In this way Steinbeck can make the reader feel the immensity of the social, historical tragedy unfolding while simultaneously he allows the reader to participate in the drama along with the Joads, to feel very personally the pain and trauma of the Joads and, thus, of all of the displaced migrants.

The first paragraphs of the novel accomplish still more. By foregrounding the seemingly irresistible forces of nature here in the beginning, Steinbeck reminds us that the human tragedies of the novel are played out against a backdrop of enduring life. Within such a setting, the seeming tragedies of humankind are reduced, made to seem transient in contrast to the regenerative power of nature. Like the people who, drawing their strength from the earth, "go on," as Ma Joad will say later in the novel, the earth cannot be destroyed. However, in the plows that "crossed and recrossed the rivulet marks," by the second sentence of the novel Steinbeck is subtly implying human responsibility for the disaster of the Dust Bowl. The plows superimpose a self-destructive human pattern—the erosion including furrows—upon the natural watershed pattern of the earth. The rivulet marks signify the continuum; their erasure is a sign of human intervention and a portent of environmental destruction. The wheels that "milled the ground" in this first chapter, and the hooves that "beat the ground" until "the dirt crust broke and the dust formed" further emphasize humanity's responsibility for the disaster that will send the Joads on the road to California.

In the weed colonies "scattered . . . along the sides of the roads" in these opening paragraphs, Steinbeck also foreshadows the colonies of migrants that will spring up along Route 66. The ant lion trap suggested in the second paragraph, a minuscule funnel of finely blown sand from which the ant simply cannot escape, also serves as a naturalistic image underscoring the sharecroppers' predicament. The cropped-out, dust-laden region offers no future for these people. Those who choose to remain, like the well-named Muley Graves, have little chance.

In these opening paragraphs, Steinbeck brilliantly establishes the dialectical pattern of the novel to follow. He introduces the implacable natural forces arrayed against his protagonists, and he hints strongly at the culpability of the sharecroppers—and all of us—in bringing about the seeming tragedy of the novel. Finally, he underscores the regenerative power of nature, foregrounding the life-force that— personified by Rose of Sharon—will triumph in the end.

NARRATIVE STRUCTURE

Steinbeck was faced with a structural dilemma in *The Grapes of Wrath:* how could he convey both the immense scope of the Dust Bowl tragedy as well as the intimate pain and suffering of the individuals caught up in the tragedy? In the preface to his documentary film, *The Forgotten Village,* Steinbeck wrote in 1941, "It means very little to know that a million Chinese are starving unless you know one Chinese who is starving."[11] His solution was to evolve the strategy of two kinds of chapters, the intercalary chapters, or interchapters, and the narrative chapters that tell the Joads' story.

Of the thirty chapters in *The Grapes of Wrath,* sixteen,

less than twenty percent of the novel's word-count, consist of intercalary chapters. Although the Joads appear in none of the interchapters, in the final third of the novel Steinbeck ensures our identification with the suffering Joads by steadily increasing the proportion of the novel devoted to the Joads' story. The first narrative (Joads) chapter of the novel, Chapter Two, is a scant eleven pages, while by Chapter Twenty the narrative chapter has grown to fifty-seven pages while the parallel interchapter, Chapter Nineteen, is only eleven pages long. Succeeding narrative chapters, telling the increasingly tense story of the Joads, will reach lengths of fifty-five (Chapter Twenty-Two) and seventy-five pages (Chapter Twenty-Six). In contrast, the final five interchapters, giving the impersonal picture of the mass of migrants, will average only four-and-one-half pages.

→   Throughout the novel, Steinbeck uses a variety of techniques to make sure that *The Grapes of Wrath* does not simply fall into two parts—narrative chapter and interchapter. Chapter One, for example, ends with a description of the sun, which "became less red" (4). Chapter Two picks up the thread of color in its first line: "A huge red transport truck stood in front of the little roadside restaurant" (4). The flaring red sun and the powerful red truck couple the twin threats of nature and machinery that confront the sharecroppers. Similarly, the first chapter has introduced the example of a faceless "walking man" lifting a thin layer of dust as he moves, and in the second chapter we first see Tom Joad as "a man walking along the edge of the highway" (5). In Chapter Three, Steinbeck begins with a description:

> The concrete highway was edged with a mat of tangled, broken dry grass, and the grass heads were heavy with oat beards to catch on a dog's coat, and foxtails to tangle in a horse's fetlocks, and clover burrs to fasten in sheep's wool; sleeping life waiting to be spread and dispersed, every seed armed with an appliance of dispersal, twisting darts, and parachutes for the wind, little spears and balls of tiny thorns, and all waiting for animals and for the wind, for a man's trouser cuff or the hem of a woman's skirt, all passive but armed with appliances of activity, still, but each possessed of the anlage of movement. (14)

Echoing the "weed colonies" that sprang up beside the road in
the first chapter, this description shows a sun-blasted landscape
surprisingly rich with life and potential life. In the next
paragraph, Steinbeck introduces a land turtle that struggles
heroically to clamber across this concrete highway. In spite of
obstacles, including a truck that attempts to run over it, the
turtle succeeds in crossing and, incidentally, in carrying the oat
seeds across the road and accidentally planting them on the
other side. In Chapter Four, Tom Joad picks up a land turtle,
perhaps the same one featured in Chapter Three, and Steinbeck links Tom further with the turtle through color— yellow
shoes and yellow underside of shell—while describing Jim Casy
in such a way that we cannot miss the preacher's resemblance to
the turtle. The not-so-subtle message is that just as the
seed-bearing turtle succeeded in crossing the road, the migrants—also possessed of the "anlage of movement"— will
succeed in carrying life "across" to the dubious Promised Land
of California. In Chapter Seven, we experience the dizzying
confusion of a used-car lot and hear the car salesman's voice
chant, "Got a Lincoln '24. There's a car. Run forever. Make her
into a truck" (68). When Tom and Casy reach Uncle John's
house, one of the first things they see is a truck, "but a strange
truck, for while the front of it was a sedan, the top had been cut
off in the middle and the truck bed fitted on" (75). Immediately, we know that the car-lot experience of Chapter Seven has
been the Joads' experience. Because the Joads' converted truck
is not a Lincoln but a Hudson, however, we also know that
theirs has been the experience of others as well. Again and
again, through interrelated details, colors, unifying imagery,
and language, Steinbeck ensures that the two kinds of chapters
will merge to form a single text.

THE BIBLE

A great deal of critical attention has been paid to biblical
elements in *The Grapes of Wrath,* so much so that there is little
need for detailed analysis here. A reader should certainly note
that the novel's title is taken from "The Battle Hymn of the
Republic" ("He is trampling out the vintage where the grapes

of wrath are stored"), and that this is itself an allusion to Revelations, in which the wine of God's wrath figures in prophecies of the Apocalypse: "And the angel thrust his sickle into the earth, and gathered the vine of the earth, and cast it into the great winepress of the wrath of God" (Rev. 14:19). So important was this title's source to Steinbeck that he insisted the entire "Battle Hymn" be printed inside the covers of the novel, saying that "in reference to this book it has a large meaning."[12] With this title, and by insisting upon the appearance of the "Battle Hymn" in the novel, Steinbeck attempted to ensure that his reader would see this novel as a work about America, about the collective self-image of a nation founded upon a biblical discourse and upon ideas of Eden and Apocalypse, of both spiritual communion (the Eucharist) and a vengeful God.

Christ in this novel is represented by Tom Joad ("Jesus Meek" in prison), Jim Casy (with his eye-catching initials and much more), and Rose of Sharon (from the Song of Solomon). Christ, it must be remembered, appeared as a herald of a new consciousness, bringing also through his commitment to humanity and his sacrifice a promise of a new beginning. Casy, like Christ, has gone into the wilderness and returned with a deep commitment to humanity. Like Christ, Casy sacrifices himself for the good of all humanity. Unlike Casy, Tom requires the experience of all he encounters on the journey to California in order to arrive at his commitment to the larger good. But it is Tom who has been called "Jesus Meek" in prison, and it is Tom whom Ma Joad describes as special and chosen. Finally, Tom takes Casy's place as a sacrificial figure.

Steinbeck deliberately blurs parallels between his characters and distinctive biblical figures. For example, Casy has baptized Tom Joad and is described at one point as "a voice out of the ground," and could very easily be compared to John the Baptist. Tom could well be described as Casy's apostle, who goes off at the end to spread the gospel. Almost invariably, throughout his fiction, Steinbeck deliberately confuses such parallels in order to make simplistic analogies impossible. It is Christ's impulse toward commitment and self-sacrifice that Steinbeck is underscoring, an impulse that must be learned by all of us, the author suggests, if we are to survive in the world.

That Rose of Sharon's name is taken from the Bible's Song of Solomon associates her clearly with Christ: "I am the Rose of Sharon, and the lily of the valleys" (Song of Solomon 2:1). Within this song is the line, "thy stature is like to a palm tree, and thy breasts to clusters of grapes" (7:7). Throughout the novel grapes have symbolized the California Promised Land—and the American Eden—and served to link this new Promised Land with the biblical Canaan. In the end, when Rose of Sharon offers her breast to the starving man, Steinbeck's message is that paradise has meaning only within the willingness of men and women to commit themselves to each other. The Garden is a place we construct out of our own consciousness, not a place we find at the end of a westward journey. The Bible's Song of Solomon is a celebration of life: "The flowers appear on the earth; the time of the singing of birds is come, and the voice of the turtle is heard in our land . . ." (2:12). And as the threatening flood waters rise about *The Grapes of Wrath*'s final scene, we should remember what the Song of Solomon promises: "Many waters cannot quench love, neither can the floods drown it . . ." (8:7). In Rose of Sharon's gesture, Steinbeck offers a symbol of compassion, commitment, and indestructible life.

Biblical imagery and allusions proliferate throughout *The Grapes of Wrath* and can be collected and analyzed with little difficulty. What is most significant, however, is the way in which Steinbeck uses biblical parallels to expand the scope of his novel. On one level the novel is the story of a family's struggle for survival in the Promised Land—a Promised Land that symbolically comprehends not only California, but all of America. On another level it is the story of a people's struggle, that of the migrants. On a third level it is the story of the way in which a nation conceives of itself and constructs itself in accordance with that conception. And on the largest scale, especially through the biblical parallels, both the allusions to Christ and those to the Israelites and Exodus, the novel becomes the story of humankind's need for commitment to humanity and to the earth itself; to what, in *The Log from the Sea of Cortez,* Steinbeck and Edward F. Ricketts holistically termed "the whole thing, known and unknowable."[13]

~ AMERICAN FAILURE

On one level, Steinbeck refuses to assess direct blame for the apparent tragedy of the Dust Bowl. As the conversation between the representative tenant voice and the "owner" voice makes clear, it is impossible to determine just who is responsible. "But where does it stop? Who can we shoot?" the tenant wonders, and the answer is "Maybe there's nobody to shoot. Maybe the thing isn't men at all" (40). Who is at fault? Steinbeck's answer is that we are all at fault as a nation, a species.

In *The Log from the Sea of Cortez,* a non-fiction treatise written just a year after the publication of *The Grapes of Wrath,* Steinbeck and Ricketts defined a philosophical posture they termed "non-teleological thinking." Teleology is defined in the glossary to the *Log* as "The assumption of predetermined design, purpose, or ends in Nature by which an explanation of phenomena is postulated."[14] The authors add:

> What we personally conceive by the term "teleological thinking" is most frequently associated with the evaluation of causes and effects, the purposiveness of events. . . . In their sometimes intolerant refusal to face the facts as they are, teleological notions may substitute a fierce but ineffectual attempt to change conditions which are assumed to be undesirable, in place of the understanding-acceptance which would pave the way for a more sensible attempt at any change which might still be indicated.[15]

Non-teleological thinking, on the other hand, "concerns itself not with what should be, or could be, or might be, but rather with what actually 'is.'"[16] This kind of thought, which the authors also term "is" thinking, is further qualified in the *Log:*

> Strictly, the term non-teleological thinking ought not to be applied to what we have in mind. Because it involves more

than thinking, that term is inadequate. Modus operandi might be better. . . . The method extends beyond thinking even to living itself; in fact, by inferred definition it transcends the realm of thinking possibilities, it postulates "living into."[17]

In *The Grapes of Wrath,* Steinbeck's non-teleological stance can be readily seen in his refusal to assess individual blame for the tragedy that sends the migrants on the road westward. Seen close up, it appears that the Dust Bowl disaster can be traced to such causes as "cottoning-out" the land, while a perspective expanding outward from an intimate point of view suggests that the tenants' evictions are caused by the tractor farming, the drought, etc. But the larger, non-blaming picture makes it clear that no one in particular is at fault. No *one* can be blamed for dry weather and no *one* can be blamed for a pattern of colonization and pattern of thinking that sent "sod-busters" to brutally displace American Indians and settle lands that were simply unsuitable to large-scale farming. The unsuitability of the land and the cycles of drought characteristic of the Great Plains caused repeated crop failures that drove the farmers further in debt to the banks. Repeated plantings of a cash crop—cotton—in order to make mortgage payments further depleted the soil, while tree-cutting and plowing caused intensified erosion. Steinbeck makes it clear that the source of the disaster is a failure to understand the ecological whole, not the culpability of individuals or even groups. Non-teleologically, once we recognize this fact we will be freed to make the "sensible attempt at . . . change" which is indicated, and the change must be on a broad, national, and global scale. We must, Steinbeck argues, radically alter the way we conceive of our relationship with the environment.

The "bad thing made by men" in this novel grows out of a pattern of thought that begins with the first European colonization. America was imagined as the New Canaan, New Jerusalem, or New Eden. Colonists such as William Bradford's pilgrims at Plymouth conceived of themselves as the chosen people and saw their situation paralleling that of the Israelites freed from bondage and newly arrived in the Promised Land. Thus Bradford, in *Of Plymouth Plantation*

(1620-50), enthusiastically compares his pilgrims to "Moyses & the Isralits when they went out of Egipte."[18] Out of this emphatically biblical consciousness—and discourse—has arisen what has come to be called the American myth, a national meta-narrative which Steinbeck explored ceaselessly throughout his life's work.

Within this self-imagining, and authoritatively biblical discourse, if America was the New Canaan, the task of the chosen people was to wrest the new paradise from the grips of wilderness and from the inhabitants of that wilderness. The colonists saw themselves as the Army of Christ embroiled in a grim wilderness battle against Satan. The Indian in the forest, appropriately outraged by the colonists' theft of lands and slaughter of Indian people, came inevitably to be seen as in league with Satan. It was within the context of such a "holy war" that, in 1653, the colonial writer Edward Johnson proposed a war of genocide against Native Americans, exhorting the Puritans to "take up your arms and march manfully on till all opposers of Christ's kingly power be abolished."[19]

Steinbeck has this national meta-narrative, or myth, very much in mind in *The Grapes of Wrath*. Within the Dust Bowl migrants' journey to the Promised Land of California exists the paradigm of Euro-America's western expansion in search of a garden that seems ever retreating. It is a pattern that might be described as the destruction of the garden in search of the garden, what Walt Whitman sums up brilliantly in his poem "Facing West from California's Shores" when he asks, "But where is what I started for so long ago? / And why is it yet unfound?" When the owner-voice in the novel intones, "Why don't you go west to California? There's work there, and it never gets cold. Why, you can reach out anywhere and pick an orange" (35), and when Grampa says, "Gonna get me a whole big bunch of grapes off a bush, or whatever, and I'm gonna squash 'em on my face an' let 'em run offen my chin" (90), Steinbeck is underscoring this biblically inspired myth. When a faceless migrant says, "Maybe we can start again, in the new rich land—in California, where the fruit grows. We'll start over" (95), Steinbeck is further underscoring the American myth of abandoning the used-up past and starting over, of self-creation free from the encumbering baggage of history. But throughout the book, Steinbeck argues that this meta-narrative that sends America ever westward in search of a retreating paradise, that excuses the slaughter of Native American Indians and the theft and destruction of land, and that promises to free us from the encumbrances of history and responsibility, is dangerously delusive and destructive.

Steinbeck refuses to pardon his suffering sharecroppers from their share of unconscious complicity in this pattern of thought. A representative migrant voice pleads for a chance to remain on the land, hoping for war to boost the price of cotton: "Get enough wars and cotton'll hit the ceiling" (32). When the owner-voice explains that corporate-scale farming is more efficient than sharecropping, the cropper exclaims, "But you'll kill the land with cotton," and the reply is "We know. We've got to take cotton quick before the land dies. Then we'll sell the land. Lots of families in the East would like to own a piece of land" (34). An eagerness for war—and death—as a means of remaining on the land and further "killing" the land with cotton seriously undercuts our sympathy for the farmer, and the owner's willingness to destroy the land for quick profit illuminates the deadly pattern of American land-use and western expansion. Steinbeck further implicates the sharecroppers in the pattern of American settlement when the representative cropper voice says, "Grampa took up the land, and he had to kill the Indians and drive them away. And Pa was born here, and he killed weeds and snakes. . . . Grampa killed Indians, Pa killed snakes for the land" (34-35).

The farmers in *The Grapes of Wrath* are integral parts of a system that has failed in a very destructive way—and that will continue to fail in the hands of banks and corporations. While we suffer with the Joads, and thus with all of the sharecroppers, as they are torn from their homes and lives, Steinbeck makes it unmistakably clear that the Joads and all of their like—and Americans as a whole—bear collective responsibility for the tragedy that has come about. Steinbeck's ideal, as it emerges in this novel and throughout his fiction, is of all men and women working together, committed to one another and to the environment in a fully conscious and responsible fashion. It is an ecological argument, and the

Joads are sent on the road to learn a new commitment that extends beyond the nuclear family to "the whole thing, known and unknowable."

DISCOURSE AND DIALOGIC

While many critics have discussed the dialectic between interchapter and narrative chapter in *The Grapes of Wrath,* the sophisticated complexity of the novel's dialogic has gone relatively unobserved.[20] In keeping with his non-teleological narrative posture, and with impressive skill, Steinbeck weaves a text in which no single voice speaks with final authority. An example of this can be found in the way Steinbeck incorporates the epic, biblical voice that recurs throughout the novel, from the broad lyricism of Genesis in the opening chapter to the admonitory tone of the biblical jeremiad of Chapter Twenty-Five. An authoritative discourse replete with prior authority, the biblical form of epic discourse is monologic, claiming absolute privilege. By situating his interchapters very clearly within this kind of discourse, Steinbeck achieves two crucial effects. On the one hand the mythic discourse tells the reader that this is a story of enormous, epic proportions, one that transcends the localized trauma of the Dust Bowl or California, or even America. The novel thus becomes a story of humanity. On the other hand, the monologic authority of the biblical discourse should remind us that the failure depicted in the novel is the result of such a single-voiced, authoritative meta-narrative. As discussed above, from the beginning of their invasion of this continent, colonizers claimed authority by situating themselves firmly within the privileged center of biblical discourse, a discourse with implications for every aspect of European domination of the so-called New World. By invoking this easily recognizable biblical voice within a context that acutely undermines the privilege and authority of that voice, Steinbeck creates a fascinating example of hybridization. Paradoxically *The Grapes of Wrath* achieves epic dimension at least partly through its invocation of biblical discourse, and thus benefits from the authority of that discourse; at the same time, however, the story itself serves to implicate that discourse in the complex tragedy being described, an effect we see perhaps most clearly in the famous jeremiad of Chapter Twenty-Five:

> The decay spreads over the State, and the sweet smell is a great sorrow on the land. . . . And the failure hangs over the State like a great sorrow. . . . Burn coffee for fuel in the ships. Burn corn to keep warm, it makes a hot fire. Dump potatoes in the rivers and place guards along the banks to keep the hungry people from fishing them out. Slaughter the pigs and bury them, and let the putrescence drip into the earth.
>
> There is a crime here that goes beyond denunciation. There is a sorrow here that weeping cannot symbolize. There is a failure here that topples all our success.
>
> . . . and in the eyes of the hungry there is a growing wrath. In the souls of the people the grapes of wrath are filling and growing heavy, growing heavy for the vintage. (p. 385)

Steinbeck's use here of a familiar form of biblical discourse— the jeremiad—often employed to move a people toward repentance is overt and unmistakable. Steinbeck is effective, however, in suggesting here, and throughout the novel, that the forms of biblical discourse and the zeal for American mythology live in dangerous political complicity. Earlier in the novel, Steinbeck implicated the westering pattern of settlement and the myth of the New Eden in the disaster that has befallen the tenant farmers. Here, while Steinbeck's jeremiad claims the *a priori* authority of biblical discourse, the facts of the novel simultaneously demonstrate the failure of America's mythic "is" self-conception to provide even minimal sustenance for a desperate people.

NOTES

1. Quoted in Jackson J. Benson, *The True Adventures of John Steinbeck, Writer* (New York: Viking Press, 1984), p. 291.
2. John Steinbeck, *Steinbeck: A Life in Letters,* eds. Elaine Steinbeck and Robert Wallsten (New York: Viking Press, 1975), p. 98; to be identified as *SLL* hereafter.

3.   *Ibid.*, p. 132.
4.   Benson, p. 336.
5.   *SLL,* p. 158.
6.   Benson, p. 376.
7.   Louis Owens, *"The Grapes of Wrath": Trouble in the Promised Land* (Boston: Twayne Publishers, 1989), pp. 11-12.
8.   Carey McWilliams, "California Pastoral," in *John Steinbeck, "The Grapes of Wrath": Text and Criticism,* ed. Peter Lisca (New York: Viking Press, 1972), p. 657.
9.   John Steinbeck, "A Letter on Criticism," in *Steinbeck and His Critics: A Record of Twenty-Five Years,* eds. E. W. Tedlock, Jr. and C. V. Wicker (Albuquerque: University of New Mexico Press, 1957), p. 52.
10.   *SLL,* p. 178.
11.   John Steinbeck, *The Forgotten Village* (New York: Viking Press, 1941), p. 5.
12.   *SLL,* p. 171.
13.   John Steinbeck, *The Log from the Sea of Cortez* (New York: Viking Press, 1951), p. 218.
14.   *Ibid.*, p. 275.
15.   *Ibid.*, pp. 138-39.
16.   *Ibid.*, p. 135.
17.   *Ibid.*, p. 150.
18.   William Bradford, *Of Plymouth Plantation,* ed. Harvey Wish (New York: Capricorn Books, 1962), p. 36.
19.   Edward Johnson, *Johnson's Wonder-Working Providence,* ed. J. Franklin Jameson (New York: Barnes & Noble, 1959), p. 30.
20.   For a much more comprehensive discussion of dialogic structure in the novel, see Louis Owens and Hector Torres, "Dialogic Structure and Levels of Discourse in Steinbeck's *The Grapes of Wrath," Arizona Quarterly,* 45 (Winter 1989), 75-94. My discussion here is drawn largely from this essay.

IV. TOPICS FOR RESEARCH AND DISCUSSION

(1)   *The Grapes of Wrath* says a great deal about our attitudes toward the natural environment, including our exploitation of and responsibilities to the environment. Explore writings by current environmentalists, including those espousing what has come to be called "deep ecology," and examine Steinbeck's arguments in *The Grapes of Wrath* in the context of contemporary ecology. To broaden your discussion, you might consider

including Steinbeck and Edward F. Ricketts's *The Log from the Sea of Cortez,* a work containing significant discussion of ecological concerns.

(2) Examine a variety of such works as R. W. B. Lewis's *The American Adam,* Leo Marx's *The Machine in the Garden,* Richard Slotkin's *Regeneration Through Violence,* Annette Kolodny's *The Lay of the Land,* Richard Drinnon's *Facing West,* and Roy Harvey Pearce's *Savagism and Civilization.* Discuss Steinbeck's treatment in *The Grapes of Wrath* of issues raised in such studies of America's conscience and consciousness.

(3) The American novel during the first half of this century falls into the period often defined as "Modernism." Using your library resources, including such texts as Louis Menand's *Discovering Modernism* as well as Warren French's essay "John Steinbeck and Modernism" found in the Ditsky collection listed in the bibliography, discuss *The Grapes of Wrath* as a modernist text. How well does it fit into paradigms associated with the modernist movement?

(4) Ma Joad and Rose of Sharon are central characters in *The Grapes of Wrath.* Incorporating published criticism that discusses these two characters—such as Mimi R. Gladstein's "From Heroine to Supporting Player: The Diminution of Ma Joad" in the Ditsky collection—as well as more general feminist criticism, explore the construction and roles of these two characters.

(5) When we first encounter Jim Casy in *The Grapes of Wrath,* the preacher has already undergone a spiritual conversion and has committed himself to the welfare of humanity. Tom Joad, on the other hand, seems dedicated primarily to his individual welfare and that of his immediate, nuclear family. Analyze Tom's evolution throughout the novel from self-interest to self-sacrifice. What experiences and impulses motivate Tom's change, and how does Steinbeck illuminate this evolution at strategic points through the course of the novel?

V. SELECTED BIBLIOGRAPHY

I have included here only collections of essays or booklength critical volumes devoted exclusively to *The Grapes of Wrath.* For additional bibliography, including individual essays, students should consult the following: Tetsumaro Hayashi, *A New Steinbeck Bibliography: 1929-1971* (Metuchen, New Jersey: Scarecrow Press,

1973), and *A New Steinbeck Bibliography: 1971-1981* (Metuchen, New Jersey: Scarecrow Press, 1983); John Ditsky, *Critical Essays on Steinbeck's "The Grapes of Wrath"* (see 2), pp. 1-21; and Louis Owens, *"The Grapes of Wrath": Trouble in the Promised Land* (see 7), pp. 111-17. Students should also be aware of the 1989 Viking Press edition of *The Grapes of Wrath* with a discursive introduction by Studs Terkel.

1. Robert Con Davis, ed., *Twentieth Century Interpretations of "The Grapes of Wrath": A Collection of Critical Essays* (Englewood Cliffs, New Jersey: Prentice-Hall, 1982). Davis provides a collection of previously published Steinbeck criticism by such noted Steinbeck critics as Warren French and Peter Lisca. Newer essays consider the novel's intercalary chapters and the role of Ma Joad as archetype.
2. John Ditsky, ed., *Critical Essays on Steinbeck's "The Grapes of Wrath"* (Boston: G. K. Hall & Co., 1989). Ditsky's volume contains a representative selection of early reviews as well as an introduction by the editor providing a comprehensive overview of *Grapes* criticism to the present time. Most valuable here are a series of original essays by Jackson J. Benson, Roy Simmonds, Carroll Britch and Cliff Lewis, Mimi R. Gladstein, and Louis Owens, as well as Ditsky's "Further Commentary" on the novel's controversial ending.
3. Agnes McNeill Donohue, ed., *A Casebook on "The Grapes of Wrath"* (New York: Crowell, 1968). In a volume most useful for an overview of the first two decades of Steinbeck criticism, Donohue provides excerpts from major criticism of *Grapes* through the mid-1960s.
4. Warren French, ed., *A Companion to "The Grapes of Wrath"* (New York: Viking Press, 1963). In this indispensable early collection, French brings together background material and critical accounts with Steinbeck's monograph on migrant worker conditions, *Their Blood Is Strong.*
5. Warren French, *A Filmguide to "The Grapes of Wrath"* (Bloomington: Indiana University Press, 1966). French discusses the direction and production of John Ford's film version of *Grapes,* with scene-by-scene analysis, summary critique, bibliography, and novel-screenplay-film comparison.
6. Peter Lisca, ed., *John Steinbeck, "The Grapes of Wrath": Text and Criticism* (New York: Viking Press, 1972). In this edition of Steinbeck's novel for the Viking Critical Library, Lisca brings together material illuminating the social and historical context

of the novel with eleven critical essays as well as original
statements about *Grapes* by Steinbeck himself.
7. Louis Owens, *"The Grapes of Wrath": Trouble in the Promised
    Land* (Boston: Twayne Publishers, 1989). A volume in
    Twayne's Masterwork Studies series, this book provides a
    chronology of Steinbeck's life, background information con-
    cerning the novel's historical context and critical reception, and
    an extensive original critical reading of *Grapes* plus a critical
    bibliography.

5. STEINBECK'S *IN DUBIOUS BATTLE* (1936)

HELEN LOJEK

I. BACKGROUND

In February of 1935, three months before *Tortilla Flat* was published, Steinbeck completed work on *In Dubious Battle,* which would appear the next year. *Of Mice and Men* was published in 1937, and *The Grapes of Wrath* in 1939. Steinbeck was clearly in a period of tremendous productivity, writing at the top of his form and producing novels which are generally still regarded as among his very best. Steinbeck, like his publishers, regarded *In Dubious Battle* as a new direction in his fiction, and he was eager to have it published quickly—in part, he said, because "I want no tag of humorist on me, nor any other kind."[1]

All his life Steinbeck advocated writing which grew from personal experience and direct observation, and *In Dubious Battle* provides a fascinating glimpse of the ways in which such direct observation stimulated his novelist's imagination. According to biographer Jackson J. Benson, Steinbeck met in the winter of 1934 two union workers who had been active in organizing farm labor in California's San Joaquin Valley. Steinbeck originally intended "to write the autobiography of a communist,"[2] apparently "a sort of diary of a communist labor organizer" from the point of view of strike leader Pat Chambers.[3] During the summer of 1934 he visited migrant camps to see and hear for himself, and picked up the material which later became the short piece "Breakfast." Throughout the year he observed, talked about, and read about a number of worker strikes which took place in the Monterey area.

At the suggestion of his agent Steinbeck decided to "reduce" his tale of strikes and organizers to fiction, and had some "trouble" recasting his "journalistic account of a strike" in novel form.[4] As he wrote, he regularly checked not just facts but language and "atmosphere" with friends who had more experience with the migrants than he did.[5] After he completed *In Dubious Battle,* Steinbeck was to spend even more time with migrants, actually travelling and working with them briefly, meeting Tom Collins, the migrant camp director to whom *The Grapes of Wrath* is dedicated, and producing an article for *The Nation* ("Dubious Battle in California," September 1936) and a series of articles for the *San Francisco News* ("The Harvest Gypsies," October 5-12, 1936). "Always Something to Do in Salinas" (*Holiday,* June 1955) comes back to the same material. Clearly his interest in the migrants and the stimulation of direct observation touched a deep creative impulse in him, an impulse which eventually resulted in *The Grapes of Wrath.*

Similarities between Steinbeck's novel and the actual history of farm labor strife in California are easy to discover. The name Steinbeck selects for his valley, Torgas, sounds quite a lot like *Tagus,* the name of a ranch near Tulare where a strike among peach pickers occurred in 1933.[6] And during the cotton workers' strike near Corcoran, land for an emergency camp was given for use by a small cotton farmer and gas station owner. To oversee sanitation, organizers brought in a doctor named, like the doctor in *In Dubious Battle,* Burton.[7] Steinbeck maintained, however, that the strike in his novel was a composite, not a depiction of an actual event.

> I have usually avoided using actual places to avoid hurting feelings, for, although I rarely use a person or a story as it is—neighbors love only too well to attribute them to someone . . . as for the valley in *In Dubious Battle*—it is a composite valley as it is a composite strike. If it has the characteristics of Pajaro nevertheless there was no strike there. If it's like the cotton strike, that wasn't apples.[8]

II. PLOT SYNOPSIS

Jim Nolan's family has been "ruined by this system"—his father is shotgunned in labor troubles; his mother dies because she has no reason to live; police provide only a token investigation of his sister's mysterious disappearance; and he is arrested and loses his job for pausing to listen to a radical park speaker. As *In Dubious Battle* opens, Jim, bitter and feeling "dead," walks away from his old life, carrying his possessions in a paper bag, and joins an organization known only as the Party. He seeks hope and a focus for his "vicious anger." "I feel dead," he tells the Party recruiter. "I thought I might get alive again."

In Dubious Battle is the story of Jim's education in Party methods, and of the new life and hope which he discovers. Although the novel does not usually reveal Jim's thoughts, it never leaves his side as he is catapulted into the troubles agitating California's farm labor in the 1930s. Alternately leading events and overwhelmed by them, Jim is cheered, beaten, shot, and finally killed, but not before he has discovered his place as part of a larger whole.

With McLeod (Mac), an experienced Party worker who acts as mentor, Jim rides the rails out of the city to the Torgas Valley, where conditions among the apple pickers are bad enough so that a strike seems possible. The Growers Association has waited until the crop tramps arrive to lower wages, knowing workers will have to pick just to earn enough money to leave. Outfinanced, outorganized, and outgunned by the forces of farm capitalism in the valley, the Party must, Mac says, "use everything." Locating a riverside jungle of worker campsites, Mac begins to teach Jim how this is done by discovering and seizing an opportunity to become part of the group. Falsely claiming medical experience, he successfully delivers a baby, a literal new birth which parallels Jim's metaphoric new birth. Simultaneously he makes the workers feel useful and initiates a group spirit by having them contribute clean rags and boiling water. Mac's motives are not altruistic.

> 'Course it was nice to help the girl, but hell, even if it killed her—we've got to use anything. . . . We made the men work for themselves, in their own defense, as a group. . . . Raising wages isn't all we're after.[9]

The grateful grandfather of the newborn is London, a muscular worker with the "power of authority" whose usefulness Mac recognizes instantly: "He's the natural leader. We'll teach him where to lead." Mac orchestrates a meeting at which London is elected leader of the workers, and he teaches London how to hold "free elections" with guaranteed results—results which match Party goals.

When the angry workers do indeed strike, Mac and Jim and their Party connections provide the necessary organization and support to make the action a real threat, hoping this strike will spread to the nearby cotton fields. Armed with a list of friendly townspeople, Dick (a "pretty" Party worker who "uses the bedroom for political purposes") arranges for the donation of tents and food. Mac and Jim ingratiate themselves with Al Anderson, the friendly Lunch Wagon owner, and then convince Al's father (a small apple grower who is being squeezed by the big owners) to allow the strikers to camp on his land, so that authorities may not force them out of the valley. And Mac sends for Doc Burton who, though not a Party member, sympathizes with the workers and keeps the camp sufficiently sanitary to meet health standards.

Mac's goal is to create out of these desperate individual workers a group animal whose anger is focused and whose actions are powerful. Mac's view is a long one, however, and he wants far more than limited improvement for the Torgas Valley crop tramps: "A strike that's settled too quickly won't teach the men how to organize, how to work together. A tough strike is good. We want the men to find out how strong they are when they work together" (38). No opportunity to encourage the emergence of the group animal is too small to seize, and Mac describes even smoking as a useful tool which allows him to "soften" strangers by offering a smoke.

Mac instructs Jim on the importance of refusing to allow human emotions to interfere with the main Party objectives, and he is always unapologetic and frequently unaware of the resulting callousness in his behavior. He notes that "every time a guardsman jabs a fruit tramp with a bayonet a thousand men all over the country come on our side . . . if we could get the National Guard called out . . . , we'd have the whole district organized by spring" (39). Mac is equally cool when a ladder gives way and Old Dan breaks his hip. "The old buzzard was worth something after all," he notes, as the

injured seventy-one-year-old becomes a symbol of the owners' failure to provide safe equipment for the workers on
whom they depend.

When, ironically, vigilantes ignite worker resistance by
killing Mac's old friend Joy, Mac has London drag the body
back to camp, where he puts it on display to enrage the
workers: "We've got to use him to step our guys up, to keep
'em together. This'll stick 'em together, this'll make 'em fight"
(169). When another worker protests that Mac is a "cold-
blooded bastard" (170) for using a pal this way, Mac defends
his desire to make a "show" of Joy: "We got damn few things
to fight with. We got to use what we can" (175).

Jim is an apt pupil, achieving what Doc calls "Pure
religious ecstasy" as he discovers his place in the group
animal: "I'm not lonely any more, and I can't be licked,
because I'm more than myself" (260). Jim is a practical as well
as an ideological striker, mastering (often evangelical) techniques of focusing worker discontent, using old playground
tricks to escape when captured by vigilantes, and citing the
Greek victory at Salamis as an indication that trapped people
sometimes fight on to victory (193).

Mac advocates detachment ("We can't waste time liking
people"), and it is a lesson Jim learns well—so well that,
ironically, he is often cooler than Mac. When Mac is sickened
by the need to beat a high school boy as a warning for others
to stay away from the strikers' camp, for example, it is Jim
who provides comfort and support: "he's not a kid, he's an
example. . . . That was like a doctor's work. It was an
operation, that's all" (278, 280). His coolness troubles Mac,
who says "You're getting beyond me, Jim. I'm getting scared
of you. . . . It's not human." But Jim feels new peace and
strength in his detachment: "I'm stronger than anything in the
world, because I'm going in a straight line. You and all the rest
have to think of women and tobacco and liquor and keeping
warm and fed" (280). Whereas Mac's indifference to the
human cost of Party techniques is layered over his humanity
(humanity which occasionally peeps out in concern for Jim or
in despair at the need to beat the high school student), Jim's
detachment becomes an inner reality.

The importance of the group animal is discussed at

various times throughout the novel by Mac, Jim, and London, all of whom are conscious both of the power of group action (ten men working together can accomplish what it would take twelve to do separately) and of the difficulty of predicting mob action. The group power theory which Mac passes on to Jim and London is questioned throughout by Doc. Doc's compassion does not yield the happiness the Party provides for Jim: "I'm awfully lonely. I'm working all alone, toward nothing. There's some compensation for you people. I only hear heartbeats through a stethoscope. You hear them in the air" (262). But he has deep and serious reservations about the violence which results from the Party indifference to individual human suffering: "in my little experience the end is never very different in its nature from the means. Damn it, Jim, you can only build a violent thing with violence." And he questions whether a victory over the Growers Association will indeed provide the victory Jim envisions: "It seems to me that man has engaged in a blind and fearful struggle out of a past he can't remember, into a future he can't foresee nor understand. And man has met and defeated every obstacle, every enemy except one. He cannot win over himself" (259).

Mac and Jim hold to the Party vision. Despite their ability to inspire the group animal, however, and despite the order created by Mac's division of the men into squads and Doc's careful layout of the campsite, the strike goes badly. Al is severely beaten and his Lunch Wagon burned. The growers manage to discourage food donations and bribe strikers to betray their friends. The strikers are increasingly hungry, listless, and apathetic, too disheartened even to kick dirt into the latrines when the lime runs out. It rains. One major strike leader is arrested, and Jim is wounded. Vigilantes burn Anderson's barn, Doc disappears, and Anderson demands that the strikers leave his land. Just as the strikers seem about to disburse in defeat, Jim is killed—a shotgun blast tearing away his face—and Mac hauls his body back to camp. The novel closes with Mac speaking over Jim's lifeless body, his words echoing those he had earlier spoken over Joy's body: "This guy didn't want nothing for himself . . ." (349).

III. CRITICAL EXPLICATION

Early readers were likely to respond most forcefully to this novel's graphic use of violence and to its treatment of labor issues and Communists (though only Doc uses that word in the novel). For contemporary readers *In Dubious Battle* continues to provide a forceful and generally believable picture of migrant labor in the 1930s. With violent labor agitation seemingly safely in the nation's past and our sensibilities dulled by seemingly endless reels of graphic film and television violence, however, we are as likely in the 1990s to respond to the novel's aesthetics as to its politics.

Steinbeck's prose in this novel is spare and uncolored, what Roy Simmonds calls an "austere, almost journalistic style . . . simple in vocabulary and syntactic construction, stripped down to bare essentials."[10] Often, in fact, it approaches the simple dramatic form he used in *Of Mice and Men,* with long passages of dialogue and brief indications (almost like stage directions) of action. Steinbeck anticipates in this novel the critical advice given by Mack in the preface to *Sweet Thursday.*

> I like a lot of talk in a book, and I don't like to have nobody tell me what the guy that's talking looks like. I want to figure out what he looks like from the way he talks. And another thing—I kind of like to figure out what the guy's thinking by what he says. I like some description too . . . but not too much of that.[11]

The absence in *In Dubious Battle* of emotional adjectives, revelation of thoughts, and extensive descriptions of setting or action is particularly noticeable in passages whose starkness contrasts with the action. When Mac beats the high school boy who will become an example for his colleagues, for example, the narration is deliberately flat and minimal.

> "Who sent you?"
> "Nobody."
> Mac struck him in the face with his open hand. The head jerked sideways, and an angry red spot formed on the white, beardless cheek. "Who sent you?"

"Nobody." The open hand struck again, harder. The boy lurched, tried to recover and fell on his shoulder.

Mac reached down and pulled him to his feet again. "Who sent you?"

The boy was crying. Tears rolled down his nose, into his bleeding mouth. "The fellows at school said we ought to."

"High school?"

"Yes. An' the men in the street said somebody ought to."

"How many of you came out?"

"Six of us."

"Where did the rest go?"

"I don't know, mister. Honest, I lost 'em."

Mac's voice was monotonous. "Who burned the barn?"

"I don't know." This time Mac struck with a closed fist. The blow flung the slight body against the tent-pole. Mac jerked him up again. The boy's eye was closed and cut. (277)

Steinbeck's very brevity and understatement in passages like this serve to underscore the force of the actions and the words. Occasionally, especially when dealing with groups of migrant workers, the description of speakers becomes (if possible) even terser and more generic, and Steinbeck identifies them with tag descriptive phrases: "Lean-face," "A short man," "Lantern-jaw."

Such spare dramatic form (once Steinbeck even introduces dialogue with character names followed by colons) led Steinbeck and Herman Shumlin briefly to contemplate turning the novel into a play, and Shumlin even talked to John O'Hara about doing the dramatization, but Steinbeck voiced some relief when the project was abandoned, observing that his attempts to block the work were "lousy . . . a re-hashed novel."[12]

But the style which Lisca describes as "harsh, factual, catalogue-like in its complete objectivity" (116) does not mean that the novel is emotionless or that the narrative is always neutral. The parallel to Milton's hell suggested by Steinbeck's selection of a title from a passage of *Paradise Lost,* for example, is reinforced by the novel's continuing pattern of dim light, dark interiors, night scenes—punctuated by flashes of red. Sometimes the red is light (neon lights, sunset, flames, gun flashes) and sometimes not (stained glass windows, eyes,

geraniums and Virginia creepers, spots in cheeks). Throughout the novel red and black, which often seem the only colors
in Torgas Valley, provide a Miltonic quality for the hellish
existence of these fruit workers. This is a novel about reds in
more than one sense of the word.

Mac's recognition that the migrants want only the
"heaven" of a blissful rural life, and Doc's insistence that Jim's
goals constitute a "vision of Heaven" (206) underscore the
pattern of hellish light which parallels Milton's descriptions of
Satan's abode. Other uses of Christian imagery extend the
pattern: Jim is "re-born" in the Party and achieves religious
ecstasy in its service, and his rhetoric resembles that of a
preacher; the workers are picking apples; Lisa and her baby
are seen as part of a "Holy Family" group; the woman
combing her hair has the "wise and cool and sure" smile of a
madonna (307);[13] and the cock crows three times before Jim's
martyrdom. The novel's pattern of Christian imagery, then, is
one way in which Steinbeck considerably modifies what may
initially seem a remarkably objective narrative style.

Occasionally there are also pieces of description whose
resonances go beyond the immediate context to become
emblematic of major movements in the novel. At one point,
for example, when Mac refills the kerosene lamp, the description of the flame parallels what the Party hopes will happen in
the mass movement: "Slowly the flame grew up again, and its
edges spread out like a butterfly's wings" (286). Later, lying
awake, London hears the roosters: "The old tough rooster
crowed first, and the young one answered" (295). That
transition parallels the passing of Party ideals from older to
younger members.

The most powerful image pattern, in addition to the use
of light and dark, is that of animals and men. This pattern is
also the most complex. *Torgas* means a yoke for hogs, and
fruit growers in the valley do indeed use the migrants like
yoked beasts. Frequently characters in the novel parallel their
experience with that of animals. Mac, for example, noticing
how he and Jim are sniffing each other out after their first
introduction, remarks, "Too bad we're not dogs, we could get
that all over with. We'd either be friends or fighting by now"
(24). Jim's training by Mac is like that of a young dog being

allowed to follow experienced hunters. And Mac compares the soldiers he knew to "good, honest, stupid cattle" (32). Old Dan describes the workers as moving about "like a bunch of hogs" (71), and Mac accuses the growers of letting the workers "live like pigs" (130). Just after Mac has returned to the camp with Joy's body, he is startled by "a hoarse, bubbling scream" (174) which initially seems human but turns out to be that of the pig the migrants are slaughtering; the parallel with Joy's death is clear though unstated. And Jim, disgusted at the disintegration evident in open attacks on London, refers to the complainers as "a bunch of swine" (305). Dakin becomes a mad dog when his truck is wrecked. Such parallels of men with animals (especially with swine and dogs) clearly emphasize situations in which men are either treated as subhuman or behave as such, and Mac defines the Party's goal as "to help you live like a man, and not like a pig" (289).

On the other hand, the Growers also appeal to the workers on the basis of their manhood. When Bolter, president of the Growers Association, comes to meet with London, his appeal to end the strike is peppered with references to Americanism (reds are, after all, un-American regardless of their genealogy), and one way he distinguishes American from non-American working men is to suggest that "American working men aren't animals" (250). It is difficult, then, to distinguish between the rhetoric of the Party and the rhetoric of the Growers, and when Mac mutters that Bolton's skill with rhetoric suggests he "ought to run for Congress" (250), the words could apply equally well to Mac himself.

If it is undesirable for individual men to act or be treated like animals, however, the unity toward which the Party is pushing these migrants is regularly described by Mac and Jim as a group *animal,* and in that context the term seems not merely descriptive, but positive. The tension in Party goals, then, is in part revealed by the fact that Mac hopes to create a group animal in an effort to eliminate the necessity for individuals to live like animals. Old Dan, whose term for the group-man is "the big guy," sounds a cautionary note about this Party optimism, and his words twist the animal imagery in yet another direction, picturing the group animal as a mad dog: "That big guy'll run like a mad dog, and bite anything that moves. He's been hungry too long, and he's been hurt too much; and worst thing of all, he's had his feelings hurt too much" (73).

The constant association of men with animals and much of the Christian imagery can coexist in this novel with a style which is accurately described as primarily objective in part because so much of the figurative language comes not from the narrative voice but from characters in the novel. In fact, the basic structure of this novel is the key factor in its final impact. Steinbeck uses Jim as the organizational focus of *In Dubious Battle,* never wandering from the young man's side, and the advantages of that choice are clear. Jim is a neophyte, new not just to the Party, but also to the country and to agriculture. He sheds his old life as an individual, his suit, his existence in the city. He becomes part of the group animal, dons jeans, and moves to the country. This is a novel of education in large part, and Mac must constantly explain the workings of California agriculture and the Party to Jim. Then Jim and Mac together explain the Party to London. And Jim and Mac debate the role of individual and group with Doc.

For a strike novel full of shootings and beatings and burnings, *In Dubious Battle* is, in fact, remarkably talky—and much of the talk is repetitious, driving firmly home key points and analogies. Attention to the novel's aesthetics and form thus leads us inevitably back to its politics, but with a firmer sense of the complex, undoctrinaire way in which Steinbeck presents those politics.

Steinbeck's letters from immediately before and after publication of *In Dubious Battle* indicate his belief that the novel would be "attacked by both sides."[14] "Communists will hate it and the other side will too," he predicted.[15] But

> [a]nswering the complaint that the ideology is incorrect, this is the silliest of criticism. There are as many communist systems as there are communists . . . the damned people of both sides . . . postulate either an ideal communist or a thoroughly damnable communist and neither side is willing to suspect that the communist is a human, subject to the weaknesses of humans and to the greatness of humans.[16]

Steinbeck's fears were in part realized when Covici-Friede, the firm which had been publishing his works, rejected *In Dubious Battle*—largely because the editor who originally read the manuscript was "strongly rooted in Marxist ideology and was certain that the book was inaccurate and that Steinbeck didn't know what he was talking about."[17] Steinbeck categorized the objections of the Covici-Friede editor as typical of "communists of the intellectual bent and of the Jewish race" and pointed out his reliance on "Irish and Italian communists whose training was in the field, not in the drawing room."[18] Covici-Friede quickly reversed its decision, however, and other critical reaction to the novel was less specifically tied to ideology, though Mary McCarthy did criticize the novel's presentation of philosophy rather harshly, calling the work

> academic, wooden, inert. . . . The dramatic events take place for the most part off-stage and are reported, as in the Greek drama, by a breathless observer. Mr. Steinbeck for all his long and frequently pompous exchanges offers only a few rather childish, often reiterated generalizations. . . . He may be a natural story-teller; but he is certainly no philosopher, sociologist, or strike technician.[19]

There is no question that the novel treats the plight of California's migrant workers with considerable sympathy. The workers are, however, by no means glorified, and there is ample evidence that they are as prone to pettiness, selfishness, laziness, violence, and sexual infidelity as the population at large. Mac and Jim, the two principal representatives of the Party, are depicted with equally obvious flaws, especially in relation to their willingness to sacrifice any number of individuals to the general goal of group unity.

On the other hand, in the Torgas Valley—where growers sacrifice individual workers not for some ideal but for personal gain—the Party is clearly the best hope the pickers have for coming a bit closer to an existence which is both human and humane. Mac more than once refers to the Valley as "organized like Italy" (200), and though it is not entirely clear what he means by the Italy connection (feudalism?

Catholicism? fascism? the mafia?), he is clearly correct about the lock on power and privilege which Torgas Valley growers have. They unhesitatingly violate both legal and ethical principles and use their full financial and military power to force both workers and small owners to conform to Growers Association mandates. In controlling the valley they use not only financial and social pressure, but also demagoguery, appealing to the general fear of lower class violence and to the belief that labor agitation is "un-American." Unlike the Party, the Growers have no vision beyond their own immediate profit; unlike Mac and Jim, the Growers are not willing to suffer personally for their beliefs.

Steinbeck's refusal either to glorify or to condemn the workers or the Party is no doubt one reason for Andre Gide's endorsement of this "remarkable book" as "the best (psychological) portrayal that I know of Communism. . . ."[20] The balanced picture which *In Dubious Battle* provides of both sides suggests that Steinbeck was indeed, as he maintained, interested in writing "a novel and not a tract."[21] The patterns of imagery are powerful reinforcements for an interpretation which does not depict one side as "good" and the other as "bad." Red is the color of the Party, but also of fire and destruction and a Miltonic hell. Animal analogies are used by both sides, and they reveal as many ambiguities as truths.

Steinbeck also builds into *In Dubious Battle* numerous indications that the events in the Torgas Valley are part of a long, cyclical, probably endless pattern. Old Dan has been a top-faller in the north woods when the Wobblies were organizing timber workers, and though the movement did "some good," making the companies "put in toilets and showers," the movement "all went to pieces"—largely because labor leaders elected by the workers betrayed them (72). Party efforts in the Torgas Valley do not strike Old Dan as original; they just remind him of the Wobblies. Similarly, Mac sees the Torgas Valley vigilantes as part of a pattern: "Mac, who in hell are these vigilantes . . . ?" asks Jim. "Why," replies Mac, "they're the dirtiest guys in any town. They're the same ones that burned the houses of old German people during the war. They're the same ones that lynch Negroes. . . . The owners use 'em . . ." (172).

It is Doc who is the most powerful spokesman in this novel for the notion that history may be repetitive rather than progressive. The first of several characters modelled after Steinbeck's good friend, biologist Ed Ricketts (Doc in *Cannery Row* and Casy in *The Grapes of Wrath* are others), Doc Burton voices the non-teleological views which Steinbeck and Ricketts discussed at great length, and which they wrote about in *Sea of Cortez,* published five years after *In Dubious Battle*. In the Easter Sunday chapter of *The Log from the Sea of Cortez,* Steinbeck explains that teleological thinking "considers changes and cures—what 'should be' in the terms of an end pattern." Non-teleological thinking, on the other hand, results from " 'is' thinking, associated with natural selection as Darwin seems to have understood it." The obvious goal here is to record external reality as it *is,* without suggesting how it *ought* to be, and without imposing traditional moral formulas. It is the impact of non-teleological thinking on his fiction which Steinbeck seems to have in mind when he writes to his agent just before publication of *In Dubious Battle* that the novel is "brutal because there is no author's moral point of view."[22] Steinbeck might more accurately have indicated that the author's point of view is not traditionally moral, that in fact it is non-teleological. It is the impact of this scientifically based non-teleological thought on Steinbeck which forms the foundation for what Jackson J. Benson has described as "a naturalism more thorough-going and a view of life colder and less sentimental than almost any other American writer we might classify as a naturalist."[23]

Doc shares with Steinbeck a preference for non- teleological thought. His goal is not achievement of a new social order, but the ability to see clearly.

> I want to see the whole picture—as nearly as I can. I don't want to put on the blinders of "good" and "bad" and limit my vision. If I used the term "good" on a thing I'd lose my license to inspect it, because there might be bad in it. Don't you see? I want to be able to look at the whole thing. (149)

What Doc's independent vision reveals to him is that there is no end—not just no end in sight, but no end.

> There've been communes before, and there will be again. But
> you people have an idea that if you can *establish* the thing the
> job'll be done. Nothing stops, Mac. If you were able to put an
> idea into effect tomorrow, it would start changing right away.
> Establish a commune, and the same gradual flux will continue.
> (149)

Because they believe that there is an achievable goal, Party
members seem to Doc to have blinded themselves to reality.
"Sometimes I think you realists are the most sentimental
people in the world" (209), he observes—thus linking his
vision with the "colder and less sentimental" view which
Benson has noted in Steinbeck's own vision.

Doc compares the actions of group-man seeking to wipe
out social injustice with Communism to the actions of
group-man in seeking to "recapture the Holy-Land" or to
make the world safe for Democracy (151). "There aren't any
beginnings," he concludes. "Nor any ends" (259). Independent, non-teleological thinking shows us that life is a flux, an
evolution not a revolution.

A good portion of Doc's authority derives from his status
as an outsider, an independent observer with no axe to grind,
and Steinbeck's use of language emphasizes Doc's outsider
status. As Jackson J. Benson points out, Doc's diction is
"pretentious, formalized"—the kind of language frequently
used by Steinbeck characters who are making "moral or
philosophical pronouncements" (Lee in *East of Eden* is another example).[24] On the other hand, Steinbeck labored to
make the language of the migrants accurate, reading much of
the novel aloud to himself to check the rhythms and maintaining that "universal rules" govern the novel's "local idioms."
The speech "may seem a little bit racy to ladies' clubs," he
acknowledged, but "I'm sick of working men being gelded of
their natural expression until they talk with a fine Oxonian
flavor."[25] (In an earlier letter to another friend he suggests
that he is "sick of the noble working man talking very much
like a junior college professor."[26])

The characters themselves recognize the distinction
revealed by their language. When Doc notes Mac's ability to
"imitate any speech you're taking part in," Mac explains the

practical advantages of such a skill. "Doc, men are suspicious of a man who doesn't talk their way." But Mac also exempts Doc from this general rule of speech: "It's not the same thing in your case, Doc. You're supposed to be different. They wouldn't trust you if you weren't" (148).

Thus Doc and Mac form a pair which Benson identifies as typical of Steinbeck's fiction.

> [A] philosophical character with whom the author's essential sympathy lies is paired with a man of action. The philosophical character seldom acts, while the man of action does not usually act very effectively or very well. Steinbeck's point seems to be that you don't act to gain results—a teleological formulation—you look in order to understand.[27]

The most powerful reinforcement of the comments from various characters who recognize the repetitive pattern of history comes, of course, from the structure of the novel itself, particularly from its ending. As Mac speaks over Jim's grossly disfigured body, the situation and the words are direct repetitions of what happened when Joy's body was displayed in an effort to ignite the workers in group effort. In a prepublication letter to his agent, Steinbeck points to the significance of the novel's end and suggests that in the disorder of the novel lies

> a terrible kind of order . . . the book ends with no finish. A story of the life of a man ends with his death, but where can you end a story of man-movement that has no end? No matter where you stop there is always more to come. I have tried to indicate this by stopping on a high point but it is by no means an ending.[28]

It is significant that the strongest emphasis on unending repetition comes from Doc. Doc is the only non-teleological thinker in this novel, and the views he expresses are very close to those Steinbeck set forth as his own in *Sea of Cortez* and in letters. Benson is probably correct when he suggests that Steinbeck is "using a Ricketts-like figure to enunciate his own perspective,"[29] and Doc is thus the closest thing to an authorial spokesman in this novel.

Steinbeck described his novel as "mostly done in dialogue thus permitting many varying opinions but keeping out any author's opinion"[30] and pointed out that "the book is about eighty percent dialogue."[31] Most critics have concurred that the novel is essentially dramatic in technique and uncolored in description. Both Mack and Jim have as much opportunity as Doc to set forth their opinions, and Steinbeck has given each powerful, though somewhat different, arguments for supporting the Party and working to organize the valley. The Growers Association has both less space in the novel and a much weaker argument: as Gide observes, the novel "leaves the capitalist and bourgeois counterpart in the shadow."[32] But Growers Association criticisms of the Party are clear and often justified. Doc's non-teleological views are by no means the only ones fully developed in *In Dubious Battle*. It is not, however, entirely true that the novel keeps out any author's opinion (for that matter, what novel does or could?). The imagery, the novel's structure, and the disinterested objectivity of Doc's analysis—an analysis unwittingly reinforced by other characters who recognize repetitive patterns—combine to give particular weight and force to what Doc says.

Much of the discussion which flows so endlessly in this novel centers around creation of the group animal (also referred to as Group-man or "the Big Guy"). It is an issue which has concerned Steinbeck before (as in the "westering" movement described in "The Leader of the People") and to which he will return in *The Grapes of Wrath*. His letters of the time frequently use the word *phalanx* to describe the unified whole he has in mind, and he referred to *In Dubious Battle* as his "phalanx novel." Letters of the time also show him referring to religion, mobs, armies, and the Jungian subconscious as examples of the phalanx, and he described art as "the property of the phalanx, not of the individual."[33]

Steinbeck's awareness of the power and unpredictability of the group animal, and his sensitivity to the tension between individual and group persisted throughout his life and throughout his writing. In 1955, in a piece for *The Saturday Review* about juvenile delinquency, he came back to the subject from yet another angle.

But also I believe that man is a double thing—a group animal
and at the same time an individual. And it occurs to me that he
cannot successfully be the second until he has fulfilled the
first.[34]

There are many ways in which the battle in the Torgas
Valley is dubious—the end may not justify the means; rebels
are both noble opponents of oppression and satanic; the
outcome is very much in doubt. One of the most central
dubious aspects of this battle, however, is that which reveals
individuals pitted against the group instinct within themselves. It is that conflict which Doc has in mind when he
suggests that "man has met and defeated every obstacle, every
enemy except one. He cannot win over himself. How
mankind hates itself" (259). Those words are echoed almost
exactly in a letter of the time which Steinbeck wrote to
express his own views: "man hates something in himself. He
has been able to defeat every natural obstacle but himself he
cannot win over unless he kills every individual. And this
self-hate which goes so closely in hand with self-love is what
I wrote about."[35]

Occasionally *In Dubious Battle* seems almost like appren-
tice work for *The Grapes of Wrath*. Both novels center on
conflicts between workers and growers in California, of
course, but there are also a number of characters in the earlier
novel who seem almost like brief pencil sketches for the full
oil portraits of Steinbeck's more famous novel. Jim Nolan's
tendency to turn the techniques of preachers to the ends of
the Party foreshadows Jim Casy's, and these two outsiders are
free to engage in the struggle more fully because they lack
families. Lisa (Elizabeth?) in her pregnancy is like Rose of
Sharon in hers. Lisa's husband Joey (Joseph?) is interested in
taking correspondence courses to enable him to become a
postman, and Rose of Sharon's husband Connie has an
unending interest in self-improvement correspondence
courses. Doc Burton is remarkably like the Weedpatch camp
manager. Strike leaders in both novels pass their ideals on to
others before dying or disappearing.

The tightness of *In Dubious Battle,* with its unity of time
and place, is a marked contrast with the expansiveness of *The*

Grapes of Wrath, but even the forms of the two novels show similarities. Steinbeck's use of emblematic flames and roosters adumbrates his use of the turtle in *The Grapes of Wrath,* as does his use of religious imagery. And the novels end equally ambiguously, with the conflicts unresolved, appearing merely to be part of the general flux of the world.

For all its similarities to *The Grapes of Wrath,* however, *In Dubious Battle* is a fully realized work in its own right, a carefully crafted novel in which—as Steinbeck had hoped—the disorder reveals "a terrible kind of order." The tight connection between aesthetics and politics, between form and idea in this novel—the impossibility of discussing one without considering the other—is merely the clearest sign of Steinbeck's achievement.

NOTES

1. *John Steinbeck: A Life in Letters,* eds. Elaine A. Steinbeck and Robert Wallsten (New York: Viking Press, 1975), p. 112. Hereafter cited as *SLL.*
2. *SLL,* p. 98.
3. Jackson J. Benson, *The True Adventures of John Steinbeck, Writer* (New York: Viking Press, 1984), p. 297.
4. *SLL,* p. 98.
5. Benson, p. 310.
6. *Ibid.,* p. 299.
7. *Ibid.,* pp. 305-06.
8. *Ibid.,* p. 298.
9. John Steinbeck, *In Dubious Battle* (New York: Covici-Friede, 1936), p. 66. Hereafter page references will be cited in parentheses following quotes.
10. Roy S. Simmonds, *Steinbeck's Literary Achievement (Steinbeck Monograph Series,* No. 6) (Muncie, Indiana: Steinbeck Society of America, Ball State University, 1976), p. 26.
11. John Steinbeck, *Sweet Thursday* (New York: Viking Press, 1954), pp. vii-viii.
12. *SLL,* p. 123.
13. Mythologist Joseph Campbell, who lived next to Steinbeck in the early 1930s, later "had the impression that some of the mythic images in [the fiction] may have come out of their

discussions, particularly in *In Dubious Battle* where the Madonna image was used." Benson, p. 223.

14. *SLL,* p. 107.
15. Peter Lisca, *The Wide World of John Steinbeck* (New York: Gordian Press, 1981), p. 114.
16. *SLL,* pp. 107-08.
17. Benson, p. 315.
18. *SLL,* pp. 109-10.
19. *Ibid.,* p. 122.
20. André Gide, *The Journals of André Gide (Vol. 2),* trans. Justin O'Brien (New York: Vintage, 1956), p. 265.
21. Lisca, p. 115.
22. *SLL,* p. 105.
23. Jackson J. Benson, "Steinbeck—A Defense of Biographical Criticism," *College Literature,* 16 (Spring, 1989), 107.
24. Benson, *True Adventures,* p. 61.
25. *SLL,* p. 105.
26. *Ibid.,* p. 99.
27. Benson, *True Adventures,* p. 249.
28. *SLL,* pp. 105-06.
29. Benson, *True Adventures,* p. 245.
30. Lisca, p. 117.
31. *SLL,* p. 99.
32. Gide, p. 265.
33. *SLL,* p. 80.
34. John Steinbeck, "Some Thoughts on Juvenile Delinquency," *Saturday Review,* 38 (May 28, 1955), 22.
35. *SLL,* p. 98.

IV. TOPICS FOR RESEARCH AND DISCUSSION

(1)   In a 1935 letter, Steinbeck said of *In Dubious Battle,*

> I have used a small strike in an orchard valley as the symbol of man's eternal, bitter warfare with himself. I'm not interested in strike as means of raising men's wages, and I'm not interested in ranting about justice and oppression, mere outcroppings which indicate the condition. But man hates something in himself. He has been able to defeat every natural obstacle but himself he cannot win over unless he kills every individual.

Does Steinbeck's description of what he hoped to accomplish
match the novel?

(2)   Andre Gide wrote about *In Dubious Battle* that "The main
character is the crowd; but from that amorphous and vague
mass there stand out various individuals. . . ." Peter Lisca
described the mob, the group-man, and the strike as "the real
protagonist and subject matter." And much criticism of the
novel has revolved around whether or not Steinbeck peoples
it with "real," "full," or "rounded" characters. Discuss Steinbeck's characterization in *In Dubious Battle*. Does this novel
have a protagonist? An antagonist? Are the characters alive
and believable?

(3)   Steinbeck was well aware that women and members of ethnic
minority groups were common in the California farm fields—
and that they often played important roles in worker organizations and strikes. Yet all the major characters in *In Dubious
Battle* are white males. When ethnic workers are mentioned,
they are Italian or Irish, despite the fact that three-quarters of
the workers on both the peach and cotton strikes he used as
models were Mexican, and despite his awareness that California growers regularly pitted racial groups (Mexican, Filipino,
black, white) against each other in order to prevent the growth
of unions (Benson, 303-04). There are a number of minor
women characters (Jim's mother and sister; Mrs. Dakin; Lisa;
the woman who invites Jim into her tent; the woman combing
her hair; the sympathizer whom Dick measures by numbers of
axe handles). Examine the implications of Steinbeck's focus on
white males and the role of women in this novel.

(4)   Like most authors, Steinbeck showed a continuing concern
with a number of central issues, and *In Dubious Battle* may be
usefully studied in relation to other works by him. Compare
Steinbeck's handling of the notion of revolution and revolutionary leaders in *In Dubious Battle* to his handling of similar
themes in one of the following: "The Raid"; *Viva Zapata!* (Elia
Kazan's 1952 film starring Marlon Brando, for which Steinbeck wrote both story and screenplay); *The Grapes of Wrath;
The Moon Is Down*. Or, apply Steinbeck's contention in *Sea of
Cortez* that "the people we call leaders are simply those who, at
the given moment, are moving in the direction behind which
will be found the greatest weight, and which represents a
future mass movement."

(5)   The relationship of farm workers to the land on which they
labor has been of continuing concern to Steinbeck and is a

theme in *Of Mice and Men* and *The Grapes of Wrath* as well as in *In Dubious Battle*. Not a lot is said about small farms or family farms in this novel, but there are glimpses (including a few lyrical descriptions of the land) which highlight much of the rest of the action. Discuss Anderson's description of his farm and Lisa's dream of the future and consider what they reveal about the farming activity which forms the bulk of the work in this novel.

(6) There are many ironies in this novel: Joy's name; the fact that it is the city dweller Jim who must teach the farm workers how to slaughter a cow; the extent to which vigilante actions designed to head off the strike in fact push it forward; the fact that Mr. Anderson (who thinks he will increase his individual profit by helping the strikers) ends up financially ruined; much of the workers' humor ("Everything's free here, food, liquor, automobiles, houses. Just move in and set down to a turkey dinner." "Figure to pick a few apples and retire on my income."). Discuss the role of irony in *In Dubious Battle*.

V. SELECTED BIBLIOGRAPHY

1. Jackson J. Benson and Anne Loftis, "John Steinbeck and Farm Labor Unionization: The Background of *In Dubious Battle*," *American Literature*, 52 (May 1980), 194-223. A detailed examination of the novel's origins and the farm labor history which forms its background. Coauthored by Steinbeck's official biographer.

2. James P. Degnan, "In Definite Battle: Steinbeck and California's Land Monopolists," in *Steinbeck: The Man and His Work*, eds. Richard Astro and Tetsumaro Hayashi (Corvallis, Oregon: Oregon State University Press, 1971), pp. 65-74. An argument that the "fascistic control of California agriculture by a handful of huge landowners" which Steinbeck portrayed in the 1930s continues in the 1970s.

3. Joseph Fontenrose, *John Steinbeck: An Introduction and Interpretation* (New York: Barnes and Noble, 1963), pp. 42-53. An exhaustive, detailed discussion of the novel's mythic parallels, especially those with Milton's *Paradise Lost*.

4. Warren French, *John Steinbeck* (New Haven, Connecticut: College and University Press, 1961) (Twayne's United States Authors Series), pp. 62-71. A basic introduction to the novel

which details the relation between the novel's use of Arthurian legends and its objective stance.

5. W. M. Frohock, "John Steinbeck: The Utility of Wrath," in his *The Novel of Violence in America* (Dallas: Southern Methodist University Press, 1958), pp. 124-43. A defense of the novel's use of "orderly" violence as an "absolute double necessity," since it contributes both to the strike and to the "growth of Jim's soul."

6. Maxwell Geismar, "John Steinbeck: Of Wrath and Joy," in his *Writers in Crisis: The American Novel Between Two Wars* (Boston: Houghton Mifflin, 1942), pp. 260-63. An analysis which focuses on the novel's "rather debonair delight in bloodshed" and criticizes Steinbeck's view of human nature.

7. Hidekazu Hirose, "From Doc Burton to Jim Casy: Steinbeck in the Latter Half of the 1930s," in *John Steinbeck: East and West,* eds. Tetsumaro Hayashi, Yasuo Hashiguchi, and Richard F. Peterson (*Steinbeck Monograph Series,* No. 8) (Muncie, Indiana: Steinbeck Society, Ball State University, 1978), pp. 6-11. This comparison sees both Burton and Casy as characters close to Steinbeck and attributes their differences to changes in Steinbeck resulting from a steadily worsening situation for migrant labor in the 1930s.

8. Peter Lisca, *The Wide World of John Steinbeck* (New York: Gordian Press, 1981), pp. 108-29. A reprint (with limited new material) of an early (1958) and important study which continues to provide a wide-ranging but concise introduction to the novel's historical background, public history, and major themes. Particularly effective discussions of the tension between group animal and individual, the treatment of strikers and Communists, language use, and early critical reaction.

9. Robert E. Morsberger, "Steinbeck's Zapata: Rebel versus Revolutionary," in *Steinbeck: The Man and His Work,* eds. Richard Astro and Tetsumaro Hayashi (Corvallis, Oregon: Oregon State University Press, 1971), pp. 51-54. A discussion of Elia Kazan's 1952 film *Viva Zapata!* (starring Marlon Brando), for which Steinbeck wrote both story and screenplay, working on the project from 1948 to 1950. Morsberger compares *Viva Zapata!*, "a study of leadership and insurrection," to *In Dubious Battle, The Grapes of Wrath,* and *The Moon Is Down.*

10. John H. Timmerman, *John Steinbeck's Fiction: The Aesthetics of the Road Taken* (Norman, Oklahoma: University of Oklahoma Press, 1986), pp. 75-94. A thoughtful consideration of the

novel's aesthetics, including the impact on the novel of Steinbeck's biographical relation to its subject matter. Careful consideration of the "impersonal" narration and the central themes of use and group man.

6. STEINBECK'S *OF MICE AND MEN* (1937)

CHARLOTTE HADELLA

I. BACKGROUND

By 1937, the year that *Of Mice and Men* was published and also produced as a Broadway play, Steinbeck had survived the poverty of his writing apprenticeship and achieved commercial success with *Tortilla Flat* (1935). *In Dubious Battle* (1936) also sold well and, to Steinbeck's surprise, received respectable critical assessments. With the popular and critical success of *Of Mice and Men* and the enormous reaction to *The Grapes of Wrath* just two years later, Steinbeck never again had to worry about making his living as a writer.

Curiously, what did concern the writer while he was composing *Of Mice and Men* was that financial security and public attention would make him unfit for his craft. In a letter to his agent, Elizabeth Otis, he characterizes the publicity generated by *Tortilla Flat* as "rather terrible."[1] He also asks Otis not to make any artistic compromises with publishers for the sake of financing. "Too many people are trapped into promises by gaudy offers," he reasons, and "we've gone through too damned much trying to keep the work honest and in a state of improvement to let it slip now in consideration of a little miserable popularity. I'm scared to death of popularity" (*SLL,* 111). After *Mice* was chosen by the Book-of-the-Month Club, Steinbeck informed Otis that the news was both gratifying and frightening. He claims, "I shall never learn to conceive of money in larger quantities than two dollars. More than that has no conceptual meaning to me"

(*SLL*, 134). Perhaps the subject matter of the novel, which took him back to his earlier, more frugal years of working on the Spreckles Sugar Company ranches, intensified Steinbeck's uneasiness with financial security. As his biographer, Jackson J. Benson, observes, the composition of *Of Mice and Men* "was certainly an exercise in humility. For an author who lived through the lives of his characters, [Steinbeck] was reminding himself on the gut level what it was to have nothing, truly, and very little hope for anything."[2] Details of the writer's financial struggles in the early years of his marriage to Carol Henning underscore the authenticity of Steinbeck's interest in marginally subsistent characters whose fiscal futures are always uncertain.[3]

Artistic uncertainty also plagued Steinbeck during the 1930s. Though there were times while he was composing *Mice* that he judged the work to be going very well, he did not allow himself to assume success (*SLL*, 123-24). Steinbeck insisted that *Of Mice and Men* was different from anything else that he had ever written. He referred to the book as an experiment, "a tricky little thing designed to teach me to write for the theater" (*SLL*, 132). The relative ease with which the novel was transformed into a playscript testifies to the validity of Steinbeck's plan; but since the form was experimental, Steinbeck maintained a note of modest skepticism whenever he commented on the project. In fact, when the earliest version of the manuscript was partially devoured by his dog, Steinbeck wrote to Otis that although he was "pretty mad," he only gave the dog "an ordinary spanking." Maintaining that "the poor little fellow may have been acting critically," Steinbeck writes, "I didn't want to ruin a good dog for a ms. I'm not sure it is good at all" (*SLL*, 124). Thus, in spite of previous accomplishments, Steinbeck's distrust of publishers and critics tempered his enthusiasm for the book.

With *Of Mice and Men* Steinbeck was breaking new ground philosophically as well as formally, a circumstance which may also have contributed to his reticence concerning its critical reception. By 1936, he had become very interested in non-teleological thinking. Benson explains that in *In Dubious Battle* the author wanted to present a conflict without taking sides. In Steinbeck's non-teleological fictions, he attempted to create situations with "no cause and effect, no problem and solution, no heroes or villains."[4] Working within this philosophical framework, which might best be described as "is" thinking, Steinbeck originally titled George and Lennie's story "Something That Happened."[5] Happily, the novel proved to be a successful marriage of form and philosophy. With the dramatic structure focusing upon the characters' dialogue and action, Steinbeck achieved a narrative intensity in the story which is largely untainted by authorial voice. Ironically, the "little book" (*SLL*, 129) which received such a tentative evaluation from its author would not only find an immediate audience, but would be recognized decades later as a minor American classic.

II. PLOT SYNOPSIS

PART I

In the late afternoon on a hot day, George Milton and Lennie Small, two migrant harvesters, tramp from the highway into a grove of willows and sycamores beside the Salinas River. They are traveling from Weed to Soledad where they have hired on as hands at a ranch. George decides to camp by the river that night and reach the ranch by noon the following day. Over a dinner of canned beans, the two men discuss their plans for the future: they will work on the ranch, save their pay, get up a stake, and buy a place of their own. Lennie wants to raise rabbits and "live off the fatta the lan'."[6]

This scene establishes the personalities of the two main characters and the relationship between them. Lennie, "a huge man, shapeless of face, with large, pale eyes, with wide, sloping shoulders" (2), is mentally deficient. He loves to pet soft, furry things, and George scolds him for carrying a dead mouse in his pocket. George, who is "small and quick, dark of face, with restless eyes and sharp, strong features" (2), has promised Lennie's Aunt Clara that he will take care of Lennie. Though George complains that he "could live so easy" (11) if he were alone, he seems committed to keeping Lennie out of trouble and going into partnership with him on a little farm of their own.

Steinbeck makes the reader aware, however, of the pattern of failure into which George and Lennie's partnership has fallen. In a moment of anger, George rails against Lennie for losing them every job they get. In Weed, for instance, Lennie had tried to touch a girl's dress because it was pretty and soft; when she screamed, he had panicked and tightened his hold. George had rescued his partner by hiding him in an irrigation ditch until dark. Now, at their campsite by the river, George makes sure that Lennie can identify the grove in case he runs into trouble at the ranch and has to flee the premises.

PART II

George and Lennie arrive at the ranch and are shown around by Candy, an old farmhand whose only job is to look after the bunkhouse since losing his hand in an accident.

Before going to work that afternoon, George and Lennie meet a number of the people who live on the ranch, including the boss and his son Curley. Though the boss is suspicious about the relationship between his two new hired men, he accepts George's explanation that they travel around together. However, Curley, a little guy who "hates big guys," insists that Lennie speak for himself (26). George tells Candy that Curley "better watch out for Lennie" because "Lennie's strong and quick and Lennie don't know no rules" (27). Candy explains that Curley treats all of the other men with suspicion now that he is married. According to Candy, Curley has married "a tart" (28).

Then Curley's wife makes an appearance, as does Slim, the jerkline skinner who is described as "the prince of the ranch" (33). The girl, who has "full, rouged lips and wide-spaced eyes, heavily made up," says that she is looking for Curley. George answers her brusquely and she leaves (31). Then George warns Lennie to stay away from the girl. The scene ends with Curley asking the men in the bunkhouse if they have seen his wife.

PART III

After dinner Slim comments to George on Lennie's incredible physical strength. George reminisces about growing up with Lennie and also explains what happened in Weed with the girl who accused Lennie of raping her. Then Lennie enters the bunkhouse with the pup that Slim has given him and George has to scold him for taking the pup away from its mother. Carlson, another ranch hand, comes in and complains about Candy's dog; he suggests that Candy shoot the cur and end its misery. Carlson persists until Candy agrees to let him take the dog away. Crooks, the black stable worker, summons Slim to the barn to put tar on a mule's hoof.

While George plays cards with Whit, the conversation turns to Curley's wife. George declares that she's "a jail bait set on the trigger" (51). Whit invites George to come along with the guys to Susy's whorehouse on Saturday night. Though George insists that he and Lennie are saving their money, he says that he might visit Susy's place just to sit and have a drink. Lennie returns from taking the pup back to the barn, and Carlson comes back to clean his gun after shooting Candy's dog. The card game ends when Curley bursts into the room looking for his wife again and inquiring about Slim. Whit and Carlson follow Curley to the barn, anticipating a fight between Curley and Slim.

Forgetting that old Candy is still lying on his bunk, George and Lennie begin talking about the dream farm that they'll buy when they have saved enough cash. Candy interrupts their reverie and offers his life's savings if they will let him participate in the enterprise. Just as they have reached an agreement, Slim enters and is followed by Curley, Carlson, and Whit. Curley is trying to apologize to Slim for accusing him of flirting with his wife. The other men chide Curley, and Lennie joins in the laughter. Curley singles out Lennie for a fight and begins throwing punches. George tells his partner to "get" Curley, and before Lennie can be stopped, he crushes Curley's fist. Slim makes Curley promise to say that his hand got caught in a machine, and then Carlson takes Curley into town to see a doctor.

PART IV

The setting shifts to Crooks's room in the barn. Crooks is the black stable buck, a "proud, aloof man," who "kept his distance and demanded that other people keep theirs" (67). It is Saturday night and George has gone into town with the other workers and Curley. Lennie, who has come to pet his puppy, sees the light in Crooks's room and wanders in. Unfriendly at first, Crooks is quickly disarmed by Lennie's childish enthusiasm over the puppy, and the two men talk for a while. Crooks scoffs at Lennie's talk of the dream farm until Candy shows up and verifies the plan. Then Crooks, too, becomes infatuated with the idea of escaping from the ranch; he offers to work on the farm just for his keep.

This convivial interlude is interrupted by Curley's wife who claims to be looking for her husband. The woman is treated with contempt by both Candy and Crooks while Lennie, fascinated, cannot resist staring at her. To counter the men's resentment, Curley's wife tells them about her dreams of Hollywood and being "in the pitchers" (78). She also threatens Crooks with lynching and reminds him of his status as a black man and stable buck on her father-in-law's ranch. Though none of the men will tell her how Curley really got injured, she deduces from the bruises on Lennie's face that he is the "machine" that crushed Curley's hand. Satisfied with her discovery, she congratulates Lennie and slips out of the barn when Candy warns her that the men have returned from town.

George comes to the barn looking for Lennie and Candy. When Candy mentions the farm plans in front of Crooks, George scowls. Crooks, sensing George's disapproval of him, withdraws his offer to go and work on the farm. The scene closes with George, Lennie, and Candy leaving Crooks alone in his room.

PART V

It is Sunday afternoon on the ranch. The men are pitching horseshoes outside while Lennie is sitting in the barn looking at his dead puppy and dreading what George will do when he discovers what has happened. While Lennie is talking to the dead dog, Curley's wife comes into the barn. Lennie tells her that he cannot talk to her because George has told him not to; refusing to go away, she tells Lennie, "I never get to talk to nobody. I get awful lonely" (86).

When the woman sees the dead puppy, she tries to console Lennie. She invites him to stroke her hair, but panics when he holds on too tightly. Her screams frighten Lennie and he shakes her violently, breaking her neck. Lennie flees, knowing that he has "done a bad thing" (91).

Candy finds the woman's body, tells George first, and then informs the rest of the men. Curley organizes a search party with orders to shoot Lennie on sight. George goes with the men in search of Lennie.

PART VI

The novel ends late Sunday afternoon in the willow grove beside the Salinas River where George and Lennie had camped just a few days earlier. Lennie sits by the river and is tormented by visions of Aunt Clara and a giant rabbit. George arrives and once again tells his partner the story of the farm. While Lennie looks across the river, comforted by the dream of owning a home and tending to rabbits, George shoots him in the back of the head with Carlson's pistol.

The search party arrives and George tells them that he took the pistol from Lennie and shot him in self-defense. As Slim and George walk away from the scene together, Slim indicates that he understands what really happened. The others remain behind. "Curley and Carlson looked after them. And Carlson said, 'Now what the hell ya suppose is eatin' them two guys?' " (107). The novel ends with this question.

III. CRITICAL EXPLICATION

The frugal text of Steinbeck's little book has inspired a wealth of critical commentary. Moreover, a number of interpretive strategies have been applied to *Of Mice and Men,* producing varied readings of the text over the last few decades. Though my discussion will highlight what has already been said about *Of Mice and Men,* my primary aim is to offer a fresh analysis by subjecting the novel to various critical probes.[7] The eclectic nature of this study suggests that productive examination of Steinbeck's work can follow any one or several critical approaches: a New Historical consideration which notes the interconnections between the work of literature and the culture of its period; interpretive strategies such as structuralist or psychoanalytic readings which assume that the text is integrally whole; and discourse analysis which views the text as open and self-conflicted.

NEW HISTORICAL

Certainly each of Steinbeck's stories about California farm workers includes realistic details which were gleaned from the writer's own experiences as an agricultural laborer and his journalistic investigations of farm labor conditions. The description of the land and the river, the names of real California towns like Soledad and Weed, the language of the men in the bunkhouse, the details of everyday life such as the horseshoe matches and the trips to town on payday, all contribute to the realistic impression of *Of Mice and Men.* Nevertheless, Steinbeck mined his sources for convincing detail, but he was primarily interested in constructing powerful metaphors. For example, in reference to *In Dubious Battle,* Steinbeck wrote, "I have used a small strike in an orchard valley as the symbol of man's eternal, bitter warfare with himself."[8]

Though *In Dubious Battle* has most often been discussed as a work of realism, recent critics have noted that Steinbeck virtually ignored the important roles played by women and minorities in the California workers' strikes in the 1930s.[9]

Likewise, Steinbeck did not attempt to draw a realistic picture of the lives of racial minorities in *Of Mice and Men*. Just before George and Lennie first enter the grove by the Salinas River, the author sets the stage with this description: "In front of the low horizontal limb of a giant sycamore there is an ash pile made by many fires; the limb is worn smooth by men who have sat on it" (2). Judging by the characters depicted in the novel, we might assume that all (or most) of the men who have sat on that sycamore limb have been white men. Crooks, the stable buck, is the sole representative of a racial minority in the story. Yet, when Steinbeck worked on the Spreckles Sugar Ranches during the 1920s (while he was on and off as a student at Stanford), most of the workers were foreign nationals: Japanese, Mexican, or Filipino. Benson identifies Spreckles Ranch Number 2, just south of Soledad on the west side of the Salinas River, as the ranch where George and Lennie hire on.[10] Of course, Steinbeck also worked alongside migrant laborers of Anglo-Saxon stock—workers like George, Lennie, Slim, Carlson, and Candy; but it is unlikely that every hired hand in the bunkhouse during haying season would be Caucasian. In fact, in a very early piece, "Fingers of Cloud," published in a Stanford literary magazine, Steinbeck tells the story of a retarded teenage girl who wanders away from home and finds refuge in the bunkhouse of a Filipino work gang.[11]

Other historical and biographical details might lead us to question Steinbeck's choice of a cast of Anglo characters for his play-novelette. Cletus E. Daniel, in *Bitter Harvest: A History of California Farmworkers, 1870-1941,* states that Mexicans had become the mainstays of the agricultural labor force in California by the mid-1920s as growers took advantage of the liberalized federal immigration policy toward Mexico and as the flow of illegal immigration from Mexico steadily increased.[12] Furthermore, Steinbeck's choice of the "land dream" as a central motif in the story may have even been inspired by his trip to Mexico in 1935 during which he witnessed the struggle of masses of poor people longing to own a piece of land. Also during this trip, the Steinbecks had observed poor, illiterate workers attending concerts and theatrical productions. Benson believes that this experience prompted Steinbeck to consider writing a play instead of a novel because his work was not reaching the people he was writing about. In keeping with this original intention, Stein-beck read his novel-as-play to the Green Street Theater Union, a group which presented works with a socialist-worker philosophy. The Union opened its new theater in North Beach, California, on May 21, 1937, with Steinbeck's *Of Mice and Men*—six months before George Kaufman produced it on Broadway.[13]

Given the multiracial configuration of the California farm labor force in the 1920s and 1930s, along with the possible Mexican influence on the form and theme of Steinbeck's novel, we must conclude that Steinbeck was not attempting to render an accurate sociohistorical picture in *Of Mice and Men*. However, the subsistence-level economy, the tensions between workers and owner, and the social marginal-ity of the migrant laborers in *Of Mice and Men* ring true to the historical details of the actual setting. Most importantly, the American Dream theme of owning a piece of land, becoming self-sufficient, and realizing a sense of place, was a realistic facet of the American psyche. By 1936, the year that Steinbeck was writing *Mice,* the technological revolution in agribusiness was threatening what little job security itinerant workers had. Anne Loftis reports that mechanical combines enabling five men to do the work of 350 men were responsi-ble for half the nation's grain harvest in 1938.[14] Cletus E. Daniel writes that

> [b]y the twentieth century, employment in California's large-scale agriculture had come to mean irregular work, constant movement, low wages, squalid working and living conditions, social isolation, emotional deprivation, and individual power-lessness so profound as to make occupational advancement a virtual impossibility.[15]

He goes on to stress that "whatever the differences of race, national origin, language, and psychology that existed among farmworkers in California from 1870 to 1930, working for wages in industrialized agriculture normally conferred mem-bership in an unhappy fraternity whose cohering force was a kinship of powerlessness."[16]

Daniel's phrase "kinship of powerlessness" aptly describes the brotherhood of George, Lennie, and Candy as they plan for their escape from the ranch to the dream farm. Thus it seems that in spite of Steinbeck's failure to render "truthfully" the racial identities of his California farmworkers, he does create an accurate social milieu in *Of Mice and Men.* Loftis contends that the "social history which [Steinbeck] had learned firsthand is woven seamlessly into the fabric of the story."[17] The rapid decline in family farming and the impersonal profile of the burgeoning agribusiness in California at the turn of the century contributed to the decline of small communities and the rise of economic class distinctions. Family farming as a way of life became even more difficult as a result of the Great Depression. Hence, when *Of Mice and Men* appeared in 1937, many Americans could identify with the powerlessness and social marginality of Steinbeck's characters.

Finally it would seem that though America has experienced uncountable cultural and economic changes since the publication of *Of Mice and Men,* the isolation of individuals in our modern society still persists. In fact, the social problems of unemployment, underemployment, and homelessness, problems of which Steinbeck was acutely aware, plague this country even as we enter the final decade of the twentieth century. Picture, if you will, the disheveled transient standing on the street corner of any large American city today with his dirty cardboard sign which reads, WILL WORK FOR FOOD. Would he not be captivated by George and Lennie's dream? Perhaps he, too, dreams of "a vegetable patch and a rabbit hutch and chickens. And when it rains in the winter, [he could] say the hell with goin' to work, and . . . build up a fire in the stove and set around it an' listen to the rain comin' down on the roof . . ." (14-15). But even if the details of the dream vary, the fact that some people have little else but dreams to sustain them has not changed.

The selection of subject and theme for *Of Mice and Men* reveals Steinbeck's understanding of basic human needs, and the author's social consciousness has appealed to a wide audience for five decades. However, to appreciate Steinbeck's achievement as a storyteller, we must go beyond the sociohistorical fabric of his novella and give some attention to its structure, its psychological framework, and the complexity of its discourse.

SYMBOL, MYTH, AND THEME: STRUCTURALIST INTERPRETATIONS

The allusive title *Of Mice and Men* signals from the outset of the story that mice symbols will appear and that the schemes of men will go astray.[18] Before the central characters delineate those plans specifically, however, Steinbeck physically associates George with mice by describing him as "small and quick, dark of face, with restless eyes and sharp, strong features" (2). Lennie's connection with mice is more obvious: he carries a mouse in his pocket because he loves to pet soft, furry things. Consequently, Lennie associates mice with the dream of owning a farm and keeping rabbits which, unlike the mice, will be able to survive his petting them.

   Of Mice and Men is a tightly structured work which unfolds as a series of scenes, each of which develops naturally from the preceding dialogue or action. In *The Wide World of John Steinbeck,* Peter Lisca analyzes recurring motifs of language, action, and symbol in *Mice.* Discussing the sense of inevitability in the novel, Lisca notes that for Lennie, the rabbits, and by extension all soft, furry things, represent the dream of owning the farm, a dream that has Edenic overtones.[19] Louis Owens, in *John Steinbeck's Re-Vision of America,* expands upon Lisca's discussion of the Eden myth in *Of Mice and Men* to show that "[t]here are no Edens in Steinbeck's writing, only illusions of Eden."[20] Steinbeck indicates the inevitable failure of the land dream by introducing a dead mouse into the opening scene of the story to show that Lennie destroys soft, furry things—as his later killing of the puppy indicates. In this symbolic system, Curley's wife is simply another nice-to-touch object that is doomed for destruction when Lennie pets her. Her death is just the "something" that was bound to happen to insure the shattering of George and Lennie's plans for escaping from their transitory existence as migrant workers.[21]

To reinforce the notion of illusive dreams, Steinbeck also has the girl recount her fantasy of escaping the lonely, restricted life of the ranch. When Candy, Crooks, and Lennie shun her company on Saturday night, she tells them contemptuously, "I could of went with the shows. Not jus' one, neither. An' a guy tol' me he could put me in pitchers . . ." (78). Curley and most of the hired men have gone into town to carouse at the saloons and whorehouses. Just "the weak ones" (77) have been left behind, and Curley's wife seeks the only companionship available to her. The next day she describes her dream again in a conversation with Lennie in the barn just before he accidentally breaks her neck. Here she tells her story "in a passion of communication, as though she hurried before her listener could be taken away" (88). With this narrative commentary Steinbeck emphasizes that being able to share one's dream with a sympathetic audience—the companionship implied by such an action—is as important as realizing the dream.

Following this same line of thought, Owens argues convincingly that loneliness is the central theme of *Of Mice and Men* and that the novel is not as pessimistic as some critics have insisted. If we accept the non-teleological premise of the story, we understand that human beings are flawed and that their hopes of regaining Eden are illusory. In Steinbeck's novel, the characters' commitment to the dream and to each other, however, is not flawed. Owens explains:

> The dream of George and Lennie represents a desire to defy the curse of Cain and fallen man—to break the pattern of wandering and loneliness imposed on the outcasts and to return to the perfect garden. George and Lennie achieve all of this dream that is possible in the real world: they are their brother's keeper.[22]

Similarly, William Goldhurst offers an allegorical reading of *Mice* as Steinbeck's parable of the curse of Cain.[23] The question "Am I my brother's keeper?" permeates the story as other characters are affected by the commitment between George and Lennie. Curley is suspicious of it, Slim admires it, and Candy and Crooks briefly participate in the brotherhood by looking after Lennie when George is not around. Although all of the plans for buying the farm are shattered when Lennie dies, Steinbeck still leaves the reader with an image of two men together as George and Slim walk away from the grove by the river where the story had begun.

THE UNCONSCIOUS

In addition to analyzing the patterns of symbol and myth in *Of Mice and Men,* we might also employ psychoanalytic strategies to interpret the action of the novel and to understand the major characters. Because Steinbeck uses animal imagery on several occasions to describe Lennie, critics often speak of Lennie as a symbol of humankind's animal nature. When Lennie drinks from the pool in the grove, he "dabble[s] his big paw in the water" (3); when he returns to the river at the end of the novel, "Lennie appear[s] out of the brush, and he [comes] as silently as a creeping bear moves" (100). Obviously, Lennie often functions on the level of the unconscious. His violent responses to fear illustrate that strong, destructive forces loom just beneath the surface of his consciousness. Even hypothetical threats, such as cats eating the rabbits on the imaginary farm, move Lennie to violent outbursts: "You jus' let 'em try to get the rabbits," he tells George. "I'll break their God damn necks. I'll . . . I'll smash 'em with a stick" (58). It is also clear that George tries to exert a conscious control over Lennie. George tells Lennie when to speak and to whom; he makes Lennie promise to return to the grove by the river if there is any trouble on the ranch. But as evidenced by the earlier incident in Weed and the fracas in the bunkhouse during which Lennie crushes Curley's hand, George's control of his partner's powerfully destructive physical strength is actually quite tenuous.

    In this interpretive frame, we might say that Lennie acts as an extension of George, a powerful id to George's ego. Mark Spilka develops this kind of Freudian reading of the novel, though he does not use the terms id and ego to describe the relationship between the two characters.[24] Clearly Lennie, without thinking about what he is doing, seems to be carrying out George's wishes when he severely injures Curley in the bunkhouse fight. Earlier in the story, George had expressed his hatred for Curley, declaring, "I'm scared I'm gonna tangle with that bastard myself" (37). George also instantly detests Curley's wife and honors her with such invectives as "bitch" and "jail bait" (32). Though Lennie responds to the girl sensually and thinks that she is "purty," that stroking her hair is "nice" (32, 91), he becomes the instrument of her destruction.

This analysis of characters and events gives a reasonable account of the partnership between the two central characters; it even suggests that George needs Lennie as much as Lennie needs George. However, it does not satisfactorily explain why George so vehemently despises Curley's wife or why he kills his partner at the end of the novel. We may come to terms with these issues by recognizing the antagonistic forces within George's psyche, forces which may be interpreted as Jungian archetypes. We know from Carol Henning, Steinbeck's first wife, that Steinbeck's friendship with the Jungian psychologist Joseph Campbell in the early 1930s had a discernible effect on the writer's intellectual development. The two men met frequently at Ed Ricketts's laboratory in Monterey where they discussed ideas and books.[25] Recognizing Steinbeck's familiarity with Jung's work, critics have noted the psychoanalytic influences in *To a God Unknown, In Dubious Battle,* and in several stories in *The Long Valley.* Likewise, Jung's ideas about the ego and the unconscious self are useful in interpreting *Of Mice and Men.* In Jungian terms, we may see Lennie as George's "shadow self" and Curley's wife as his "anima," archetypes which invade the personal unconscious of one's ego personality.[26]

Jung describes both the shadow and the anima or animus as projections which "change the world into the replica of one's unknown face."[27] The shadow is always of the same sex as the subject and may even be recognized as the subject's evil nature. But the contrasexual figure—the animus of a woman, and the anima of a man—represents the face of "absolute evil" and is usually not recognized by the subject as part of his or her own psyche.[28] One face of a man's anima is the seductress, a projection which embodies the negative, unconscious, and unlived aspects of the psyche to which a man responds with fear. At the same time that the anima arouses libidinal drives within the psyche, a patriarchal consciousness strives to repress the feminine force.[29]

Curley's wife represents a mysterious and autonomous force which stimulates George's sexual consciousness, challenges his manhood, inspires self-doubt, and taunts him for his meanness. At various times throughout the story, George gives conscious expression to these feelings. For instance, he admits that it is mean of him to lose his temper over Lennie's wanting ketchup with his beans (12); and he tells Slim about the tricks that he played on Lennie when they were youngsters (40). Also, George seems reluctant to express himself sexually, and when Whit tries to interest him in visiting Susy's place on Saturday night, he insists that if he does go to the whorehouse, it will only be to buy whiskey. The overt sexuality of Curley's wife is an inversion of George's puritanical nature, and as George's anima she sparks an intensely negative reaction from him. She also serves as a conscious reminder of his longing to "live so easy and maybe have a girl" (7), the dream that he represses because of his association with Lennie.

The shadow, on the other hand, is a lower level of personality than the ego. Jung explains that the shadow self is a projection of the ego's dark characteristics, inferiorities of an emotional, obsessive, or possessive quality. Jung writes: "On this lower level with its uncontrolled or scarcely controlled emotions one behaves more or less like a primitive, who is not only the passive victim of his affects but also singularly incapable of moral judgment."[30] We see Lennie at once as a primitive entity who responds instinctively to various stimuli and is incapable of moral judgment. Yet, it just so happens that Lennie manages to harm the people towards whom George harbors animosity. At times George even expresses an extreme dislike of Lennie. He complains that because of Lennie he can't keep a job, or "[g]et a gallon of whiskey, or set in a pool room and play cards or shoot pool" (11). Ultimately, Lennie brings about the circumstances which allow George to rid himself of the illusive land dream and the responsibility of taking care of his mentally deficient partner.

If we look closely at the text, we see that in the opening scene Steinbeck subliminally defines Lennie as George's shadow. But first the author draws our attention to the river, a symbol of the Jungian collective unconscious. Then as Lennie follows George into the sycamore grove, Steinbeck underscores the fact that they are dressed exactly alike; they walk single file down the path, "and even in the open one stayed behind the other. . . . The first man stopped short in the clearing, and the follower nearly ran over him" (2-3). After both of them have had a drink of water from the pool, George

> replaced his hat, pushed himself back from the river, drew up his knees and embraced them. Lennie, who had been watching, imitated George exactly. He pushed himself back, drew up his knees, embraced them, looked over to George to see whether he had it just right. He pulled his hat down a little more over his eyes, the way George's hat was. (3-4)

The shadow motif is unmistakable in this scene which serves as our introduction to the main characters.

That Lennie has survived as long as he has testifies to George's conscious commitment to his care. George, however, has a violently aggressive nature. Both fearing and repressing the primitive impulses in himself, he projects them onto Lennie. The dream farm represents a haven in which George's aggressive nature (represented by Lennie) can be repressed. George devises the plan to escape from the real world of migrant life—bunkhouses, rough men, whiskey, and whorehouses—because he is disturbed by the qualities in himself that such a life brings to the surface. Unconsciously, he projects these disturbing qualities onto his shadow self and feels the need to control that self by isolating it in the safe haven of the Edenic dream farm. Meanwhile, George inadvertently directs Lennie towards disaster by staying at the ranch even after the trouble with Curley, and by making Lennie afraid of Curley's wife. Though George realizes that Lennie will eventually do something so terrible that he will

have to be incarcerated or destroyed, he does not take him
away from the ranch because of an unconscious desire to rid
himself of his shadow. Not until Lennie's death is George
really free to join the community of men represented by Slim.
As the only character in the novel who understands that
George did not kill Lennie in self-defense, Slim expresses his
approval of George's actions. Then he offers to buy George a
drink, and together they walk away from the river grove
where Lennie has died.

This Jungian interpretation of *Of Mice and Men* highlights
the conflict of personalities and priorities in the story. It hints
that there is more to the characterization of Curley's wife than
has previously been assessed, and it suggests that the novel
does not simply relate the story of disillusioned dreamers. By
focusing on the conflicting forces in George's life, we discover that the text itself may be ambiguous and self-
conflicted.

DISCOURSE ANALYSIS

Several times in the novel, George expresses the desire to
change his life. Sometimes he imagines himself free of the
responsibility of looking after Lennie: he could keep a job and
not always have to be on the move; maybe he could have a girl,
or he could go into town with the guys whenever he wanted to;
he could shoot pool, drink whiskey, etc. At other times, he
talks about buying a little farm where he could raise a garden,
and Lennie could tend rabbits. These "dreams" have several
elements in common: each represents a change from the status
quo and each holds forth some form of freedom for George.
Nevertheless, the two scenarios are mutually exclusive.

In a sense, George's dreams compete throughout the
text for actualization and verbalization; and though they are
voiced by the same character each time, they are spoken in
different "voices." The narrative expletive attached to
George's speech about life without Lennie is, "George
exploded" (11). His description of living "so easy" comes out
in anger; the words spew forth in an unrehearsed explosion.
In contrast, when George tells Lennie about the dream farm,

his voice "became deeper. He repeated his words rhythmically as though he had said them many times before" (13). The signal is clear: we are not experiencing George's "voice" as we had been in the present-tense situation of the story, and the words of his speech may not even be his own. Eventually, we learn that George's partnership with Lennie and the notion of living in a place where he can keep Lennie safe from the real world are the results of a promise made to Lennie's Aunt Clara. The plan reflects the illusion of the American Dream and the mythic innocence of prelapsarian Eden.

This close examination of the narrative syntax in the passages related to the competing dreams reveals that Steinbeck consciously creates dialogic tension in the text. To explain this dialogic tension, or double-voicedness, in *Of Mice and Men,* I am borrowing from Mikhail Bakhtin's theory of discourse as dialogue between a speaker and a listener, about a hero or subject.[31] In verbal and written utterances, the subject becomes an active agent, interacting with the speaker "to shape language and determine form," and the subject (or hero) often becomes the dominant influence.[32] Dialogic tension exists in all discourse because words, the elements of the dialogue, are loaded with various social nuances which influence each other and perhaps even change as a result of the association. According to Bakhtin, "Each word tastes of the context and contexts in which it has lived its socially charged life; all words and forms are populated by intentions. Contextual overtones . . . are inevitable in the word."[33]

The contextual overtones of the dream-farm passages in *Of Mice and Men* are twofold: mythical and communal. Sometimes the description of the land dream is delivered as if it were a religious incantation, as when George deepens his voice and speaks rhythmically. Sometimes the story is related as a dialogue or as a chorus of two or more speakers who combine their "speech acts" (Bakhtin's term) to create a composite image. This happens when Lennie interrupts George's recitation and is coaxed into completing the story himself (14). Later, in the bunkhouse, after George has agreed to a partnership with Candy, Steinbeck notes that "each mind was popped into the future when this lovely thing would come about" (60). With their minds on the future,

Lennie, George, and Candy discuss their plan, each one adding a specific detail to the description of life on the farm. Lennie, of course, mentions feeding the rabbits; Candy asks if there will be a stove; and George imagines taking a holiday and going to a carnival, a circus, or a ball game (60-61).

Notice that both Lennie's and Candy's comments deal with specific details of farmlife. On the other hand, George's contribution to this idyllic picture focuses on activities which would take him away from the farm, not on the farm itself. Though his comments are in keeping with the spirit of camaraderie which flows through the conversation, the narrative shift to non-farm activities is a subtle clue that George's version of the future does not coincide with his partners'. What George seems to be doing in this speech is reconciling the mythic vision with the more personal vision of how he would live his life if he did not have to look after Lennie. Though George gives lip service to the dream-farm myth, it is possible that he is not really committed to it. After all, the primary reason for acquiring the farm is to remove Lennie from the everyday working world in which he cannot seem to stay out of trouble. While Lennie's presence necessitates keeping the dream alive, his uncontrollable strength and outbursts of violence virtually assure that the dream will not come true.

By introducing both of George's dreams in the opening scene of the story, and by emphasizing the differences in the way they are "voiced," Steinbeck highlights the dialectical nature of the narrative. From scene to scene, as George appears to be working conscientiously toward achieving the land dream, he is actually moving closer and closer to the competing dream which is not a dream at all, but a rather realistic description of the bunkhouse life which might be possible for George if he did not have to worry about Lennie.

Through the dialogical structure of the text, Steinbeck maintains narrative tension without imposing moral judgments. George is neither unreasonable nor unrealistic when he imagines himself unencumbered by his promise to Lennie's Aunt Clara. Any moral judgments which might influence our interpretation of the final scene must come from outside of the text. Lennie's death, of course, leads to the inevitable resolution of the narrative tension, but Steinbeck offers few syntactical clues to help the reader decide exactly what motivates George to kill Lennie. As George calmly tells Lennie about the farm, he hesitates to raise the pistol even after he hears the footsteps of Curley and the other men. Steinbeck prolongs the inevitable resolution of the crisis with this comment: "The voices came close now. George raised the gun and listened to the voices" (106). Though Steinbeck lets the reader decide which George speaks through the pistol—the one who creates the world of protected innocence or the one who expresses a desire for freedom—he makes one thing very clear: George's pulling the trigger is a reaction to the voices of cruelty from which neither he nor Lennie can escape any longer.

NOTES

1. John Steinbeck, *Steinbeck: A Life in Letters,* eds. Elaine Steinbeck and Robert Wallsten (New York: Viking Press, 1975), p. 111. Subsequent references to the letters are from this edition and are cited in the text as *SLL* with page number.
2. Jackson J. Benson, *The True Adventures of John Steinbeck, Writer* (New York: Viking Press, 1984), p. 326.
3. *Ibid.,* pp. 163-413.
4. *Ibid.,* p. 327.
5. Louis Owens, *John Steinbeck's Re-Vision of America* (Athens: University of Georgia Press, 1985), p. 103.
6. John Steinbeck, *Of Mice and Men/Cannery Row* (New York: Viking Penguin, 1986), p. 14. Subsequent references to the novel are from this edition and page numbers are cited parenthetically in the text of my essay.
7. For the structure of this critical explication, I credit Eugene K. Garber, " 'My Kinsman, Major Molineux': Some Interpretive and Critical Probes," in *Literature in the Classroom,* ed. Ben F. Nelms (Urbana, Illinois: NCTE, 1988), pp. 83-104.
8. Benson, p. 304.
9. Benson refers to the Mexicans and the Mexican-Americans involved in the 1933 cotton strike (p. 304). Also, Louis Owens discusses the role played by women and minorities in

the strikes in " 'Putting Down the Thing': Irony of *In Dubious Battle,*" a paper delivered at The Third International Steinbeck Congress in Honolulu, Hawaii, on May 30, 1990.

10. Benson, p. 39.
11. *Ibid,* p. 61.
12. Cletus E. Daniel, *Bitter Harvest: A History of California Farmworkers, 1870-1941* (Berkeley: University of California Press, 1982), p. 67.
13. Benson, pp. 326, 351.
14. Anne Loftis, "A Historical Introduction to *Of Mice and Men,*" in *The Short Novels of John Steinbeck,* ed. Jackson Benson (Durham, North Carolina: Duke University Press, 1990), p. 39.
15. Daniel, p. 64.
16. *Ibid.*
17. Loftis, p. 41.
18. The allusion is to Robert Burns's poem, "To a Mouse."
19. Peter Lisca, *The Wide World of John Steinbeck* (New Brunswick, New Jersey: Rutgers University Press, 1958; reprint, New York: Gordian Press, 1981), pp. 136 (page references are to the reprint edition).
20. Owens, p. 101.
21. Lisca, pp. 136-38.
22. Owens, p. 102.
23. William Goldhurst, "*Of Mice and Men:* John Steinbeck's Parable of the Curse of Cain," in *The Short Novels of John Steinbeck,* ed. Benson, pp. 48-59.
24. Mark Spilka, "Of George and Lennie and Curley's Wife: Sweet Violence in Steinbeck's Eden," in *The Short Novels of John Steinbeck,* ed. Benson, pp. 59-70.
25. Benson, *True Adventures,* pp. 223-25.
26. Carl G. Jung, "Aion: Phenomenology of the Self," in *The Portable Jung,* ed. Joseph Campbell (New York: Penguin Books, 1976), pp. 139-62.
27. *Ibid.,* p. 147.
28. *Ibid.,* p. 148.
29. Bettina L. Knapp, *Women in Twentieth-Century Literature: A Jungian View* (University Park: Pennsylvania State University Press, 1987), pp. 164-65.
30. Jung, p. 146.
31. M. M. Bakhtin, *The Dialogic Imagination: Four Essays,* ed. Michael Holquist, trans. Caryl Emerson and Michael Holquist (Austin: University of Texas Press, 1981), pp. 314-15.

32. Charles I. Schuster, "Mikhail Bakhtin as Rhetorical Theorist," *College English,* 47 (October 1985), 595.
33. Bakhtin, p. 293.

IV. TOPICS FOR RESEARCH AND DISCUSSION

(1) This study merely introduces students to some of the critical commentary that *Of Mice and Men* has generated since its publication. A broad survey of the criticism published about the novel could accomplish several objectives:
   (a) it would lead to a better understanding of *Of Mice and Men;* and
   (b) it would shed light on the variety of critical approaches and the shifts in literary theory which have occurred over five decades.

(2) For a critical survey which is more focused than the one above, examine thoroughly the historical/cultural dimensions of *Of Mice and Men.* Try to answer some of the following questions:
   (a) Why was *Of Mice and Men* popular in 1937?
   (b) What kind of international reading audience has Steinbeck's work attracted and what accounts for his international appeal?
   (c) Why is the novel still in the curriculum for high school and college English classes today?

(3) *Of Mice and Men* has been recognized as a tightly structured work of fiction. Choose one element of the novel—narrative structure, theme, characterization, setting—and show how that element contributes to the unity of the story and the effectiveness of the narrative.

(4) Consider Steinbeck's stated goals when he began composing *Of Mice and Men:* he wanted to write a novel in play form. After the novel was published, Steinbeck reworked the manuscript to produce a playscript. Compare the two texts, noting similarities and differences. Give special attention to the expanded role of Curley's wife and/or the difference in endings.

(5) Lennie is commonly discussed as a symbol of primeval innocence or as an inarticulate Everyman. He may also represent uncontrollable violence. Investigate the meaning of Lennie's character by examining two of his predecessors in Steinbeck's fiction: Tularecito in Chapter 4 of *The Pastures of*

Heaven, and Johnny Bear in the story "Johnny Bear," which appears in *The Long Valley* anthology.

V. SELECTED BIBLIOGRAPHY

1. Jackson J. Benson, *The True Adventures of John Steinbeck, Writer* (New York: Viking Press, 1984). Benson details the history of the composition of *Mice,* and sets the biographical context for the novella.

2. William Goldhurst, *"Of Mice and Men:* John Steinbeck's Parable of the Curse of Cain," *Western American Literature,* 6 (Summer 1971), 123-35; reprint, in *The Short Novels of John Steinbeck,* ed. Jackson Benson (Durham, North Carolina: Duke University Press, 1990), pp. 48-59. Goldhurst details evidence in Steinbeck's novella which supports a reading of *Mice* as a modern version of the biblical story of Cain's curse. The failure of fraternal order in *Of Mice and Men* can also be seen as a critique of the Hebrew-Christian ethic which mutilates man's nature, dividing the self between reason (represented by George) and appetite (represented by Lennie).

3. Howard Levant, *The Novels of John Steinbeck: A Critical Study* (Columbia: University of Missouri Press, 1974), pp. 133-44. Levant analyzes the dramatic elements of *Mice* and evaluates it as a play-novelette. He discusses Steinbeck's attention to simplification of character and event.

4. Peter Lisca, *The Wide World of John Steinbeck* (New Brunswick, New Jersey: Rutgers University Press, 1958); reprint (New York: Gordian Press, 1981), pp. 130-43 (reprint ed.). Lisca analyzes recurring motifs of language, action, and symbol in the novel. His discussion focuses upon the inevitability of events given the pattern of symbols and action.

5. Anne Loftis, "A Historical Introduction to *Of Mice and Men,"* in *The Short Novels of John Steinbeck,* ed. Jackson Benson, pp. 39-47. Statistics on itinerant workers in the early twentieth century place Steinbeck's novella in its historical context. Loftis details the author's personal experiences as a harvester and summarizes a story which Steinbeck published in the *Stanford Spectator* twelve years prior to the publication of *Mice* about a runaway girl who seeks shelter in a bunkhouse. Loftis outlines differences between the novella, the play, and the film versions of the work and ends with a brief summary of comments by critics.

6. "Men, Mice and Mr. Steinbeck," *New York Times,* December 5, 1937; reprint, in *Conversations with John Steinbeck,* ed. Thomas Fensch, (Jackson: University Press of Mississippi, 1988), pp. 8-10. In this interview, Steinbeck describes the real-life prototype for Lennie.
7. Louis Owens, *John Steinbeck's Re-Vision of America* (Athens: University of Georgia Press, 1985), pp. 100-06. Owens discusses the author's exploration of the themes of disillusionment and commitment as they pertain to the American Dream motif in all of Steinbeck's fiction, including *Of Mice and Men.*
8. Mark Spilka, "Of George and Lennie and Curley's Wife: Sweet Violence in Steinbeck's Eden," *Modern Fiction Studies,* 20 (Summer 1974), 169-79; reprint, in *The Short Novels of John Steinbeck,* ed. Benson, pp. 59-70. Spilka argues that misogyny dictates Steinbeck's characterizations of George, Lennie, and Curley's wife.
9. John Steinbeck, *Steinbeck: A Life in Letters,* eds. Elaine Steinbeck and Robert Wallsten (New York: Viking Press, 1975), pp. 154-55. Steinbeck mentions *Of Mice and Men* in several letters discussing his experimental approach to writing a novel that will read like a play. Also, his comments to Claire Luce about the real-life prototype for Curley's wife may be of particular interest to feminist critics.

7. STEINBECK'S *THE PEARL* (1947)

Patrick W. Shaw

I. BACKGROUND

The idea for the pearl story is first explained in *Sea of Cortez,* Steinbeck's book about sea life which he wrote with the help of his biologist friend Ed Ricketts. In March 1940 their boat, *The Western Flyer,* stopped at the Mexican town of La Paz, famous for oyster beds that produced superb pearls. As Steinbeck points out, the pearls had for many years drawn men from all over the world, and "the terrors of greed were let loose on the city again and again."[1] Here in La Paz Steinbeck heard the story of the Indian boy who finds a fabulous pearl:

> He knew its value was so great that he need never work again. In his one pearl he had the ability to be drunk as long as he wished, to marry any one of a number of girls, and to make many more a little happy too. In his great pearl lay salvation, for he could in advance purchase masses sufficient to pop him out of Purgatory like a squeezed watermelon seed. In addition he could shift a number of dead relatives a little nearer to Paradise. He went to La Paz with his pearl in his hand and his future clear into eternity in his heart. (*Log,* 102)

The boy's illusions are shattered, however, when the pearl agents try to cheat him out of the pearl, and he is clubbed by robbers trying to steal it. He heads inland to avoid those who would kill him for the pearl, but he is captured and tortured. He creeps back to La Paz, takes his pearl from its hiding place beneath a stone, and throws it back into the ocean. As Steinbeck relates the story, the Indian boy was "a free man again with his soul in danger and his food and shelter insecure. And he laughed a great deal about it" (*Log,* 103).

Steinbeck thought the story was probably true, very much like a parable, but he felt that the Indian boy was "too heroic, too wise," and acted "contrary to human direction" (*Log,* 103).

In late 1943, during World War II, Steinbeck was seriously injured on the beach at Salerno, Italy, when he went ashore with American troops. Emotionally and physically traumatized, Steinbeck returned to America, feeling "mean" and "sadistic"[2] and much in need of recuperation. In January 1944, he and his second wife Gwyn returned to La Paz for a vacation. He remembered the story of the Indian boy and his pearl, and he began an outline for a movie based on the story to be filmed in Mexico. Because of a series of events in his personal life, however, immediate plans for the film did not work out; but in November 1944, in Monterey, California, Steinbeck began work on the story—"sitting in his unheated woodshed and writing by kerosene lantern" (Benson, 560).

A few weeks later his novel *Cannery Row* was published and received bad reviews, which did nothing to cheer Steinbeck. Moreover, the bums, prostitutes, and generally unsavory characters he celebrated in *Cannery Row* were not appreciated by the people of the Monterey area. The citizens' anger was one of the reasons Steinbeck was anxious to leave California for work on the film in Mexico (and also one of the reasons he would soon leave his beloved home state altogether and take up permanent residence in New York). Moreover, his wife was pregnant and Steinbeck was concerned about his impending fatherhood. In face of all his tensions and troubles, Steinbeck began to doubt that the film of the pearl story would ever be completed (Benson, 565). Nonetheless, in January 1945 he managed to finish a 125-page draft of the story, and plans were resumed for filming in Mexico.

Worried by the feeling that the movie was "just another perverse detour from the real use of his talent" and that he had "not tackled anything really substantial in years" (Benson, 569), Steinbeck's agent and publisher suggested that he turn the pearl story into a novelette, to be combined with two other such short works about Mexico and published in a single volume. Steinbeck liked the idea, and set about converting the film script into a short novel. Although the plans for a one-volume collection of the Mexican stories did not materialize, the pearl story was completed and first published in the *Woman's Home Companion* as "The Pearl of the World" in December 1945. It was published separately as a short novel in 1947 as *The Pearl*. The movie version was also released in 1947.

II. PLOT SYNOPSIS

The Pearl is divided into six chapters, preceded by a brief comment by an unidentified narrator. The words spoken by this narrator are italicized, and the speaker suggests that the story is a parable from which "everyone takes his own meaning."[3] The story tells of the fisherman Kino, his wife Juana, and their baby Coyotito, and of the great pearl Kino finds.

CHAPTER I

Kino awakens in his brush house near the beach. Juana lies beside him and Coyotito is sleeping in a hanging box. Mixed with the outside sounds of roosters, pigs, and birds, Kino also hears songs in his head. These are old songs, and this morning he hears what he calls the "Song of the Family," which tells him his life is "Whole." Suddenly he and Juana see a scorpion moving down the rope into Coyotito's box, and the song Kino now hears is the "Song of Evil." Juana repeats some ancient magic and mutters a Hail Mary, while Kino tries to grab the scorpion. Despite Kino's efforts, the scorpion stings the baby. The villagers and Kino are surprised when Juana decides she wants a doctor for Coyotito, for they know the doctor only takes care of the rich people in the nearby "stone and plaster" town and will not come to the brush huts (477). Juana demands, therefore, that Coyotito be taken to the town. The beggars in the town know the doctor for "his ignorance, his cruelty, his avarice, his appetites, his sins" (478). He is of a foreign race who conquered Kino's people four hundred years ago. Kino has only eight "misshapen seed pearls" (480) to pay for the doctor's services, so the doctor refuses to see Coyotito.

CHAPTER II

In the gulf fishing village, his canoe is the only thing of value Kino owns. It has been passed down from Kino's grandfather. Juana prays that her husband can take the canoe and go out to find a pearl large enough "to hire the doctor to cure the baby" (482). Hearing the "Song of the Pearl," Kino dives into the oyster beds and finds "the great pearl, perfect as the moon. . . . It was the greatest pearl in the world" (484). Meanwhile Juana has put a seaweed poultice on Coyotito's shoulder, and Kino returns to see that the swelling is going down and the poison is receding from his son's body.

CHAPTER III

News spreads quickly about Kino's pearl. The town's shop-keepers suddenly think of clothes they need to sell, the priest remembers repairs the church needs, and the doctor now announces that he is treating Coyotito for a scorpion sting. All the pearl buyers (who actually work for only one agent) start to calculate the "lowest price" (486) for which they can get the pearl from Kino. Kino thinks that now he and Juana can be married properly. He also dreams of a new harpoon and a Winchester carbine, and of Coyotito's going to school. The priest visits and then the doctor. Although "the baby is nearly well," the doctor tells Kino and Juana that Coyotito will die unless he takes quick action. He forces the baby to take some white powder and a capsule of gelatin, and promises to return in an hour. Suddenly the baby gets "very sick" (493), and though Kino is suspicious, he lets the doctor give Coyotito more of the white powder. Juana adores the doctor. That night someone enters the hut to try to steal the pearl, and though Kino chases the intruder away, he is struck on the head and wounded. Juana tells him the pearl is evil and wants it destroyed, but Kino cannot give up what the pearl promises.

CHAPTER IV

Kino is going to the town (La Paz) to sell the pearl, and the pearl buyers are excited by their conniving to get the pearl at the lowest possible price. Juan Tomás, Kino's brother, cautions Kino about being cheated. Kino's people have been taught by the church and four hundred years of repression not to try new ways to sell the pearls or "leave their station" (500). The dealer tells Kino the pearl is too large, and like fool's gold it has no value. He offers Kino 1,000 pesos, though Kino knows it is worth at least 50,000. Three other buyers, pretending they are not part of the scheme, also tell him the pearl is valueless. In a rage, Kino tells them he will take the pearl to the capital to sell. Juan Tomás warns him that he has defied "the whole structure, the whole way of life, and I am afraid for you" (505). That night, rising to check outside his brush house, Kino is again attacked, suffering a slash from ear to chin. Once more Juana asks him to destroy the evil pearl, but Kino vows that nothing can take their good fortune from them.

CHAPTER V

Later Kino awakens to see Juana remove the pearl from its hiding place under a fireplace stone. He follows her as she moves toward the ocean, knocks her down with his fist, and takes the pearl. Going back to his hut, he is again attacked by someone wanting the pearl. He stabs one of the attackers, and the pearl is saved only because it rolls into the sand. Juana, bruised and in pain, comes upon her husband and the man he has killed, and finds the pearl. She knows "that the old life was gone forever" (509). Kino decides they must flee, but he discovers that someone has knocked a great hole in the bottom of his canoe. Moreover, while they have been struggling over the pearl, someone has burned their brush house. Juan Tomás hides Kino for the night and tells the neighbors his brother has drowned in the gulf. The following night Kino, Juana, and Coyotito set off afoot. Kino's eyes are now "hard and cruel and bitter" (513).

CHAPTER VI

In the windy darkness Kino and his family head through "the brushy country toward Loreto where the miraculous Virgin has her station" (514). Kino is careful to eliminate their tracks as they go, and now the music of the pearl is sinister and evil to him. He soon discovers that despite his efforts to hide their trail, three trackers are following them, one on horseback. Kino thinks of giving himself up, but Juana reminds him that the trackers will kill them all if they catch them. Kino then decides to head for the mountains. Juana is resolute about not leaving Kino, and refuses to hide while he distracts the three men. Fighting heat and fatigue, they make their way to a spring in the mountains. The trackers follow, and Kino, Juana, and Coyotito climb into a small cave about thirty feet above the spring. By evening the trackers reach the spring and make camp below Kino and his family. That night Kino removes his clothing so he cannot be seen and climbs down to confront the men. He moves "like a slow lizard down the smooth rock" (524). Just as he is about to attack with his knife, Coyotito makes a small cry and one of the men fires a rifle toward the cave. Kino kills the man, grabs the rifle, crushes the head of the second man with it, then shoots the third. When he is finished, he hears "the cry of death" (525) from the cave above.

The people in La Paz now retell Kino's story. Kino and Juana returned to the village, Kino carrying the rifle and Juana carrying Coyotito's body. They "walked through the city as though it were not there" (526), paying no attention to Juan Tomás or anybody else. When they reached the gulf, Kino looked at the pearl and saw "Coyotito lying in the little cave with the top of his head shot away" (527). He offered the pearl to Juana to throw, but she told him to do it. He threw the pearl as far as he could into the water. The pearl settled to the bottom and a passing crab raised a little cloud of sand which covered it. "And the music of the pearl drifted to a whisper and disappeared" (527).

III. CRITICAL EXPLICATION

As shown in the background discussion of *The Pearl,* Steinbeck first conceived of the story as a parable. Indeed, on the surface it is a very straightforward moral tale, pointing out the dangers of human greed. It is an antimaterialistic and anti-intellectual statement which celebrates the virtues of the simple, primitive life. As a parable, *The Pearl* may be viewed as a retelling of the Garden of Eden story, and much of its continued popularity rests upon its simplicity. As Steinbeck's publisher Pat Covici noted when the story was first presented to him, it is composed in "rich blacks" and "dazzling whites."[4] If we look beneath that apparent simplicity, however, we realize that while the text of the story is presented in black and white, its subtext offers a variegated, subtle narrative about human relationships.

The problem lies in how to gain access to this subtext. Critics have analyzed *The Pearl* from numerous perspectives, seeing it (for example) as Jungian psychology, as a modern version of medieval allegory, and as a flagrant effort to make money.[5] The analysis which follows owes much to those who have commented on *The Pearl,* and while space does not permit an extensive overview of existing Steinbeck criticism, I try in the "Selected Bibliography" to show that recent criticism to which I am most directly indebted. I do, however, avoid overly specific or "hobby horse" interpretations of the short novel, and my mode of analysis follows the principle which Warren French (quoting John Cawelti) acknowledges in his "Introduction" to Howard Levant's *The Novels of John Steinbeck: A Critical Study:* "A good plot model should provide a basis for explaining why each event and character is present in the work, and why these events and characters are placed in the setting they occupy."[6] With this general guide in mind, I believe the best way to access and understand the subtext of *The Pearl* is via an orderly examination of those narrative devices which Steinbeck uses to convey his intent.

SETTING

As we have seen in the "Background" discussion, Steinbeck first encountered the pearl story in La Paz, Mexico, and thereafter identified it completely with its Mexican origin, both in story and film. The tale of Kino and the pearl could be set in few other places, for the setting must be a locale near an ocean with pearl-bearing oysters, in a village in which individuals still venture forth without the aid of sophisticated diving equipment and seek to harvest the pearls. The village must be part of or close to a larger, more "modern" town. Aside from the literal requirements of the setting, however, Steinbeck wants to relocate his audience back to a time which is both more primitive and more innocent than the "real" time of the early 1940s, when the story was composed. We need to recall that World War II was raging when Steinbeck began the story, that he himself had recently been seriously injured in that war, and that in August 1945, just before the story was completed and published in December 1945, the atomic bomb had devastated Hiroshima and Nagasaki, Japan. Clearly it was a time when modern science and technology seemed to threaten the world. Steinbeck purposely does not reveal precisely when Kino's adventure takes place, but we do know that it is in some past era, away from this dangerous present, in a town without machines, electricity, or any other form of modern industrialization. Even in the fictive present of the story, La Paz is primitive and pristine by standards which would be applied by "progressive" civilizations. In today's terminology, we would refer to it as a "Third World" community. Only in such an "old" or premodern situation is the story of one small family's struggle against the forces of evil believable. In a sense, Kino and Juana's fight is a face-to-face confrontation with recognizable, definable enemies—the ocean, the scorpion, the night robbers, the crooked pearl agents, the pursuers. Against such substantive threats individuals can take clear-cut defensive actions. The outcome of those actions is, of course, problematic, but the agents which cause the actions are definite. Such an ironic luxury is not possible for a modern society which must face the impersonal threats of mass bombings and the possibility of instant annihilation, and a society for which the war erased clear-cut definitions of good and evil. Especially in the late 1940s would such a feeling of personal helplessness have held true.

POINT OF VIEW

Steinbeck subtly and effectively combines this exotic setting with his omniscient, objective point of view. Technically the point of view is limited omniscient, for Steinbeck focuses most often on Kino, giving us his thoughts and letting us see the world as he sees it. But Steinbeck moves us outside of Kino's limited vision, letting us see other characters such as Juana, the doctor, the beggars, and even the town itself as a kind of organism. Howard Levant is correct in noting that "the entire fishing village" is part of the microcosm which Kino's family represents;[7] and the same can be said for the town of La Paz. Steinbeck therefore gives us a double perspective on the actions and events which comprise the story. First is the view which we receive from Kino (his literal seeing of his surroundings and his rather simplistic thoughts); and second is the larger view which we receive from a narrator who seems to be removed from the events, translating them for us in unemotional, objective terms. It is, for instance, through Kino's eyes that we see the "lightening square which was the door," "the hanging box where Coyotito slept," and Juana's "blue head shawl over her nose and over her breasts" (473). On the other hand, it is the removed, objective narrator who informs us that "Kino was young and strong and his black hair hung over his brown forehead" (475) and that "The town lay on a broad estuary, its old yellow plastered buildings hugging the beach" (481). The illiterate, unschooled Kino, for instance, would probably not know such a word as "estuary" and could not therefore use it credibly (473).

Such a dual perspective immediately places us as audience in a position which Steinbeck intends for us to occupy, and which he has helped set up by using La Paz as the setting. Steinbeck is assuming—perhaps with too much faith in the existence of an audience that appreciates good literature—that his reading audience is a relatively intelligent, sophisticated entity who will view the primitive village and its naive inhabitants with an awareness which Kino and the other fictive characters do not possess.[8] That is, the audience will know of the war, the bomb, the unspeakable potential horrors facing a modern, technological society. In fact, this contrast which Steinbeck immediately establishes between his reading audience and his fictive personae constitutes the first or dominant conflict in the narrative: the dramatically ironic conflict between an informed, modern, and perhaps highly skeptical audience and a naive, innocent set of characters living their lives in a non-industrialized world and still retaining faith in things other than the "gods" of science and the machine. (It is in this light, for instance, that Kino's obtaining his rifle and the violent way he gains it are seen as being so troubling—a point we will return to later.) Thus, by quickly establishing this contrastive relationship between "real" audience and fictive personae, Steinbeck simultaneously establishes the complex ambiguity of what superficially seems to be a straightforward parable. Steinbeck's point of view management forces us to view everything from more than one perspective, forces us to feel that we as "enlightened" audience are supposed to perceive things about Kino and the other characters that they may not realize about themselves. By inculcating this dual point of view into the essential structure of his narrative, Steinbeck, in turn, sensitizes us to the variety of possible meanings which all other factors in the story possess.

SYMBOLISM

Symbols and images combine with Steinbeck's dual point of view to help give us access to the many possible meanings of *The Pearl*. We can determine rather easily that the pearl itself is the dominant symbol, since Steinbeck is careful through repetition and other means of emphasis to make certain that the pearl is most obvious to us. As for images, Michael J. Meyer argues that "light versus darkness" is "the first major image Steinbeck uses" to give evidence of "the morally ambiguous state of the narrative."[9] He goes on to explain the pearl itself as part of this light-dark imagery. Meyer's discussion is a good example of how Steinbeck uses symbols and images, and from it we can extrapolate other image patterns in the narrative: land versus water, the mountains versus the flat lands, those who quest for treasure versus those who seek treasure through swindle and thievery. To the pearl as central symbol, we can add the symbolism of the ocean, the mountain spring, the mountains themselves, the rifle, the various animals, and the songs. This brief essay does not permit a full discussion of each of these, but a close analysis of the pearl symbolism will serve to exemplify Steinbeck's careful management of these elements.

As we have noted in background discussion, and as John H. Timmerman phrases it, Steinbeck was originally attracted to the pearl story because it coincided with his contemplations "on human greed, materialism, and the inherent worth of a thing."[10] It is not surprising, therefore, that the foremost symbolic function of Kino's pearl is to convey human greed or the human desire to possess "things" to which other humans attach value and for which they are willing to pay great costs. As Steinbeck shows through other elements in the narrative, the essential human needs are food, shelter, health, a sense of communal and familial love, and faith in a power which transcends the self. Through the pearl, he shows that each of these essential values is corrupted. Although the oyster from which the pearl comes is a valuable source of food, it is cast aside in order to get what Steinbeck describes as that "layer of smooth cement" which surrounds the irritating grain of sand in the oyster's flesh (482). The divers destroy dozens of edible and nutritious oysters in search of that one "accident" which creates a pearl. Ironically, pearls will kill the oysters unless they are washed free "in some tidal flurry" (482)—just as the big pearl ultimately threatens the lives of Kino and his family. Brought into his home, the pearl leads ultimately to the destruction of that home when the brush hut is burned by those who will have the pearl at any cost. Moreover, the pearl can do nothing to restore Coyotito's health after the scorpion bite, and in fact leads to the doctor's giving the baby a powder which sickens rather than cures and which is the indirect cause of Coyotito's death in the cave. The priest—far from being sincerely concerned about Kino's soul—is interested less in faith than in how many repairs to the church the pearl might finance. His first thought is "what the pearl would be worth" (485). The point is that the pearl, no matter how large or of what quality, has no intrinsic value, and the buyers are ironically correct when they tell Kino the pearl is like "fool's gold" and worthless (502). Any value the pearl possesses derives only from the fact that few others like it exist and humans desire that which their neighbors do not or cannot have. Were it common and available to everyone—like the ocean sand which created it in the first place—it would be utterly valueless in the monetary sense because everyone could possess it. Owning such a common thing would not distinguish the owner or make him appear superior to his neighbors. It is such greed for the pearl that stands as a microcosm for the greed that precipitated the world war which was being fought when Steinbeck wrote *The Pearl*—a greed that drives humans to kill their neighbors, whether that killing occurs in a small village in Mexico or in the great cities of Europe and Asia. Steinbeck invokes this comparison between the events in La Paz and World War II when he states that such pearls "had raised the King of Spain to be a great power in Europe in past years, had helped to pay for his wars" (482). Kino's pearl, therefore, epitomizes the worst qualities of the human animal—violence, bloodshed, betrayal of transcendent values.

Viewed from another perspective, however, the pearl symbolizes beauty and the potential for happiness which humans fail to realize. Aside from what other values the pearl may or may not have, it is aesthetically beautiful. "It captured the light and refined it and gave it back in silver incandescence." It is "perfect as the moon" (484). In that incandescence Kino sees his dreams, those things "he had considered in the past and had given up as impossible" (487). Signifi-

cantly, the first vision the pearl brings to Kino is of himself
and his family kneeling "at the high altar" of the church (487),
of his being able to legitimize his marriage to Juana, thus to
get his soul better prepared to meet his God. This initial
vision is, of course, later superseded by thoughts of clothes
and guns and pleasure boats, but the purity of the first vision
serves to remind us of the innate human goodness which
greed and materialism have corrupted. In its association with
the ocean, the moon, and light generally, the pearl symbolizes
the natural life forces which control the universe and which
Steinbeck greatly appreciated—though he himself had by
1947 been removed from his native California and its ocean,
the simple boyhood he enjoyed there, the pleasure he took in
exploring the biology of the ocean currents with his friend Ed
Ricketts. Famous, wealthy, taken by Hollywood and its
glamour, living in New York, traveling first class all over the
world, his wife resentful of his absences and of having to care
for two children (she demanded a divorce in early 1948
[Benson, 616]), and his writing being devastated by critics,
Steinbeck may well have seen visions of his own life reflected
in Kino's pearl. The literal beauty of the pearl indicates
(contrary to what John Keats may have felt) that a thing of
beauty is not a joy forever.

Thus the pearl symbolizes and continues the paradox we
see in the point of view and in the narrative generally: that
which appears beautiful may be evil; that which seems simple
may be immensely complicated. There are no "dazzling
whites" or "rich blacks" (to borrow Covici's words). In
questions of human behavior and morality, there is only that
grayness symbolized by the "gray oysters" and "the haze,
riding over the oyster bed" (482).

CHARACTERIZATION

As John H. Timmerman points out, "The danger of allegory
to many modern authors is that the characters in the narrative
may become wooden signposts pointing toward their individual allegorical meanings." Such is not the case with Steinbeck
in *The Pearl*, Timmerman correctly concludes, because

"Steinbeck's involvement with allegory operates on the level of a rich suggestiveness in story, but with characters and thematic plot development coming first."[11] Indeed, it is through the people of the story that *The Pearl* attains most of its universal appeal. As Howard Levant recognizes, Steinbeck worked consciously on the characterizations, adding more complexity to the original story he heard in La Paz by shifting "from an Indian boy to an Indian family," thereby attaining "more complexity" than a simple parable would allow.[12] Michael J. Meyer is correct in his overall evaluation of Steinbeck's protagonists, Kino and Juana:

> These primitive natives undergo an initiation rite . . . similar to what Adam and Eve experienced when they ate from the tree of knowledge of good and evil. This initiation destroys the couple's naive concept of what man and the world are like and leaves them bereft but wiser in their knowledge of themselves and of their society. Their discovery dispels the illusions of the "good" that surrounds them but also frustrates them as they struggle to cope with a reality which almost always involves a paradoxical yoking of opposites.[13]

Let us examine how Steinbeck manages Kino and Juana's initiation into life's harsh dualities.

Perhaps the best clue to the alterations that occur in Kino's personality is the contrasting images we have of him at the beginning and end of the narrative. On the first page of *The Pearl,* Kino awakens (not unlike Adam opening his eyes to his first dawn). His first impressions are of the shining stars above, and he is comforted by the familiar crowing of roosters, the sounds of pigs feeding, the chitter of little birds. His wife lies beside him, and his baby son sleeps peacefully in his hanging box. In his imagination, Kino hears the ancestral "Song of the Family" (473-74). Clearly, he is in tune with nature, his family, and himself. Juana, too, awakens from a peaceful sleep beneath her blue shawl and with apparent contentment works to prepare the morning cakes. She softly sings "an ancient song" which assures her that "this is safety, this is warmth, this is the *Whole*" (475).

At the end of the short novel, however, we see Kino and

Juana quite differently. They return to the village looking as if "they carried two towers of darkness with them." No longer wearing her blue shawl, Juana now carries it "like a sack over her shoulder," and it is "crusted with dried blood." Her face is "hard and lined and leathery with fatigue." Juana and Kino "moved a little jerkily, like well-made wooden dolls, and they carried pillars of black fear about them" (526). As such contrasting descriptions show, Kino and Juana change significantly within the span of several days. From youthful, healthy innocents secure in their own home, they change to tired, fearful wanderers. They have been initiated into the realities of a world motivated by selfishness, greed, and violence. Coyotito's death is to them a very real (albeit to us highly symbolic) manifestation of the death of innocence and a harsh proof of the fragility of human happiness. The naivete which Kino and Juana display early in the story simply cannot endure in the face of life's reality.

Yet, positive factors result from the experiences which so radically alter Kino and Juana's personalities. Especially in Juana do we see transitions which make her appear more admirable to us. For the moment these changes may seem to destroy the happiness she has early in the story, but viewed from the dual perspective which Steinbeck insists we as audience maintain (as discussed above), Juana's changes clearly better suit her for life's realities. They make her psychologically tougher, more independent, and far less willing to suffer the abuse of those who would dominate her. We note that early in the narrative Kino surveys his domain, including Juana, "with the detachment of God" (474). Then, when the pearl enters their lives, we see Kino physically attack Juana, who (with considerable foresight) tries to throw the evil thing back into the gulf. In fury, he strikes "her in the face with his clenched fist" and kicks "her in the side." She is "like a sheep before the butcher" (508). Moreover, she naively adores the corrupt doctor; though he is purposely making her son ill in order to convince her that his services are needed, she "looked at him with adoration" (494). Yet her contact with the pearl and the events surrounding it force Juana to remove herself as much as possible from those forces which squelch her native instincts and wisdom. Though never resorting to open rebellion or violence such as that which has driven Kino to murder, Juana is firm in her refusal to let Kino continue the journey without her (519). Moreover, she is the one who logically assesses the situation and explains to Kino that the pursuers will kill them all, even if they get the pearl (518). And when she and Kino return to the town, she walks beside him as an equal (526), not subserviently trotting "behind him" trying to "keep up" as she did when they left their village (514).

It is significant that at the end of *The Pearl* events are not presented to us through Kino's eyes, as they were in the opening paragraphs. Events are described, instead, through the eyes of the objective narrator. This change in perspective implies a significant alteration in Kino's character. Kino changes from essentially self-centered, naive male to a man sensitized and humbled by life's experiences. For finding the pearl and for killing the scorpion which stings his son, Kino is elevated to a kind of "hero" status. But he learns how ephemeral such adulation is and how quickly the simplest of human actions can precipitate the most violent and threatening reactions. His stubborn inflexibility, his refusal to listen to advice from Juana and his brother Juan Tomás, his clinging to a dream of owning a boat and a gun and fancy clothing endanger not only himself but his wife and lead to the death of his infant son. Even his "heroic" killing of the men who pursue them and kill Coyotito cannot alter the tragic consequences of his actions. His gesture at the conclusion of the story of offering Juana the opportunity of throwing the pearl back into the gulf indicates his recognition of the new role which she has assumed and his acceptance of her individual significance. Moreover, it is an act of contrition. That Juana refuses to accept his offer and tells him to throw the pearl is a sign of her understanding, her composure, and her forgiveness.

The changes which occur in both Kino and Juana illustrate that though initiation into life's harsh realities may not be pleasant, the knowledge gained through those experiences compensates for the naive peace of mind that has been lost. Though the villagers (still relatively naive and uninitiated) think the returning Kino and Juana seem "to be

removed from human experience" (526), it ironically has
been direct involvement with such experience that has so
altered the couple. Kino comes back from their journey
looking as if he is "as dangerous as a rising storm" (526), a
simile which suggests that he no longer will be prone to the
exploitation which his previous ignorance and naivete allowed. For four hundred years he and his people have been
exploited and humiliated by foreigners, represented in the
story by the priest, the church, the physician, and the pearl
buyers. By casting away the pearl, Kino symbolically rejects
the materialism and greed which seem to be the dominant
values of these non-native forces, and the rifle he now carries
suggests that he will be willing in the future to fight for the
values which he and Juana have so painfully learned to
appreciate—values which put them back in tune with nature.
The "Song of the Family" has reasserted itself in Kino's ears as
"a battle cry" (526), while the music of the damnable pearl has
"disappeared" (527). Kino and Juana have recognized that the
once alluringly bright, incandescent pearl is, in fact, "gray,
like a malignant growth," its music "distorted and insane"
(527), and they have cast it away.

Steinbeck does not suggest in the story that Kino and
Juana's future will be without struggles and problems. Quite
the contrary. The same signs which symbolize their independence also foreshadow potential trouble. The rifle symbolizes
the "machine" which has helped subjugate Kino's people for
four hundred years and the violence which lurks in Kino's
personality—the same rifle and the same violence which has
"shot away" the top of Coyotito's head (527). The "rising
storm" that the people see in Kino implies this same potential
violence. As a biologist and a naturalistic writer, and as a
recent participant in World War II, Steinbeck would never
deny the role that violence plays in all life processes—from
the lowest sea creature to humans. And he certainly does not
deny its presence in Kino's personality. The hope is that the
violence can be controlled and directed for good rather than
evil and that the difference between the two is recognized.
That Kino and Juana now stand as equals, toughened by
mutual experience, and no longer separated by fighting

between themselves as they have been in the past is a positive
indication of what the future may hold for them.

NOTES

1. John Steinbeck, *The Log from the Sea of Cortez* (New York:
   Viking Press, 1951), p. 102. All further references to this
   work will appear in the text.
2. Jackson J. Benson, *The True Adventures of John Steinbeck,
   Writer* (New York: Viking Press, 1984), p. 540. All further
   references to this work will appear in the text.
3. John Steinbeck, *The Pearl*, in *The Short Novels of John Steinbeck*
   (New York: Viking Press, 1963), p. 473. All further references to this work will appear in the text.
4. Quoted in Benson, p. 569.
5. For comments about Steinbeck's monetary concerns relative
   to *The Pearl*, see Warren French, *John Steinbeck* (New York:
   Twayne, 1961), p. 137. Michael J. Meyer gives a good brief
   review of critical attitudes toward *The Pearl* in his article
   "Precious Bane." For annotations on Meyer's and other
   relevant critical commentaries, see the "Selected Bibliography."
6. Warren French, "Introduction," in *The Novels of John Steinbeck: A Critical Study.* ed. Howard Levant (Columbia: University of Missouri Press, 1974), p. xix.
7. Levant, p 188.
8. Warren French, for instance, in his introduction to Howard
   Levant's *The Novels of John Steinbeck,* suggests that the audience which appreciates good literature and which earlier
   critics of Steinbeck took for granted may no longer exist. "We
   cannot assume that many people today love literature" and
   "before we can now talk about books and authors we must
   redevelop an audience interested in books and authors" (p.
   xvii).
9. Michael J. Meyer, "Precious Bane: Mining the Fool's Gold of
   The Pearl," in *The Short Novels of John Steinbeck,* ed. Jackson J.
   Benson (Durham, North Carolina: Duke University Press,
   1990) p. 163.
10. John H. Timmerman, *John Steinbeck's Fiction: The Aesthetics of
    the Road Taken* (Norman: University of Oklahoma Press,
    1986), p. 196.
11. *Ibid.,* p. 197.

12.   Levant, p. 186.
13.   Meyer, p. 163.

IV. TOPICS FOR RESEARCH AND DISCUSSION

(1)   *The Pearl* may be read as a parable. A parable is a story which
      is meant to teach a lesson or point up a moral. It usually deals
      with the conflict between good and evil in human actions.
      Analyze the ways in which *The Pearl* serves as a parable.
      Consider these and other questions: What moral lesson does
      The Pearl teach us?; how does it compare to other famous
      parables, such as those from the Bible?; do Kino and Juana
      learn the same lesson that their story is meant to teach us as
      audience?; and how is its moral lesson relevant or not relevant
      to our lives in the late twentieth century?

(2)   Peter Lisca noted some years ago that Steinbeck's fictional
      women seem to have but two choices: homemaking and
      prostitution. On the other hand, Mimi R. Gladstein refers to
      Juana as an "indomitable" heroine. Compare Juana with
      several other female characters in Steinbeck's short fiction,
      such as Curley's wife in *Of Mice and Men* or Elisa Allen in "The
      Chrysanthemums," in order to arrive at your own evaluation
      of Steinbeck's attitude toward women. Do the women charac-
      ters you have chosen substantiate either of the opposing views
      noted above? How do you account for such a difference of
      opinion about Steinbeck's women?

(3)   If we see Kino as the protagonist of *The Pearl,* who or what is
      the antagonist? In answering the question, consider that
      Steinbeck never identifies the people who invade Kino's
      house, who pursue him on the trail, and who ultimately cause
      the death of his son. On the other hand, Steinbeck devotes
      considerable time to identifying the pearl merchants, the
      greedy physician, and others. Is Kino's enemy to be found
      somewhere in these various characters, or is he his own worst
      enemy?

(4)   Steinbeck seems to prefer primitive or rustic individuals as the
      major characters in much of his fiction. Compare Kino and
      Juana to similar characters from such Steinbeck works as *The
      Grapes of Wrath, Of Mice and Men,* or *Cannery Row.* What
      human values does Steinbeck find in such individuals to cause
      his admiration of them? On the other hand, what shortcomings
      does Steinbeck recognize in such individuals? Does anything

in his own life help explain his interest in these primitive/rustic protagonists?

(5) In *The Pearl,* Steinbeck carefully constructs the settings. He uses both general or natural settings (the ocean, the mountains, the cave) and specific or artificial ones (Kino's hut, the town of La Paz). Analyze the ways in which Steinbeck uses these various settings to help characterize the people who inhabit them and as a reflection of the "messages" he wishes for his parable to convey. Note, for example, the implications of Kino and Juana's movement from one type of setting to another and their eventual return to La Paz.

V. SELECTED BIBLIOGRAPHY

1. Keith Ferrel, *John Steinbeck: The Voice of the Land* (New York: M. Evans and Co., 1986). This book does not attempt a significant analysis of *The Pearl,* but does offer interesting comments about the circumstances relevant to the story's origins and the events of Steinbeck's personal life during the time of its being written and filmed.

2. Mimi Reisel Gladstein, "Steinbeck's Juana: A Woman of Worth," in *Steinbeck's Women: Essays in Criticism,* ed. Tetsumaro Hayashi (*Steinbeck Monograph Series,* No. 9) (Muncie, Indiana: Steinbeck Society of America, Ball State University, 1979), pp. 49-52. In this brief article Gladstein argues that like Ma Joad, Juana is one of the most positively depicted female characters in Steinbeck's fiction. She serves as the "epitome of strength and devotion" and stands as a positive force against the otherwise dark message that Steinbeck offers.

3. Tetsumaro Hayashi, "*The Pearl* as the Novel of Disengagement," *Steinbeck Quarterly,* 7 (Summer-Fall 1974), 84-88. Hayashi discusses how *The Pearl* draws its narrative flow from a process of commitment to false values and a "disengagement" from those values. The pearl is a symbol of moral bankruptcy. Kino is at first fascinated, then obsessed by the pearl. When he loses his real "Pearl" (Coyotito), he recognizes the dual nature of the pearl as an image of life and death. By looking at evil, Kino is made aware of the true nature of humans and of their lonely fate. He is restored when he renounces the pearl.

4. Howard Levant, "The Natural Parable," in his *The Novels of John Steinbeck: A Critical Study* (Columbia: University of Missouri Press, 1974), pp. 185-206. Discusses *The Pearl* as a

noting that in comparison to Steinbeck's other allegorical and partially allegorical novels it is more successful as "objective, credible narrative, . . . capable of expanded belief." Levant goes on to discuss Steinbeck's use of irony, imagery, point of view, and other narrative techniques that demonstrate how "the harmony of its parts" makes *The Pearl* a singular success.

5. Michael J. Meyer, "Precious Bane: Mining the Fool's Gold of *The Pearl*," in *The Short Novels of John Steinbeck*, ed. Jackson J. Benson (Durham, North Carolina: Duke University Press, 1990), pp. 161-72. Meyer denies that *The Pearl* is a simple black-white allegory, as some critics have seen it, and tries to show that it is a story showing the good-evil "duality that undergirds all of man's actions." Meyer focuses mostly on the light versus darkness imagery that Steinbeck uses and demonstrates that the short novel "possesses archetypal significance" and "offers a deep moral lesson to conscientious readers."

6. Louis Owens, *John Steinbeck's Re-Vision of America* (Athens: University of Georgia Press, 1985), pp. 35-46. Focuses on the importance of the setting, especially the mountains, and argues that they are the thematic and symbolic center of the novel. He says that Kino challenges the unknown, primarily symbolized by the mountains, and thereby achieves a form of greatness. The undefined threat of the dark figures suggests the isolation that Kino has brought upon himself and the fact that he must now face such forces alone. He does not win, but he triumphs in defeat.

7. Roy S. Simmonds, "Steinbeck's *The Pearl:* Legend, Film, Novel," in *The Short Novels of John Steinbeck*, ed. Benson, pp. 173-84. After a brief background of how Steinbeck came to be interested in the pearl story, Simmonds states that Steinbeck's recent experiences during World War II made him want to write books that were "more overtly moralistic" than his previous ones. Moreover, Steinbeck's recent experiences with films made him decide to make the pearl story into a movie, feeling it would reach a larger audience more immediately. If Steinbeck failed in *The Pearl* (as either film or novel), it is because he "tried to encompass not only three quite distinctive narrative forms (cinematic, realistic, and fabular) but also an overwhelming preponderance of identifiable symbols, metaphors, and philosophies for so slight a story."

8. John H. Timmerman, *"The Pearl,"* in his *John Steinbeck's Fiction: The Aesthetics of the Road Taken* (Norman: University of Oklahoma Press, 1986), pp. 194-209. The book offers a brief

background to Steinbeck's writing of the story, then tries to demonstrate how the symbols "emerge naturally and power-fully from a carefully arranged symbolic environment cast in the narrative framework." It discusses the contrast between the primitive and civilized worlds, animal imagery, and other narrative techniques to show how Steinbeck succeeded in his theme of "pitting the individual and his dreams against the threat of social power structures."

9. Edward E. Waldron, "*The Pearl* and *The Old Man and the Sea:* A Comparative Analysis," *Steinbeck Quarterly,* 13 (Summer-Fall 1980), 98-106. Waldron argues that *The Pearl* and *The Old Man and the Sea* are the essence of their authors in theme and style. Both concentrate on primitive people, both depict men setting goals and trying to achieve them, and both have a sparse, "stilted" prose style that tries to duplicate a foreign language. Waldron notes the similarity of imagery, the use of refrains, and the motif of triumph in face of overwhelming adversity.

8. STEINBECK'S *THE RED PONY* (1945)

PATRICK W. SHAW

I. BACKGROUND

The Red Pony consists of four short stories, each originally published independently over a period of approximately five years. "The Gift," which tells of the red pony, was published in the *North American Review* in November 1933. "The Great Mountains" was published in the same journal the following month. The third story, "The Promise," was published in *Harper's* magazine in October 1937. "The Leader of the People" was not published in America until 1938, in *The Long Valley,* a collection of Steinbeck's short stories. It had previously been published in the English magazine *Argosy* in August 1936. The four stories were brought together as a novella in 1945, when they were published as *The Red Pony* in a special illustrated edition. All four of the stories, however, were written in the early 1930s. Steinbeck also wrote a movie script for *The Red Pony*—significantly different from the short novel—which was produced in 1949.

The "pony story," as Steinbeck called it, was written under rather unusual circumstances, beginning in the spring of 1933. In the early 1930s the entire country was in the midst of the Depression, and Steinbeck himself was not yet famous and had little money. He was much influenced by the biologist Ed Ricketts and was developing a serious interest in biology. His mother was dying, and he and his wife Carol moved back to the family home in Salinas, California, to help care for her. The letters he wrote as *The Red Pony* was taking shape offer an excellent account of its composition. Steinbeck was trying to come to terms, as he says, with the fact that

"Half of the cell units of my mother's body have rebelled."[1] Because of his mother's incontinence, Steinbeck personally had to change her bedclothes. "There are terrible washings [of 9-12 sheets] every day. . . . I wash them and Carol irons them" (82). The pony story which he began was based loosely upon his own childhood experience with a sick pony. Writing on a dining-room table just outside his mother's sick-room door, Steinbeck would compose a few lines or a paragraph, then be interrupted to go empty her bedpan or change her sheets (83). Contemplating his mother's death and the experiences surrounding it, he tried to "sneak in a little work" (82) and to put events "into the symbolism of fiction" (76). In a letter written in June 1933, he refers to the experience as "a very long siege" that could "last for years," and a "sentence" which he could not leave (78). He longed for time to spend a few hours at the beach or to go camping with friends.

Confined to home by his mother's paralysis, Steinbeck began to form a thesis of life itself—a thesis that "takes in all life, and for that part, all matter" (79). Steinbeck tried to explain his thinking to a friend:

> A further arrangement of cells and a very complex one may make a unit which we call a man. That has been our final unit. But there have been mysterious things which could not be explained if man is the final unit. He also arranges himself into larger units, which I have called the phalanx. The phalanx has its own memory—memory of the great tides when the moon was close, memory of starvation when the food of the world was exhausted. Memory of methods when numbers of his units had to be destroyed for the good of the whole, memory of the history of itself. (79-80)

Elucidating his theory in another letter, Steinbeck noted that "the group is an individual as boundaried, as diagnosable, as dependent on its units and as independent of its units' individual natures, as the human unit, or man, is dependent on his cells and yet is independent of them" (75). Steinbeck realized his theory was not without its faults, explaining that he was "neither scientist nor profound investigator," and that he was trying to understand his mother's dying in terms of a "tremendous and terrible poetry" (81).

As the months wore on, Steinbeck's father also began to break under the strain; and Steinbeck worried that his father would end up "in the same position as my mother" (88). The elder Steinbeck lost his eyesight, and was "like an engine" shaking "itself to pieces" (88). "Death," Steinbeck wrote, "I can stand but not this slow torture wherein a good and a strong man tears off little shreds of himself and throws them away" (89). On top of all this, Steinbeck's dog Tillie died and was replaced by another dog named "Joddi" (87-88)—a name similar to that he gave the boy protagonist of *The Red Pony*. As his biographer Jackson J. Benson writes, "Writing had always been in part for [Steinbeck] an escape; now escape became a way of surviving."[2]

Under such circumstances, Steinbeck wrote "The Gift" and "The Great Mountains." His mother died shortly after Christmas 1933, and in the early spring of 1934 Steinbeck wrote "The Promise" and "The Leader of the People," which would eventually serve as the final stories for *The Red Pony*.

II. PLOT SYNOPSIS

The Red Pony consists of four stories: "The Gift," "The Great Mountains," "The Promise," and "The Leader of the People." The setting for each of the stories is the Carl Tiflin ranch, near Salinas, California. In addition to the usual house and outbuildings, prominent landmarks on the ranch are a cold water spring and a great black kettle under a cypress tree. Here pigs are killed and scalded. No definite dates are given in the stories, but certain details such as the lack of electricity and the absence of motorized vehicles suggest the early twentieth century. The events of all four stories cover approximately two and one-half years, beginning in the summer of Jody's tenth year, but the sequence in which the stories appear may not be the same sequence in which the events of Jody Tiflin's life occur.

Jody Tiflin is an obedient little boy, "with hair like dusty yellow grass" and "shy polite gray eyes."[3] Billy Buck, the middle-aged ranch hand, is "a broad, bandy-legged little man" whose eyes are "watery gray" and whose hair protrudes from beneath his Stetson hat like spikes (137). Carl Tiflin is a "disciplinarian" and a "tall stern father" (138). Mrs. Tiflin is given no specific description, and is referred to only once as "Ruth."

I. "THE GIFT"

Jody returns home from school one day to discover that his father and Billy Buck have brought him a red pony colt and a red leather saddle back from their trip to Salinas. He is very excited about the pony and is admired and envied by his school-mates, who know "instinctively that a man on a horse is spiritually as well as physically bigger than a man on foot" (143). He names the pony "Gabilan," which means "hawk" and which is also the name of the nearby mountains. In the ensuing months Jody is diligent in caring for and training the pony, with Billy Buck's guidance. Seeing the progress his son has made with the pony, Mr. Tiflin promises him he can ride Gabilan by Thanksgiving, three weeks away. Jody worries about how ashamed of him everybody will be if he does not ride well.

Before Thanksgiving, the weather turns cold and rainy. Jody is careful to make sure Gabilan is kept dry in his stall. When the sun returns, Billy Buck assures Jody that he can safely leave Gabilan out in the corral during the school day. He promises Jody he will watch Gabilan and put him back in the barn if the rain should return. While Jody is at school, the rain returns, and though Jody wants to run home to check his pony, he is afraid of doing so because of the punishment he knows he would receive for leaving school. After school he hurries home to "see Gabilan standing miserably in the corral" (150), cold and wet. He accuses Billy Buck of being wrong about his assurance that it would not rain, and Billy feels guilty.

Despite all of Billy's efforts to help Gabilan, the colt gets worse. His "eyes were half closed" and "thin fluid ran from his nostrils" (152). A large lump forms under his jaw, a sign of "strangles," and Billy Buck must slash it open with a knife to keep the colt from suffocating. During the night the wind and rain return, and Jody runs to the barn to find that the colt has once again left his stall and wandered out into the storm. This time Billy Buck has "to open a little hole" in Gabilan's windpipe to allow him to breathe. Jody watches as the "blood ran thickly out and up the knife and across Billy's hand" (157).

At daylight Jody awakens to find that the barn door has swung open and that the pony is gone once again. He easily tracks Gabilan through "the frostlike dew on the young grass" (158). A buzzard is sitting "on the pony's head and its beak had just risen dripping with dark eye fluid" (159). Jody grabs the bird and smashes its head with a piece of white quartz rock, but not before the buzzard vomits "putrefied fluid" (159). Billy Buck and Carl Tiflin find Jody by the pony, and his father asks him if he knows that "the buzzard didn't kill the pony" (159). Billy Buck lifts Jody to carry him home, looking back at Carl Tiflin to say "'Course he knows it. . . . Jesus Christ! man, can't you see how he'd feel about it?'" (160).

II. "THE GREAT MOUNTAINS"

It is midsummer and Jody destroys swallow nests, sets rat traps so the ranch dogs will get their noses snapped, and kills a thrush with his slingshot. After beheading and disemboweling the bird, he washes the blood from his hands in the tub filled by the spring. Then he thinks about the mountains in the distance and how little he knows about them. He remembers asking his father what lies between the mountains and the ocean which is on the other side. Though his father tells him "nothing," Jody knows "something was there, something very wonderful" (162). Yet he is afraid of the "terrible" mountains. Turning to face the east, he then sees the Gabilans, which are "jolly mountains, with hill ranches in their creases" (162). He remembers that "battles had been fought against the Mexicans on the slopes" (162).

Jody returns to the house just as a bony old man dressed in worn cowboy clothing arrives. "I am Gitano," he tells Jody, "and I have come back" (163). Jody runs to get his mother, and Gitano then explains to them that he was born in an old adobe house on the ranch and that he has returned to stay until he dies. Jody then gets his father from the barn, and Carl Tiflin tells the old man that he cannot stay and will have to leave tomorrow.

Jody shows Gitano to the bunkhouse, and finally gets up enough nerve to ask him if he is from the "big mountains." The old man tells him he has been in the mountains only once, when he was a little boy accompanied by his father. He tells Jody he cannot remember what was there. "I think it was quiet—I think it was nice," he tells Jody (166).

Among the horses on the ranch is one with yellow teeth, protruding rib bones, and painful movements. Jody explains to Gitano that it is old Easter, the first horse his father ever had. Jody's father says that such old things should be shot and put out of their misery. Billy Buck tells him that after having worked all their lives, animals should be allowed to rest and "just walk around" (167). Jody realizes that Carl Tiflin is "probing for a place to hurt in Gitano" (167). After Carl Tiflin and Billy Buck leave, Jody apologizes to the old man, while Easter lets Gitano rub his neck and mane.

That night after supper Jody returns to the bunkhouse to find Gitano holding a "lovely rapier with a golden basket hilt" (169). Gitano is angry at the intrusion and will not let the boy examine the sword. He will only tell Jody that he got it from his father. Leaving the bunkhouse, Jody realizes that he "must never tell anyone about the rapier" because to do so would "destroy some fragile structure of truth" (170).

Next morning Jody arises to learn that both Gitano and old Easter have disappeared. Later, a neighbor, Jess Taylor, informs the Tiflins that early that morning he saw an old man riding an old horse without a saddle, and holding something shiny like a gun in his hand. He was headed into the mountains. Carl Tiflin tells the neighbor that Gitano's stealing the old horse will just save him the cost of having to bury it. Jody thinks about the towering mountains, the rapier, and old Gitano. He lies down in the "green grass near the round tub" at the spring, filled with longing and a "nameless sorrow" (171).

III. "THE PROMISE"

Jody is returning from school one spring day, pretending to lead an army and collecting grasshoppers and other creatures. When he reaches home, his mother informs him that his father is waiting to see him. Fearing punishment for some misdeed, Jody goes to find his father in the pasture. Carl Tiflin tells Jody that he can take the mare Nellie to a neighbor's ranch to be bred, if he will accept responsibility for her and the colt she will throw, and if he will work off the $5.00 stud fee. Though his insides are "shriveling," Jody calmly tells his father that he will accept the responsibility. That evening, with bats and nighthawks flying about, Billy Buck explains to Jody that it will take nearly a year before the colt is born. Jody promises he will not get tired of waiting. Next morning he takes Nellie to be bred and is almost killed when the stallion Sun Dog breaks loose and charges down the hill to meet Nellie.

Jody wants Billy Buck to promise that he will not let anything happen to Nellie's colt, but Billy remembers the red pony and says that he cannot promise anything. Jody often goes to the spring, to think and be soothed. But he thinks also of the pigs that are slaughtered near the black cypress tree and scalded in the black pot.

Christmas passes. Then January. By February, Nellie still has not given birth. Finally, Jody is awakened one night by Billy Buck, telling him the colt is about to be born. They run to the barn to find Nellie "standing rigid and stiff" (185). Realizing something is wrong, Billy Buck takes a horseshoe hammer and crushes Nellie's skull. He then cuts her stomach open with a pocket knife, plunges his hands into the hole, and drags out "a big, white, dripping bundle" (186). With his teeth he tears open the birth sac and lays a black colt at Jody's feet. "There's your colt," Billy says. "I promised. And there it is" (186). Leaving the barn to get water which Billy has demanded, Jody tries to be happy, but "the haunted, tired eyes of Billy Buck hung in the air ahead of him" (186).

IV. "THE LEADER OF THE PEOPLE"

Billy Buck is raking the last of the old year's hay. Jody is interested in the mice that live in the haystacks and vows that he will now kill "those damn mice" (188). Billy warns him that he must first get his father's permission. Carl Tiflin returns home on horseback, carrying a letter from Mrs. Tiflin's father which says he will arrive today for a short visit. Carl Tiflin is not pleased with the news, complaining that all the old man can talk about is Indians. Mrs. Tiflin is at first angry with her husband's attitude, but then quietly explains that her father's leading a wagon train "clear across the plains to the coast" was the "big thing" in his life and after he had done it, there was nothing left for him to do (189).

Jody, who is excited by his grandfather's visit, goes out to meet the "old man," who is dressed in black and has a white beard and "sternly merry" blue eyes (191), and he arrives in a horse-drawn cart. Jody announces that he is going on a mouse hunt tomorrow and asks Grandfather to come with him. "Have the people of this generation come down to hunting mice?" Grandfather chuckles. He says that in the past when "the troops were hunting Indians and shooting children and burning teepees" it was like a mouse hunt (192). Billy Buck comes out of the bunkhouse to meet them, for he holds Grandfather "in reverence" (193). Grandfather knew Billy's father, Mule-tail Buck, a man whom he respected. At dinner, Grandfather begins to retell his frontier stories, and Carl Tiflin reminds him that everyone at the table has heard them "lots of times." Jody knows how his grandfather feels "collapsed and empty" inside, and encourages him to continue his Indian stories (194). Billy Buck, Carl Tiflin, and Mrs. Tiflin sit at the table but do not listen.

Jody gets permission from his father to kill the mice the next day, then goes to bed and thinks of his Grandfather on a huge white horse, "living in the heroic time" (196). He arises next morning eager to kill the mice, but at breakfast Grandfather overhears Carl Tiflin complain about having to hear Grandfather's tales "over and over" (197). Carl Tiflin apologizes, but Grandfather tells him that he is probably right. Jody is no longer interested in killing the mice, but sits instead on the porch with Grandfather. Grandfather explains to Jody that he feels that the crossing was not worth doing. It was not getting to the coast that mattered, he says. The important thing was "movement and westering" (199). Now, he says, "There's a line of old men along the shore hating the ocean because it stopped them" (199). Westering is done, and there is no place left to go. Jody then offers to make Grandfather a glass of lemonade, but when his mother asks if he wants one for himself, he declines.

III. CRITICAL EXPLICATION

As most previous analyses recognize, the stories which comprise *The Red Pony* detail Jody Tiflin's initiation into death and his awakening to the need for human compassion. As R. S. Hughes phrases it, "Steinbeck focuses on the progress of Jody's initiation into the reality of death" by objectively presenting "graphic descriptions of suffering, violence, and death."[4] This initiation is a fundamental and significant element in the stories, but Steinbeck seemed to have most in mind an experiment in point of view. He describes his intent during the early stages of writing *The Red Pony:*

> It is a very simple story about a boy who gets a colt pony and the pony gets distemper. There is a good deal in it, first about the training of horses and second about the treatment of distemper. This may not seem like a good basis for a story but that entirely depends upon the treatment. The whole thing is as simply told as though it came out of the boy's mind although there is no going into the boy's mind. It is an attempt to make the reader create the boy's mind for himself. (*SLL,* 71)

In my analysis of *The Red Pony,* I will focus upon the interrelationships among the initiation motif, the point of view that tries to "make the reader create" Jody's mind, and Steinbeck's characteristic use of symbols.

Howard Levant is correct in noting that whereas the "objective events" of the story "are self-contained," they are presented to the reader through Jody's "innocent point of view." Levant goes on to explain that "each episode begins with a focus on Jody's childish faith in adults or a child's world." In this process, "death and imperfection are everywhere" and "nature is a merely neutral element."[5] It is important for us to keep in mind that while the story is not presented from the first person point of view, the narrative focus is indeed upon Jody, for it is through his experiences that we as readers must form our evaluation of the various narratives that make up *The Red Pony*. Moreover, recognizing that Jody is indeed a child forced to cope with life in an exclusively adult environment which is frequently narrow and unfriendly is important to our understanding of Steinbeck's intent. Brian Barbour correctly anticipates this conflict when he notes that Jody's father personifies cruelty, inhumanity, and a near total lack of compassion.[6]

A reader unfamiliar with *The Red Pony* may come to it expecting to find a children's tale or a story of pastoral innocence. The title suggests the happy story of a boy who gets his heart's desire, a pony. This tone of innocent contentment is continued in the first two paragraphs of the story, with Billy Buck's taking care of the animals, the mother's call to food and warmth of the breakfast table, the summer weather, and Jody's carefree obedience. From such a beginning a reader may well anticipate a nostalgic, escapist account of "good" actions set in a past era. Such benign expectations are soon negated, however, and the contrast between what the title and opening paragraphs may connote and what Steinbeck actually describes is a major element in the impact which *The Red Pony* has upon us as audience. Far from a happy tale of innocent experiences on a western ranch, Steinbeck gives us what superficially seems to be an unrelieved account of disappointments, meanness, and death. There is nothing idyllic about any of the four stories. Only in the subtext of the narrative can we discover the philosophical positives which counterbalance the textual negatives.

What Steinbeck gives us in the narrative context of the stories is the objective account of a ten-year-old boy who is being reared in geographical and psychological isolation. That is, Jody is physically isolated on a ranch in the Salinas Valley of California and psychologically isolated in that he has no contact with the cosmopolitan world of cities and large numbers of people. His only contact with the world off the ranch is at his school, and Steinbeck only briefly mentions this part of Jody's life, thus suggesting its relative insignificance in the formation of Jody's responses to the world. The lessons

Jody learns are from life, not from books. The distance of
other families or neighbors is indicated when Jody takes
Nellie to be bred and has to walk steadily for an hour before
reaching the road that leads to Jess Taylor's ranch. Having no
brothers or sisters, and having only brief contact with his
schoolmates, Jody is surrounded by adults—isolated, that is,
in a world that is psychologically "foreign." Within the space
of a relatively short period of time, he is forced to deal with
the realities of sexuality (epitomized by the breeding frenzy
of the horses); with human cruelty (his father's harsh treatment of Jody's grandfather and Gitano); and death (the red
pony and Nellie). As a child, therefore, he is a kind of
stranger in a strange land of adults and adult problems. That
the final scene in the short novel shows Jody acting with
loving kindness toward his aging grandfather does not prove
that he has transcended these problems, but it does suggest
that Jody is preparing to enter his own adulthood with more
understanding and compassion than the adults with whom he
has been reared.

In light of Jody's compassion, we need also to note the
dominance of the "male" attitudes in Jody's life—attitudes
which too often seem coldly pragmatic and lacking in compassion. We see this masculine hardness in both Carl Tiflin and
Billy Buck. Though Jody's father is capable of giving and of
parental love, he seems more prone to squelch those emotions.
As the narrator of the story says, "Carl Tiflin hated weakness
and sickness, and he held a violent contempt for helplessness"
(151). Moreover, his harsh, sarcastic condemnation of Jody's
grandfather in "The Leader of the People" shows a meanness of
spirit which few readers can condone. The ranch hand Billy
Buck is less prone to such hard treatment of others than is his
boss, but he, too, is ultimately hard and practical. His devoted
nurturing of the sick colt Gabilan is ironically counterbalanced
by his bloody killing of the mare Nellie to save the second colt.
Billy well knows that he can save the mare by "tear[ing] the colt
to pieces to get it out" (178), but he chooses instead to save the
colt and sacrifice the mare. That this colt is male, as shown by
the masculine pronouns Billy uses (186), and that Billy does not
hesitate to kill the mare to save it symbolize the dominance of
the male in the value system which determines the rural life in

which Jody must mature. Further, practically all the male characters in the novella are conspicuously named (Billy Buck, Carl Tiflin, Gitano, Jody Tiflin), but the only human female in the novel (Jody's mother) is identified almost exclusively as "Mrs. Tiflin" or "his mother." Such a naming device suggests her subservience to her husband and to the male patriarchy in general, and significantly emphasizes her lack of individual identity. Even her displeasure at Carl Tiflin's harsh attitude toward her father is implied by gesture, never by direct outspoken opposition, though clearly she has good cause to express her anger at such churlish behavior. In passing, we might note also that her father is a man who does not fit into the hard, pragmatic mold which Carl Tiflin and Billy Buck epitomize. He is a man of compassion and understanding, as shown in his awareness that "hunting Indians and shooting children and burning teepees" shows a lack of human love like the pointless killing of mice (192). And similar to his daughter in the story, he is given no specific identification. He is designated only as "Grandfather."

Jody must choose between this masculine, pragmatic hardness and the compassionate nurturing usually identified as feminine. We are never told of Jody's choices overtly in the story, for as I have noted, the style remains predominantly objective and non-judgmental; and the overall tone reflects the same hard pragmaticism we have associated with the masculine world of the ranch. That is, Steinbeck passes no substantive judgments against the male attitudes which are part of a pattern of behavior adopted to cope with a nature that is often violent, bloody, and unforgiving. As Steinbeck himself has pointed out, he never takes us inside Jody's mind. Yet, rather subtly, Steinbeck's management of the feminine elements in the short novel suggests what the harsh life of the rural ranch can do to an individual: it can render him insensitive to the emotional needs of others and remove him from the nurturing compassion that is important in human relationships if humans are to be anything other than predators and vultures and mere victims to those who are physically stronger. We see this predator-victim life symbolized by the circling buzzards, the quail Jody wants to shoot, the cows and pigs which are slaughtered, and (ironically) in the name "Gabilan," which means hawk.

That Steinbeck had the conflict of the feminine- masculine sensibilities in mind while writing *The Red Pony* is substantiated by "The Chrysanthemums," a short story he published in the same year as "The Promise," which would become part of *The Red Pony.* "The Chrysanthemums" focuses upon a woman who is isolated on a Salinas Valley ranch (like Jody) and whose femininity is repressed if not totally destroyed by a male-dominated society. It is probably Steinbeck's best short story and clearly demonstrates his subtle management of the theme of artistic sensibility at odds with a hard, pragmatic world, the same theme we see in *The Red Pony* when Jody's innocence and innate compassion must confront a world in which such qualities have little value. As John H. Timmerman wisely points out in a footnote to his own comments about "The Chrysanthemums," it is a mistake "to pass modern liberation theories onto Steinbeck,"[7] but certainly he was innately, if not consciously, sensitive to the issues arising when any individual is squelched by a prevailing social bias.

Keeping to his objective style and unemotional tone, Steinbeck does not reveal to us which way Jody will go—toward the "stern" hardness of his father and bloody pragmatism of Billy Buck or toward the kinder, more compassionate, and ultimately perhaps more humanitarian way personified by his mother and Grandfather. Yet, as I note above, by the simple fact that Jody decides at the end of "The Leader of the People" to forego the killing of the mice and spend time on the porch with his despondent grandfather, Steinbeck suggests that Jody is moving toward an understanding of the human predicament which neither his father nor Billy Buck has attained. Grandfather's experience during his visit to the Tiflin ranch has taught him that if the life epitomized by Carl Tiflin's attitude is typical of the settlement of the country, then the fight for the land and the crossing of the continent "wasn't worth doing" (199). "Westering," that dream of adventure and a belief in the unstoppable progress of the human animal (the phalanx as Steinbeck called it), somehow "died out of the people" (199). Grandfather knows the Pacific

Ocean halted the dream of the westward migration, and "There's a line of old men along the shore hating the ocean because it stopped them" (199). Yet we as audience, as perhaps will Jody as he further matures, realize that it is only the physical movement that has been halted, the geographical, literal limitations that have been reached. The psychological or emotional "frontiers" are left to be explored, and the ocean which Grandfather sees as a barrier can serve just as easily as a symbol for the limitless mystery of human life that is yet open to exploration. (We recall that Steinbeck himself was nursing his dying mother as he wrote *The Red Pony* and that with his biologist friend, Ed Ricketts, he would soon set sail to explore the oceans, both literally and symbolically.) John H. Timmerman summarizes *The Red Pony* in this way: "Working through the major themes of death and renewal, of dreams such as Grandfather's and the confines of civilization upon it, is also the theme of freedom and constraint that especially marks the tension between Carl and Jody Tiflin."[8] Timmerman is correct, for indeed Jody quietly insists that he have the freedom to dream of a life which transcends the harsh confines of the ranch and the narrow-minded attitudes personified by his father.

We should note, however, that Jody does not rebel against the realities that are forced upon him. He adjusts. This ability to adapt to adverse conditions— this "toughness"—is Jody's great strength, and the positive balance to what otherwise appears to be the harsh negativism of the story. He moves from a boy too ready to kill and dismember birds to a young man who forgoes the needless clubbing of mice. It is not a romantic, sentimental misunderstanding of nature's design which leads Jody to appreciate life. He is surrounded by death constantly, and he himself inflicts death. At no point does Steinbeck's management of point of view lead us to believe that either the author or his young protagonist believes in a benevolent natural purpose. Humans die as surely as pigs and ponies and old horses. Death is part of the natural cycle, just as are the seasons which appear in the stories. Like Grandfather and Gitano, Jody will grow old and die. Nature can be violent, bloody, and unforgiving. But against those qualities stands the potential of human compassion, the one human trait which separates humans from the buzzards that symbolize survival by dependence on death and carnage. As Howard Levant notes, "in feeding on carrion, buzzards mark the point at which death becomes an ugly imperfection that cannot be accepted serenely."[9] Jody senses but cannot articulate that there must be more satisfying approaches to coping with the impending death which nature forces upon all living things. Old Gitano's ascent into the mountains on a horse conspicuously named "Easter" symbolizes this spiritual potential and offers to Jody a kind of epiphany, a suggestion that there is something beyond the mere biological processes of birth and death. Human existence does not cease in the stomach of a hungry buzzard.

We noted earlier Steinbeck's theory of the phalanx, his idea that human individuals arrange themselves into larger units, like cells in the body (see the "Background" discussion). Some readers of *The Red Pony* feel that Steinbeck compromises his point of view management by trying to work the phalanx theory into the narrative design. R. S. Hughes, for instance, argues that Grandfather's comments about "the big crawling beast," which presents the phalanx idea, do not "fit thematically" into "The Leader of the People."[10] Viewed in terms of *The Red Pony* as a narrative unit, and in light of the theme of Jody's continued initiation and maturity, however, Grandfather's awareness that the individual must see himself or herself as part of a larger unit of humanity becomes an integral part of Steinbeck's purpose. The failure to make this association between the individual and humankind collectively is what renders Carl Tiflin such an insensitive, cruel man. Moreover, it is Billy Buck's determination to keep his promise about the second colt and not to lose face as a man that leads him to kill the mare Nellie, the symbol of life's continuity. And later, though Billy Buck has some admiration for Grandfather, he ceases to listen to the lessons the old man is trying to impart through his tales. While Grandfather talks, Billy idly "watched a spider crawling up the wall" (195). Only Jody listens, though he, too, has heard the tales before. Jody is yet too young to articulate what he learns from Grandfather's experiences, but the last scene we have in the short novel is Jody taking a lemon from his mother to make lemonade for Grandfather. This visual image which groups Mrs. Tiflin, her father, and Jody separates them in our minds from Billy Buck and Carl Tiflin and suggests that Jody's future alliance will be with those who represent artistic sensibilities and humanity. Thus Grandfather's lesson about the unity that took many individuals to the ocean (the phalanx) is an important part of Jody's increasing awareness. Grandfather's ideas offer him an alternative to the hard, bloody life into which Carl Tiflin and Billy Buck have initiated Jody. Jody has learned the literal lesson from Gabilan who leaves his stall and wanders beyond the confines of his corral that if one steps beyond the narrow confines of fences, he risks death. Grandfather's experiences with a wider, multi-ethnic world beyond the ranch give Jody an alternative to that "fenced" mentality. As Grandfather teaches, it is the "westering" that matters, the questing, the searching, the going beyond apparent confinements. He fears that it "has died out of the people" (199), but in Jody we see some hope that the questing spirit can be revived. As I noted earlier, Steinbeck's intent is not a message of Pollyanna optimism, but he does want to suggest that Jody (and each of us) has choices that transcend the mere acceptance of the cold, final deaths we see in the red pony, Nellie, the buzzards, and in Carl Tiflin's indifferent crushing of the moth that tries to fly to the light (194).

Finally, in contrast to the death images that dominate the narrative, we need briefly to analyze Steinbeck's symbols of the life force. The spring and the ocean are the most apparent of these symbols. We have already mentioned the ocean and how Grandfather views it as a barrier, though it serves equally as a symbol of life itself. We can elucidate the point that the ocean serves as a symbol of the mysterious, spiritual force by noting Jody's earlier dream of the ocean that lies beyond the great mountains which he imagines old Gitano crossing (171). Significantly, Jody is lying near the spring when he imagines the mountains and the ocean, a point we will return to in a moment. Here in "The Great Mountains" the mountains (not the ocean) serve as barriers. One reaches the freedom of the ocean only after surmounting the mountains, which Jody imagines as towering "ridge after ridge after ridge" (171).

Jody, however, does not envision the mountains as being either insurmountable or negative. In fact, he longs to enter them and move, like Gitano, toward the great ocean that lies beyond. The mountains symbolize the life experience Jody must acquire (sexually, morally, experientially) before he can move into the more abstract, mysterious, psychological realm emblematized by the ocean. He cannot, of course, articulate the ideas at such a young age, but his innate or instinctive awareness of the literal and spiritual quests which await him are the cause of the "nameless sorrow" (171) which fills him as he contemplates the mountains and the distant ocean.

That Jody is associated with the life force and not the death force symbolized by the buzzards and other similar images we have already noted is witnessed by the fact that Jody is lying in "the green grass" near the spring (171). The spring and the tub it fills with water so "cold that it stung his mouth" (154) are first mentioned in "The Gift," the story which is otherwise so dominated by death and death symbols. Quite literally, when Jody pops the bloody tick between his thumbnails, he washes the death away in the cold spring (158)—a minor act of salvation. Immediately following this cleansing of the blood from Jody's hands, we are given the scene in which he discovers his pony dead, its eyes being punctured by the buzzards (159). With this juxtaposing of contrasting scenes, Steinbeck makes a point about seeing and not seeing. Jody has literally seen much; now he must learn to see in the sense of understanding. He must commence to see beyond the literal, to comprehend the lessons that his experiences have taught him. It is in light of this transition which is taking place for Jody that placing "The Great Mountains" immediately after Jody's finding his dead pony makes sense. From the small act of washing the tick's blood off his hand in the cold spring, Jody now sees the approach of human death in the form of old Gitano and must contemplate the larger concept of a transcendent spiritual life as symbolized by the great ocean.

Steinbeck reiterates the important symbolic connection between the spring and ocean by mentioning the spring early in "The Great Mountains" and repeating a similar blood/hand image. In angry frustration at his pony's gruesome death, Jody has killed and dismembered a thrush, itself a symbol of natural beauty and love.

> The hills were dry at this season, and the wild grass was golden, but where the spring-pipe filled the round tub and the tub spilled over, there lay a stretch of fine green grass, deep and sweet and moist. Jody drank from the mossy tub and washed the bird's blood from his hands in cold water. Then he lay on his back in the grass. . . . (161)

Again the spring symbolizes the source of Jody's absolution; but in this instance the reiterated scene serves also to remind us that Jody is about to move a step closer to an awareness of the interconnected quality of all life, further away from being a senseless destroyer of life. It is while lying beside the spring, his hands literally and symbolically cleansed, that he becomes aware of the distant mountains and begins to contemplate their "secret" (160). Old Gitano then enters Jody's life and will soon thereafter enter the mountains to await the end of his own life, thereby connecting the spring-mountain-ocean symbols. Thus, the end of the short novel, when Jody chooses not to kill the mice but chooses instead to bring his grandfather a drink, serves not only to connect the various stories within the story by reminding us of the spring from which Jody has drunk; it suggests also that Jody seems to have learned the lesson implied by the spring-ocean symbolism.

Ironically, the life force implied by the spring-ocean symbology stands in contrast to the other important water symbol Steinbeck employs. Rain throughout the novella symbolizes death. This is not a unique symbolic usage (Ernest Hemingway, for instance, uses rain extensively in *A Farewell to Arms* to symbolize death), but Steinbeck does use the symbol quite effectively to make the point that like water from the earth (the spring) and water from the sky (rain), life and death are natural processes. Steinbeck limits the rain symbology to "The Gift" and "The Promise," the two stories dealing with the horses and in which death is most graphically depicted. The rain motif is especially dominant in

"The Gift." Jody wishes that "it might not rain before Thanksgiving," (149) when he is scheduled to ride Gabilan for the first time, but the rain does come. Billy Buck then promises Jody that it will not rain again, so Jody "went to school [and] left Gabilan standing out in the corral" (150). But Billy is wrong, for again the rain returns, soaking the pony and causing the illness that leads to his death. Ironically, the rain that is usually welcomed on a dry-land ranch here is ominous and threatening, a foreshadowing of disaster. Then in "The Promise," when the mare Nellie is about to give birth to the colt that is to replace the dead Gabilan, Steinbeck uses the rain again as a symbol of impending death: "The night was black and thick. A little misting rain fell. The cypress tree and the bunkhouse loomed and then dropped back into the mist" (183). Coupled with the black cypress tree under which the hogs are slaughtered, the rain is doubly ominous. Keeping the symbolic integrity of the rain, Steinbeck then has Billy Buck kill Nellie in order to save the colt and thereby keep his promise to Jody.

When Billy Buck yells to Jody to get "the water" (186) to wash the blood from the foal, the water symbology shifts from the fatal rain to the cleansing waters of redemption, as established by the spring symbol and Jody's hand washing. Because of the rain, Billy Buck has broken his solemn promise and allowed the red pony to die, and with the birth of Nellie's foal he tries to redeem his honor, to keep his "promise." That he shouts the profane term "God damn you" (186) to Jody suggests both that Billy desires *not* to be damned for his failed promise and that he harbors some anger at Jody for forcing him into killing the mare in order to obtain forgiveness. Redemption is clearly on Billy Buck's mind. Yet, the fact that the foal is "black"—the color of the deadly cypress tree—indicates that Billy's sacrifice may not have been for the good cause he anticipated. His face remains "bloody" and his eyes "haunted" and "tired"; and though the black colt is alive and apparently well, Jody is not elated. "He tried to be glad," but Billy's image "hung in the air ahead of him" (186). In a world in which there are no absolutes, no clear-cut divisions between salvation and damnation, and in which life and death merge into an almost indistinguishable process, Jody has moved one step further toward an understanding of the human predicament. It is this step that helps prepare him for the encounter with his grandfather in "The Leader of the People" and for the compassion which he demonstrates in that concluding story.

NOTES

1. John Steinbeck, *Steinbeck: A Life in Letters*, eds. Elaine Steinbeck and Robert Wallsten (New York: Viking Press, 1975), p. 76. All further references to this work will appear in the text.
2. Jackson J. Benson, *The True Adventures of John Steinbeck, Writer* (New York: Viking Press, 1984), p. 264.
3. John Steinbeck, *The Red Pony*, in *The Short Novels of John Steinbeck* (New York: Viking Press, 1963), p. 137. All further references to this work will appear in the text.
4. R. S. Hughes, *Beyond "The Red Pony": A Reader's Companion to Steinbeck's Complete Short Stories* (Metuchen, New Jersey: Scarecrow Press, 1987), p. 91.
5. Howard Levant, "John Steinbeck's *The Red Pony*: A Study in Narrative Technique," in *The Short Novels of John Steinbeck*, ed. Jackson J. Benson (Durham, North Carolina: Duke University Press, 1990), p. 85.
6. Brian Barbour, "Steinbeck as a Short Story Writer," in *A Study Guide to Steinbeck's "The Long Valley,"* ed. Tetsumaro Hayashi (Ann Arbor, Michigan: Pierian Press, 1976), p. 125.
7. John H. Timmerman, *John Steinbeck's Fiction: The Aesthetics of The Road Taken* (Norman: University of Oklahoma Press, 1986), p. 282.
8. *Ibid.*, p. 74.
9. Levant, pp. 85-86.
10. Hughes, p. 102.

IV. TOPICS FOR RESEARCH AND DISCUSSION

(1) By consulting biographies and other sources such as John Steinbeck's letters, develop an awareness of what Steinbeck's

personal life was like during the composition of the stories which became *The Red Pony*. You will note as you study Steinbeck's life during the composition period and compare it to the stories that he does not write directly about the events which occupy his time and attention as he writes. Instead, he transfers those private events into symbols, themes, and actions which indirectly reflect what is on his mind as he composes the stories. Based upon your knowledge of Steinbeck's private life and of the elements of the stories, discuss the ways in which Steinbeck transfers his personal experiences into the stories. Consider, for example, why Steinbeck uses a child as a protagonist, why he places Ruth Tiflin (the mother) into such a seemingly unimportant role, why symbols of death are so prominent, and whether the short novel ends on a note of hope or pessimism.

(2) *The Red Pony* has frequently been termed an "initiation" story, or the account of how a child becomes an adult by facing the painful realities of death. Analyze this process of maturation in Jody. In this process of becoming aware of life's hard realities, does Jody simply become obsessed by death itself or does he let the awareness of life's termination make him equally aware of other values or potential for human happiness? If so, what specifically are these values? You might want to consider, too, that some commentators criticize Steinbeck for presenting a story which is so bleak and pessimistic. Do you agree with such an assessment or do you believe Steinbeck is more optimistic than the facts of the story may at first make him appear?

(3) Steinbeck uses the horse throughout the stories, not only as a plot device but for its symbolic power: Gabilan, Nellie, Easter, the horses which underlie Grandfather's "westering" stories. Analyze the ways in which Steinbeck uses the horse to unite the stories and the way the horse serves as a thematic symbol. Think of how appropriate the horse is to the early twentieth-century ranch setting, how a boy such as Jody would desire his own pony (much as a young person today wishes for a car), how valuable horses are to families such as the Tiflins, and why an old Indian such as Gitano would want to take his last journey on a horse. Beyond these considerations, think of what the horse symbolizes: freedom, questing, power, even sexuality. You may want also to recall famous horses from history and fiction: Pegasus, Man of War, Trigger, Silver, Don Quixote's Rocinante, Tonto's Scout, and others.

(4) Other than Jody, Billy Buck may be the most important human character in *The Red Pony*. Analyze Billy's character. What, for instance, do the names "billy" and "buck" suggest and how do they fit the overall symbolic structure of the short novel? What is the significance of the physical characteristics Steinbeck describes for Billy? (Does Steinbeck give similar details for other characters?) What values or philosophies does Billy personify? Does Billy offer an example of adulthood for Jody to emulate, or is his code of life too narrow and simple? You might want to compare Billy with similar rustic, men-of-the-earth characters from other Steinbeck fiction, such as George Milton in *Of Mice and Men*.

(5) The elements which unify the four stories of *The Red Pony* are relatively easy to recognize: Jody Tiflin as protagonist, the ranch setting, repetition of symbols such as the black cypress and the mountains, and the theme of death, plus other elements. Each story in the short novel, however, was originally written as a separate short story and is therefore distinguished by its own "personality." Concentrate on any one of the four stories which make up *The Red Pony* and discuss selected elements that distinguish it from the other three stories. Two of the stories, for instance, have characters that appear in none of the other three stories. One of the stories mentions an idea (westering) which is not named in any of the other three. Two of the stories concentrate on dead horses. Moreover, certain symbols appear in one story but not another. There are, of course, other distinguishing characteristics which you can discover. By analyzing the individuality of your chosen story, you should come to some conclusion about the way all the stories come together to form a unified work of fiction. (As a somewhat different exercise, you might want to compare *The Red Pony* with other short novels to see how it is unusual if not unique in its structure. Ernest Hemingway's *The Old Man and the Sea*, Philip Roth's *Goodbye, Columbus*, Katherine Anne Porter's *Noon Wine*, and Steinbeck's *The Pearl*, plus many other short novels, offer good possibilities for comparison.)

V. SELECTED BIBLIOGRAPHY

1. Max L. Autrey, "Men, Mice, and Moths: Gradation in Steinbeck's 'The Leader of the People,' " *Western American Litera-*

ture, 10 (November 1975), 195-204. Autrey's thesis is that in this story Steinbeck is mainly concerned with humankind's position in the universe and the impact which this relative positioning has on various levels of society. We can understand Jody relative to his "chain of being" relationship with other life forms. The Indians whom Grandfather mentions, for instance, are as helpless against the cavalry as the mice are against Jody. Jody himself is subservient to the adults. Grandfather has descended to the level with his horse. Autrey believes that Steinbeck seems to have accepted the limiting potential of humankind, rather than the human potential for growth and improvement.

2. Jackson J. Benson, *The True Adventures of John Steinbeck, Writer* (New York: Viking Press, 1984). An essential book for any Steinbeck study, this biography is perhaps the best summary of information relating to the composition of *The Red Pony* and of the details of Steinbeck's life during the writing of the four stories. Perhaps more than any other example of Steinbeck's fiction, these stories come most immediately out of personal experiences and thus offer good examples of how life is transformed into art.

3. Warren French, "*The Red Pony* as Story Cycle and Film," in *The Short Novels of John Steinbeck,* ed. Jackson J. Benson (Durham, North Carolina: Duke University Press, 1990), pp. 71-84. An overview of the chronology of the four stories which make up *The Red Pony* and a comparative analysis of the short novel and the movie. French points out that the film script is the only instance in which Steinbeck was solely responsible for writing a movie version of one of his earlier works. More than half of the movie derives from "The Gift," with the pony's death coming near the end of the movie. Nothing is used from "The Great Mountains," and Jody's relationship with his grandfather is moved to early in the film. Moreover, the mare Nellie (Rose in the film) gives a normal birth, and at the end the family is gathered around, beaming blissfully. Though possessing some merit, the film misses the point of Jody's initiation and is not as forceful as the original short novel.

4. Mimi R. Gladstein, " 'The Leader of the People': A Boy Becomes a 'Mensch,' " in *Steinbeck's "The Red Pony": Essays in Criticism,* eds. Tetsumaro Hayashi and Thomas J. Moore (*Steinbeck Monograph Series,* No. 13) (Muncie: Indiana: Steinbeck Research Institute, Ball State University, 1988), pp. 27-37. Gladstein draws parallels between "The Leader of the

People" and Ernest Hemingway's stylistic techniques and compares Jody to Nick Adams. Unlike most Hemingway protagonists, however, Jody does not develop his sense of manhood through the violence of hunting and war but through "respect and compassion." By the end of *The Red Pony,* as shown especially in his kindness toward Grandfather, Jody has become a "mensch"—a Yiddish term which means "person" but which connotes an individual characterized by dignity, integrity, and compassion.

5. R. S. Hughes, *Beyond "The Red Pony": A Reader's Companion to Steinbeck's Complete Short Stories* (Metuchen, New Jersey: Scarecrow Press, 1987), pp. 90-103. Hughes quickly reviews the circumstances surrounding the composition of the stories and briefly summarizes previous critical opinions of them. His discussion consists of short plot summaries and noting of common interpretations of the stories.

6. Robert S. Hughes, Jr., "The Black Cypress and the Green Tub: Death and Procreation in Steinbeck's 'The Promise,' " in *Steinbeck's "The Red Pony": Essays in Criticism,* eds. Tetsumaro Hayashi and Thomas J. Moore, pp. 9-16. Hughes repeats the circumstances surrounding the composition of the pony stories and their publication history and Steinbeck's personal situation. He states again that *The Red Pony* is a story of Jody's initiation into death. The value of this essay is the fairly close textual analysis Hughes offers of various symbolic themes, such as sexuality, seasonal changes, and death. The black cypress tree and the green tub are opposing symbols of death and procreation.

7. Louis Owens, *John Steinbeck's Re-Vision of America* (Athens: University of Georgia Press, 1985), pp. 46-58. Owens notes that *The Red Pony* does not neatly fit the category of initiation stories to which it is frequently assigned. He then discusses each of the four stories in the order in which they appear in the short novel. He concludes that the pattern of the four stories is to present Jody's various experiences with death, ending with his encountering the abstract values of his grandfather. Grandfather, Owens states, represents a person who avoids commitment and runs away from responsibility—a trap into which Jody must not fall if he is to continue his own growth. Owens concludes that "The pattern of non-commitment illustrated by the westering impulse in American history is in direct contrast to and a contradiction of the values Steinbeck asserts throughout his writing."

8. Roy S. Simmonds, "The Place and Importance of 'The Great Mountains' in *The Red Pony*," in *Steinbeck's "The Red Pony": Essays in Criticism,* eds. Tetsumaro Hayashi and Thomas J. Moore, pp. 17-26. Simmonds discusses the apparent chronological and thematic problems which "The Great Mountains" presents within the overall structure of *The Red Pony* and notes Steinbeck's uncertainty about the place of this story in the short novel. Simmonds argues for the thematic importance of "The Great Mountains" by noting that it presents a significant change in Jody's attitude toward death and a symbolic statement about human affirmation and hope.

9. John Steinbeck, *Steinbeck: A Life in Letters,* eds. Elaine Steinbeck and Robert Wallsten (New York: Viking Press, 1975). An indispensable source of original material for any element of Steinbeck's life, especially for the circumstances surrounding the composition of the pony stories. Steinbeck wrote numerous letters to various people during the composition period, and they reveal much about his thought processes as he created *The Red Pony*.

10. Thomas M. Tammaro, "Erik Erikson Meets John Steinbeck: Psychosocial Development in 'The Gift,' " in *Steinbeck's "The Red Pony": Essays in Criticism,* eds. Tetsumaro Hayashi and Thomas J. Moore, pp. 1-9. Tammaro believes that "The Gift" is perhaps Steinbeck's finest short story and that it traces the various levels of awareness that Jody passes through as he moves toward responsibility and independence. Tammaro parallels Jody's growth with the ideas of psychosocial development presented in Erik Erikson's "Eight Stages of Man" theory. Erikson divides human growth into eight stages and argues that we must successfully meet the crises and requirements of each stage before mental and emotional stability is accomplished. Tammaro notes that the weakness of his thesis is that Erikson's theory was published twenty years after Steinbeck wrote "The Gift."

9. STEINBECK'S *TRAVELS WITH CHARLEY* (1962)

BARBARA HEAVILIN

I. BACKGROUND

The scholar's best background for *Travels with Charley in Search of America* is *Steinbeck: A Life in Letters,* edited by Elaine Steinbeck and Robert Wallsten. Together with the editors' elucidating commentaries, these letters place Steinbeck's journey and the subsequent writing task in perspective. While writing *The Winter of Our Discontent,* "already he was looking ahead to the trip around the United States that would provide material for *Travels with Charley.*"[1] In a May 25, 1960, letter to Mr. and Mrs. Frank Loesser, whom he addressed as "Frank and Fatima," he discusses progress on *The Winter of Our Discontent* and states his already determined purpose for the proposed trip:

> I'm going to learn about my own country. I've lost the flavor and taste and sound of it. It's been years since I have seen it. . . . I just want to look and listen. What I'll get I need badly—a re-knowledge of my own country, of its speeches, its views, its attitudes and its changes. . . . It will be a kind of rebirth.[2]

Steinbeck looks forward to learning, looking, listening on this trip, to gaining "a re-knowledge" and experiencing "a kind of rebirth."

In this letter he also provides the particulars of the proposed journey, to begin "right after Labor Day." He describes the pickup truck and its homey conveniences. He plans out a general itinerary—"out toward the West by the northern way but zigzagging through the Middle West and the mountain states . . . down the coast from Washington and Oregon and then back up through the Southwest and South and up the East Coast but always zigzagging." And he determines that he will "avoid cities, hit small towns and farms and ranches, sit in bars and hamburger stands and on Sunday go to church."[3]

On December 3, 1959, he had experienced what appeared to be a "minor stroke," after which "he was in the hospital nearly two weeks."[4] Although Elizabeth Otis, Steinbeck's agent and friend, had encouraged him to make such a trip, both she and his wife Elaine were concerned about his going alone in his truck for fear of another attack. But in June 1960 Steinbeck writes Otis, telling her why he feels that he must go alone "as a wandering car and eye," the "true" and the "right" way for him at this time:

> I am trying to say clearly that if I don't stoke my fires and soon, they will go out from leaving the damper closed and the air cut off. . . . Between us—what I am proposing is not a little trip of reporting, but a frantic last attempt to save my life and the integrity of my creative pulse.[5]

Otis's response to Steinbeck's appeal, in which she approves his plans, "made a very great difference," Steinbeck writes in his next letter to her, for now Elaine is no longer "dead set" against his going.[6]

Because some find his journey "Quixotic," on June 20, 1960, he writes Pascal Covici that he is calling it "Operation Windmills" and naming his truck "Rocinante" after Don Quixote's horse. In this letter he reiterates his purpose for going:

> There are people who would like to contract for writing about it in advance. But since I don't know what it will be, I think any agreement might have a governing effect and I should want to see and hear what is there, not what I expect to be there. I nearly always write—just as I nearly always breathe. So there will be writing in it but I don't know what. That's one of the reasons I am so excited about it. I will not shape it. It must make its own form.[7]

"To see and to hear what is there," then, is the genuine goal from the outset.

Because of Hurricane Donna, his trip is delayed until September 23, 1960. On October 1 he writes Elaine that he has "no thoughts" but that he has "impressions."[8] For example, he has a sense of foreboding about the accumulation and disposal of waste materials and a kind of depressed curiosity about "mobile homes" and the people who live in them, whom he describes as "Martians":

> I wanted to ask them to take me to their leader. They have no humor, no past, and their future is new models. Their present is exactly that of the White Leghorns that produce the eggs in batteries. Maybe I've finally found it. We live in batteries and any product is no better than the chemicals we take in.[9]

Always the emphasis is on these impressions, on seeing and hearing.

On October 11, 1960, he writes Elaine again: "I know E. O. [Elizabeth Otis] wouldn't approve of the speed with which I am covering ground but I'm sure seeing lots and hearing lots."[10] He describes for her his impressions of truckers as "a set apart bunch of men," the Bad Lands as a place "it would be possible to fall in love with," the grandeur of Montana, a trailer park in which the people are like the trailers because they are "warm" and "comfortable," the purchase of a "narrow-brimmed stockman's hat" which provides him anonymity, and the "little air leaks" behind the refrigerator which he has plugged with "Kleenics."[11] The letters to Elaine stopped at this point because she began joining him "for a few days at a time along the way," and the next recorded correspondence deals with the task of writing.[12]

Discouraged by critics who view *The Winter of Our Discontent* as "less than a work of art," plagued by family "matters impossible of solution," and faced with a publication date, Steinbeck has "great difficulty getting back the rhythm and flow of the Travels piece."[13] He has difficulty in discovering design in what he has seen and heard. His major impression of America gained on this journey is one of decay, a sickness for which he cannot find a name:

No, it was a sickness, a kind of wasting disease. There were wishes but no wants. And underneath it all the building energy like gasses in a corpse. When that explodes, I tremble to think what will be the result. Over and over I thought we lack the pressures that make men strong and the anguish that makes men great. The pressures are debts, the desires are for more material toys and the anguish is boredom. Through time, the nation has become a discontented land.[14]

Comparing his own times with those of Isaiah, the Old Testament prophet, he laments that "We have no prophecy now, nor any prophets."[15]

    Travels with Charley in Search of America is a record of what Steinbeck sees and hears and feels as he travels. He is storing up impressions from which he will draw conclusions in *America and Americans*. The relationship between these two works, therefore, is similar to the relationship between Thoreau's journals and *Walden*. The one, which is basically private discourse, provides a sense of immediacy—the opportunity to look at the world through the writer's eyes—and the other provides a sense of distance and retrospection—the opportunity to meditate on the design he makes of what he has seen.

II. PLOT SYNOPSIS

Travels with Charley in Search of America is divided into four parts: Part One, with fourteen pages, serves as an introduction to the trip; Part Two, with one hundred pages, deals with the beginning of the trip up to his arrival in Chicago, where Elaine is to meet him; Part Three, with one hundred and one pages, covers the trip from Chicago to California and back to the Continental Divide; and Part Four with fifty pages covers from Texas back to his home in New York and also serves as an epilogue.

    Part One is a meditative piece on Steinbeck's own propensity for travel and on the nature of journeys, each of which has its own "personality, temperament, individuality, uniqueness."[16] He then outlines his purpose for this particular trip—"to look again, to try to rediscover this monster-land," and furnishes the particulars of his preparations for it, ranging from the outfitting of his truck and naming it Rocinante to his choice of companion: Charles le Chien, "an old French gentleman poodle known as Charley" (6-9). The remainder of the opening section describes Steinbeck's battle with Hurricane Donna in rescuing his boat, the *Fayre Eleyne*.

Part Two opens with a discussion of one of Steinbeck's "main but secret reasons for going at all"—to reassert his own manhood after a threatening illness. With "a feeling of gray desolation," he leaves his wife Elaine, taking Rocinante on ferries at the onset of the journey in order "to avoid New York traffic" (20-21). On the ferry he discusses submarines with a young sailor. Remembering "burned men pulled from oil-slicked sea" during World War II, Steinbeck despises submarines as instruments of "mass murder, our silly, only way of deterring mass murder," but he determines not to put his own "memories and fears" on this young man who views his own submarine service as "just a job with good pay and a future" (21-23).

Leaving the ferry, on back Connecticut roads he encounters a liquor store owner, "a young-old man with a gray face," who looks longingly at Rocinante—a look Steinbeck "was to see so many times on the journey"—and expresses his desire "to go anywhere," regardless of the destination (25). In contrast, in Massachusetts Steinbeck meets a dairy man with a Ph.D. in mathematics and "some training in philosophy" who "liked what he was doing" and had no desire "to be somewhere else—one of the few contented people" he encounters (27). Settled comfortably at the table in Rocinante with cups of hot coffee spiked with applejack, in New Hampshire he discusses politics and philosophy with a farmer, musing afterwards that human beings have to have time "to develop the means to think, for man has to have feelings and then words before he can come close to thought and, in the past at least, that has taken a long time" (33). Afterwards he feels at last that his journey has actually started.

The farther north he goes, the more "advertising for Florida real estate" he hears on the radio. Declaring that a "good climate" is boring, he asks a New Hampshire woman whether she ever becomes accustomed to autumn: "It is a glory," she said, "and can't be remembered, so that it always comes as a surprise" (35-37). Resting at a New Hampshire picnic place, he takes out Richard Addison's *The Spectator* and writes some two and a half pages in an imitation of Addison's style, discussing his work, his beard, and his attire before he is interrupted by Charley's romantic inclinations for "a rather stout and bedizened Pomeranian of the female persuasion" and the ensuing protests by her owner, "a rather stout and bedizened woman" (41).

In New England he marvels at "the thousands of antique shops along the roads, all bulging with authentic and attested trash from an earlier time" and at the auto court and restaurant where "everything was done in plastics—the floors, the curtain, table tops of stainless burnless plastic, lamp shades of plastic . . . the table linen, the butter dish. . . . Even the waitress wore a sponge-off apron" (43-46). At indescribable and strangely beautiful Deer Isle, Maine, he stays at the home of Elizabeth Otis's charming friend Miss Eleanor Brace and her irascible old gray cat, ironically a female named George. Continuing his journey, he protects himself and Charley as best he can from the "rolling barrage" of hunters in Maine, wrapping "Charley's tail in red Kleenex" which he fastens "with rubber bands" (58). He feels "very fortunate" to meet some Canucks, workers who pick up "potatoes and place them in barrels," and to share a bottle of cognac with them in Rocinante, a time so special that as a result "Rocinante took on a glow it never quite lost" (64-70). On his last day in New England, he attends "a John Knox church" in Vermont, where the minister "spoke of hell as an expert, not the mush-mush hell of these soft days, but a well-stoked, white-hot hell served by technicians of the first order" (77-78).

Crossing into New York State at Rouses Point and staying close to Lake Ontario because he wants to see Niagara Falls, Steinbeck muses on the "individual prose style" of each state, which is "made sharply evident in its highway signs" (79). Although he had planned to go into Canada, he discovers that he cannot because he does not have a "certificate of rabies vaccination" for Charley and goes instead toward Erie, Pennsylvania. As he travels on U.S. 90, bypassing Buffalo and Erie, he observes that "when we get these thruways across the whole country, as we will and must, it will be possible to drive from New York to California without seeing a single thing" (89-90). At Madison, Ohio, he takes "the equally wide fast U.S. 20 past Cleveland and Toledo, and so into Michigan" (89-95).

His impressions of the Middle West as he drives through Ohio, Michigan, and Illinois are that the population has increased enormously and that "an electric energy, a force, almost a fluid of energy so powerful as to be stunning in its impact" pervades the area (105). "Almost on crossing the Ohio line," he finds the people "more open and outgoing" (105). While resting beside a lake and trying to sort out his impressions ("Maybe understanding is possible only after," he decides), he encounters a young man whom he describes as "the guardian of the lake" and as "a lonely man, the more so because he had a wife" (108-13). Declining an opportunity to meet the lovely lady, whose ambitions will spoil her husband's life, Steinbeck heads for Chicago where Elaine is to meet him. Part Two closes with his musings about "Lonesome Harry," who had preceded him in his room at the Ambassador East, leaving behind evidences of an affair of the heart: "Three things haunted me about Lonesome Harry. First, I don't think he had any fun; second, I think he was really lonesome, maybe in a chronic state; and third, he didn't do a single thing that couldn't be predicted—didn't break a glass or mirror, committed no outrages, left no physical evidence of joy" (119).

Part Three purposely leaves out the visit with Elaine in Chicago because "it would only contribute a disunity," centering rather on Steinbeck's leaving Chicago on "a fair autumn day . . . crisp and clean" with a freshly groomed and clipped Charley (125). He marvels at the beauty and richness of Wisconsin, surprised to discover "the greatest distributor of sea shells in the world—and this in Wisconsin, which hasn't known a sea since pre-Cambrian times," and to see "the weird country sculptured by the Ice Age" in the Wisconsin Dells and a "valley floor . . . carpeted with turkeys" (126-27).

Inundated by traffic which struck him "like a tidal wave" on Highway 10, he does not see St. Paul or Minneapolis, ending up "on an Evacuation Route" designed for escape in case of an atomic attack (129).

Going through Sauk Centre, the birthplace of Sinclair Lewis, "pounding on to Detroit Lakes" to spend the night, he muses: "The only good writer was a dead writer. Then he couldn't surprise anyone any more, couldn't hurt anyone any more" (133-34). The next day he discovers that Fargo, North Dakota, "the east-west middle of the country," which he had envisioned as "the coldest place on the continent" on a cold day and the hottest place on a hot day, seems "no different from Minnesota over the river" (135-36). As he and Charley set up housekeeping "on the Maple River, not far from Alice," he jots down "some notes on the nature and quality of being alone," observations based on his present experience after leaving Elaine in Chicago and on his past experience "in the Sierra Nevada mountains on Lake Tahoe" as "a caretaker of a summer estate during the winter months when it was snowed in" (136-37). In a conversation with Charley he assesses what he is learning about America, tentatively questioning and hypothesizing rather than asserting: (1) of food: "Can I then say that the America I saw has put cleanliness first, at the expense of taste?"; (2) of "books, magazines, and papers": "If this people has so atrophied its taste buds as to find tasteless food not only acceptable but desirable, what of the emotional life of the nation?"; (3) of "local radio": "And apart from a few reportings of football games, the mental fare has been as generalized, as packaged, and as undistinguished as the food"; and (4) of politics: "Those whom I had met did not talk about the subject, didn't seem to want to talk about it" (140-42). An actor camps near them, and they become acquainted.

He is amazed when he arrives at the Missouri River at Bismarck, North Dakota:

> Here is the boundary between east and west. On the Bismarck side it is eastern landscape, eastern grass, with the look and smell of eastern America. Across the Missouri on the

Mandan side, it is pure west, with brown grass and water scorings and small outcrops. (154)

He is similarly unprepared for the Bad Lands, which filled him with "foreboding." But their transformation by a spectacular sunset and a lovely night, in which the stars are "close" and starlight makes "a silver glow in the sky," causes him to change his view: "In the night the Bad Lands had become Good Lands. I can't explain it. That's how it was" (154-57).

Steinbeck describes "the next passage" in his journey as "a love affair . . . with Montana" (158). He finds the state "a great splash of grandeur" and its people warm and humane. Next he visits Yellowstone, and discovering that the normally docile Charley has a killer instinct for bears, cuts his tour of the park short and does not spend the night there. Returning to Montana to cross "The Great Divide," he gets out of the car and straddles it, observing that "it had a strange impact" on him that rain on his right side would go into the Pacific Ocean and that rain on his left side "would eventually find its way after uncountable miles to the Atlantic" (166). As they drive across "the upraised thumb of Idaho and through real mountains that climbed straight up," it snows lightly, but the air seems "softer," perhaps because of the "warm airs from over the Japanese current" (167). Getting a cabin for the night, he intervenes in the proprietor's argument with his son, who wants to be a hairdresser. He assures the father that "the hairdresser is the most influential man in any community," and the son thanks him for giving him "a hand up" (175). Charley becomes ill in the middle of the night, and the next day Steinbeck drives to Spokane to a veterinarian, an alcoholic whom they both distrust. They stay for awhile in Seattle, where Charley rests and Steinbeck investigates the city he once knew but which has undergone "frantic growth, a carcinomatous growth" (181). On a Sunday afternoon in Oregon Rocinante blows "a right rear tire," which he repairs in a downpour of rain. His "faith in the essential saintliness of humans" is reinforced by a service station attendant, an "evil-looking man," who finds him a tire to replace the one on the left rear, which "might go at any moment" (184-87).

He introduces Charley to the majesty of the California redwoods before going to his home in northern California where "progress" has altered Salinas, where growth approaches "a saturation point" (196). San Francisco puts on a "show" for him as he crosses the Golden Gate Bridge in the afternoon sunlight and sees it as a "gold and white acropolis rising wave on wave against the blue of the Pacific sky." In Monterey he sends off his absentee ballot and argues politics with his sisters, who "are still Republicans," and visits Johnny Garcia's bar, where he discovers the truth in Thomas Wolfe's title *You Can't Go Home Again* (198-204). On Fremont's Peak he tells Charley some of his childhood memories before hurrying "away from the permanent and changeless past" (206-08).

Leaving California "by the shortest possible route . . . from Salinas to Los Banos, through Fresno and Bakersfield, then over the pass and into the Mohave Desert," he stops in the desert to give Charley some water, contemplates killing two coyotes he sees there, and decides not to shoot them—instead opening two cans of dog food to leave "as a votive" (213-14). Satiated with "seeing" and "hearing," Steinbeck laments that he has passed his "limit for taking it . . . like a man who goes on stuffing in food after he is filled." He makes Charley a birthday cake of hotcake mix with "plenty of syrup and a candle on top," and Charley assures him that he has probably started seeing again, an insight that proves true as Steinbeck finds "a good little new-split stone with a piece of mica in it" and pockets it before they go to bed (221-24).

Part Four covers from Texas back to his home in New York and also serves as an epilogue. In Amarillo, Texas, Charley's illness recurs, and Steinbeck finds a good veterinarian who keeps him for four days' treatment for prostatitis. Elaine joins him for what he calls his "Thanksgiving orgy in Texas" (235-42). In New Orleans he observes "the Cheerleaders" and the crowd gathered to heckle "the littlest Negro girl you ever saw" and "the white man who dared to bring his white child to school" (256-59). Too sickened by the "show" to enjoy one of New Orleans' fine restaurants, he buys a sandwich to eat by the side of the Mississippi River. Monsieur Ci Git, a "neatly dressed man well along in years, with a Greco face and fine wind-lifted white hair and a clipped white mustache" joins him, and they discuss racial problems in the South (260-66). Leaving, Steinbeck offers a ride to "an old Negro who trudged with heavy heels in the grass-grown verge beside the concrete road," who feigns ignorance of racial tensions. The next day he offers a ride to a man in "a light gray suit that was travel-wrinkled and stained" (269). Sickened by the man's prejudice and hatred, Steinbeck pulls Rocinante over to the side of the road and insists that he get out. His final "passenger between Jackson and Montgomery" is "a young Negro student with a sharp face and the look and feel of impatient fierceness" (272). They agree that a change is coming in the South, but Steinbeck is worried about "the dreadful uncertainty of the means" (273).

The final short chapter of *Travels with Charley* serves as an epigraph and comes full circle to discuss once more, as he had discussed in the introduction, the nature of journeys, in particular Steinbeck's "own journey," which started long before he left and ended before he returned (274-75). Near Abingdon, Virginia, the journey ends for both Steinbeck and Charley, their longing for home consuming their attention. Arriving in lower New York during rush hour traffic, Steinbeck typically gets lost, pulling "to the curb in a no-parking area" (276-77). A police officer offers to give him directions, "and that's how the traveler came home again" (277).

III. CRITICAL EXPLICATION

Critics have variously described and cataloged Steinbeck's *Travels with Charley*. In "Travels with Steinbeck: The Laws of Thought and the Laws of Things," Richard Astro describes it literally and accurately as "the published result of the novelist's journey in a camper across the United States with his French poodle Charley."[17] In "Steinbeck's *Travels with Charley:* The Quest That Failed," John Ditsky calls it "the record of a failed venture, a quest 'in search of America.' "[18] In "Lost in America: Steinbeck's *Travels with Charley* and William Least Heat Moon's *Blue Highways,*" Thom Tammaro classifies the work as a travel book which is a "failed success" in "unity,

coherence, pace, emphasis, balance, its architectonics."[19] Echoing Joseph Addison and taking an opposing tactic from those
who describe and classify his works, Steinbeck himself writes:
"In regarding my Work, some Readers profess greater Feeling
for what it makes than for what it says" (39).

Steinbeck is concerned with what his works "make," but
he is vitally concerned also with what they say. Reminiscent of
Ralph Waldo Emerson's "A foolish consistency is the hobgob-
lin of small minds," Steinbeck writes further that since a
suggestion from the master writer Addison "is a Command
not unlike Holy Writ," he intends to "digress and comply at
the same time" (39). In spite of this reference to "Readers"
and concern for what his works say, *Travels with Charley* is
essentially private discourse, and, as such, it is neither a
"failed venture" nor a "failed success." For an analysis of this
work's mode of discourse, that is, of Steinbeck's intended
audience and purpose in writing, including his writing strategies and style, reveals achievement and fulfillment. In *Travels
with Charley* Steinbeck did what he said he was going to do.

MODE OF DISCOURSE

Travels with Charley is essentially private discourse even
though Steinbeck had a contract to write what proved to be a
very salable book. Somewhat in the nature of the French
pensée, in the opening chapter he meditates on "the urge to be
someplace else" which has been with him since youth and
concludes: "I set this matter down not to instruct others but to
inform myself" (3). Having settled the matter of his own
natural inclination to succumb to "the virus of restlessness,"
to explore "the road away from Here" which seems so "broad
and straight and sweet," he provides another personal reason
for his journey and for the book. He has discovered that he
does not know his "own country" any longer, that he is
"working from memory," and determines "to look again," to
try to rediscover this "monster land" so that he can regain his
ability to "tell the small diagnostic truths which are the
foundations of the larger truth" (6, 7). His journey, then, is

not so much a travelogue as it is a quest in search of the essence of this land, of "the small diagnostic truths."

This emphasis on the author's own looking and seeing provides a leitmotif which runs through the book from beginning to end—from the opening determination "to look again," to a reminiscence of a farm in Denmark that looked like the "lovely little farm" in "a looking egg" that he received "long ago at Easter," to his satiety with "hearing" and "seeing," "the stuffed and helpless inability to see more" and fear that he may even have "stopped seeing," and finally to his sharp insights on his own and Charley's longing for home and on New York City (36-37, 221, 274-77). In one of his dialogues/soliloquies with Charley immediately after this statement of fear that he may not be able to see any more, Charley reassures him that maybe he has already started seeing again. Following this reassurance are sharply deline-ated and insightful vignettes depicting Texas, the racial tensions in the South at the time, and his arrival home in New York during rush hour traffic when "every evening is Pam-plona" (276).

The portraits of and imaginary dialogues with Charley, the French poodle, are also private discourse, somewhat in the nature of soliloquies or monologues. These descriptions and dialogues are explorations. Steinbeck explores the nature of things: "Driving the big highway near Toledo I had a conversation with Charley on the subject of roots" (103). He explores the nature of dogs: "Charley is a mind-reading dog," "a gallant dog," an "old fool" who plays with a "plastic bath mat like a puppy" (12, 47). And he explores the nature of human beings: Charley "doesn't belong to a species clever enough to split the atom but not clever enough to live in peace with itself" (269).

Steinbeck's purpose in writing *Travels with Charley,* then, is personal—to inform himself. Another of his "main but secret reasons for going at all," however, is also per-sonal—to reassert his manhood after becoming "seriously ill with one of those . . . difficulties which are the whispers of approaching age" (19). Although Steinbeck's aim is to see clearly and objectively, the viewpoint is essentially subjective with an emphasis on discovery, on Steinbeck's own ability to see clearly, to understand, and to interpret what he sees. "What I found was closely intermeshed with how I felt at the moment," he declares (209). "This monster of a land, this mightiest of nations, this spawn of the future, turns out to be the macrocosm of microcosm me" (209).

WRITING STRATEGIES

Writing essentially for himself, seeking to inform himself and to see clearly, Steinbeck writes informally and with a sense of immediacy in a first person narrative. His major writing strategies are vignettes, brief character sketches, dialogues, anecdotes, rhetorical questions, and meditative *pensées* in which he expounds on a topic. In vignettes he describes "the roadside stands" in the White Mountains of Vermont and New Hampshire which are "piled with golden pumpkins and russet squashes and baskets of red apples so crisp and sweet that they seemed to explode with juice" and a "valley floor" in Wisconsin so "carpeted with turkeys" that the earth "seemed to move and pulse and breathe," rippling "like a black liquid" (127). On occasion these vignettes reveal Steinbeck as a Romantic, a mystic who sees beyond the physical into the metaphysical, into the essence of things. His encounter with Wisconsin is such an occasion:

> I never saw a country that changed so rapidly, and because I had not expected it everything I saw brought a delight. I don't know how it is in other seasons, the summers may reek and rock with heat, the winters may groan with dismal cold, but when I saw it for the first and only time in early October, the air was rich with butter-colored sunlight, not fuzzy but crisp and clear so that every frost-gay tree was set off, the rising hills were not compounded, but alone and separate. There was a penetration of the light into solid substance so that I seemed to see into things, deep in, and I've seen that kind of light elsewhere only in Greece. I remembered now that I had been told Wisconsin is a lovely state, but the telling had not prepared me. It was a magic day. The land dripped with

> richness, the fat cows and pigs gleaming against green, and, in
> the smaller holdings, corn standing in little tents as corn
> should, and pumpkins all about. (126)

Here the physical "butter-colored sunlight" becomes metaphysical insight into universal mysteries, "a penetration of
light into solid substance" so that he seems "to see into things,
deep in" (126).

The brief character sketches are masterful condensa-
tions, capturing an essence tersely, sometimes almost epi-
grammatically. For example, consider his encounter with a
waitress at an auto court near Bangor, Maine:

> She wasn't happy, but then she wasn't unhappy. She wasn't
> anything. But I don't believe anyone is a nothing. There has to
> be something inside, if only to keep the skin from collapsing.
> This vacant eye, listless hand, this damask cheek dusted like a
> doughnut with plastic powder, had to have a memory or a
> dream. (46)

After talking with her, however, he believes that "this dame"
is one of those people "who can drain off energy and joy, can
suck pleasure dry and get no sustenance from it," spreading
about them "a grayness in the air" (46, 47). He concludes with
the epigrammatic statement that "a sad soul can kill you
quicker, far quicker, than a germ" (48). In essence, Steinbeck's waitress is a sad, gray, joyless human being like Al
Capp's Gloomy Gus who takes his cloud of misery with him
wherever he goes.

His sketch of Miss Eleanor Brace's cat George on Deer
Isle in Maine is similarly terse. Similarly also, through
empathy he captures the particularity and essence of the cat:

> I never did rightly see George, but his sulking presence was
> everywhere. For George is an old gray cat who has accumu-
> lated a hatred of people and things so intense that even hidden
> upstairs he communicates his prayer that you will go away. If
> the bomb should fall and wipe out every living thing except
> Miss Brace, George would be happy. That's the way he would
> design a world if it were up to him. (51)

Because of Steinbeck's mystical tendencies and his affinity with the Romantics who see in nature metaphysical truths, even the descriptions of the redwoods become character sketches:

> The feeling they produce is not transferable. From them comes silence and awe. It's not only their unbelievable stature, not the color which seems to shift and vary under your eyes, no, they are not like any trees we know, they are ambassadors from another time. They have the mystery of ferns disappeared a million years ago into the coal of the carboniferous era. They carry their own light and shade. The vainest, most slap-happy and irreverent of men, in the presence of redwoods, goes under a spell of wonder and respect. Respect—that's the word. One feels the need to bow to unquestioned sovereigns. (189)

The book is rich in such sketches: truckers compared to sailors because both have "little contact" with the world through which they travel; the "guardian of the lake" who is "a lonely man, the more so because he had a wife"; Steinbeck's surmises about "Lonesome Harry," the man who precedes him in the hotel room in the Ambassador East in Chicago; and others (93, 112, 114-19).

Steinbeck's reported dialogues with many of those he encounters on the journey serve also as character sketches as well as adding to the sense of immediacy. With a New Hampshire farmer whose name he politely refrains from asking because "there's a gentility on the road" and "a direct or pertinent question is out of bounds" (30), he discusses national issues:

> Khrushchev was at the United Nations, one of the few reasons I would have liked to be in New York. I asked, "Have you listened to the radio today?"
> "Five-o'clock report."
> "What happened at the U.N.? I forgot to listen."
> "You wouldn't believe it," he said. "Mr. K. took off his shoe and pounded the table."
> "What for?"
> "Didn't like what was being said."
> "Seems a strange way to protest."

> "Well, it got attention. That's about all the news talked about."
>
> "They should give him a gavel so he could keep his shoes on."
>
> "That's a good idea. Maybe it could be in the shape of a shoe so he wouldn't be embarrassed." He sipped the applejack with a deep appreciation. "That's pretty nice," he said. (30)

The book is rich with such exchanges and with the descriptions of the speakers. Some of them become universal: "This man, this store," which "might have been anywhere in the nation, but actually it was back in Minnesota" (142). This representative storekeeper he portrays further as having "a kind of gray wistful twinkle in his eyes as though he remembered humor when it was not against the law" (142). The dialogue between them is humorous, highlighting the human tendency to find a scapegoat to blame when things go wrong:

> "Yes, sir," he said with growing enthusiasm, "those Russians got quite a load to carry. Man has a fight with his wife, he belts the Russians."
>
> "Maybe everybody needs Russians. I'll bet even in Russia they need Russians. Maybe they call it Americans."
>
> He cut a sliver of cheese from a wheel and held it out to me on the knife blade. "You've given me something to think about in a sneaking kind of way." (143-44)

While the dialogues provide a sense of immediacy, Steinbeck's personal anecdotes look sometimes at the immediate past of the journey's events and sometimes through reminiscences at his roots, his own personal heritage. Running as a humorous thread throughout the entire book is Steinbeck's dislike of heavy traffic and his tendency to panic and get lost when he encounters it. In an anecdote he tells how such traffic prevented him from seeing "the noble twin cities of St. Paul and Minneapolis" (128-29):

> First the traffic struck me like a tidal wave and carried me along, a bit of shiny flotsam bounded in front by a gasoline truck half a block long. Behind me was an enormous cement

mixer on wheels, its big howitzer revolving as it proceeded. On my right was what I judged to be an atomic cannon. As usual I panicked and got lost. Like a weakening swimmer I edged to the right into a pleasant street only to be stopped by a policeman, who informed me that trucks and such vermin were not permitted there. He thrust me back into the ravening stream. (129)

At ease with himself—including this tendency to panic and get lost in heavy traffic—Steinbeck takes advantage of the opportunity to view himself objectively, humorously, and honestly in these anecdotes. His imagination takes over in this particular anecdote as he finds himself on an "Evacuation Route" designed as "the planned escape route from the bomb that hasn't been dropped":

> Here in . . . the Middle West an escape route, a road designed by fear. In my mind I could see it because I have seen people running away—the roads clogged to a standstill and the stampede over the cliff of our own designing. (129)

To illustrate "how the myth wipes out the fact," Steinbeck tells the story of the man in his hometown who said that he remembered him as "a peaked, shivering child," with his "inadequate overcoat fastened . . . with horse-blanket pins" (81). "This in its small way is the very stuff of myths," he writes, "the poor and suffering child who rises to glory, on a limited scale of course" (81). He then characterizes his mother as a person who is actually "a passionate sewer-on of buttons," who considers "a button off" as "a sin," who "would have whaled" him for pinning his coat (81). On another occasion, having shown Charley the valley in which he grew up and recounting some of the family stories, he concludes:

> I printed it once more on my eyes, south, west, and north, and then we hurried away from the permanent and changeless past where my mother is always shooting a wildcat and my father is always burning his name with his love. (208)

The past and the far past thus mingle in some of these anecdotes as Steinbeck reminisces on his rich family heritage.

Interspersed throughout *Travels with Charley* are *pensées*, brief and thoughtful expositions on a topic. Some of these *pensées* are in the nature of word studies:

> In Spanish there is a word for which I can't find a counterword in English. It is the verb *vacilar*, present participle *vacilando*. It does not mean vacillating at all. If one is *vacilando*, he is going somewhere but doesn't greatly care whether or not he gets there, although he has direction. My friend Jack Wagner has often, in Mexico, assumed this state of being. Let us say we wanted to walk in the streets of Mexico City but not at random. We would choose some article almost certain not to exist there and then diligently try to find it. (63)

Other *pensées* deal with a variety of topics, such as Steinbeck's own propensity for wandering, the nature of a journey, mobile homes, his almost mystical experiences with the redwoods, "the Texas problem." These strategies of writing—vignettes, character sketches, dialogues, anecdotes, and *pensées*—are the devices of a master storyteller. And Steinbeck uses them in *Travels with Charley* in order to store his experiences, informing himself, entertaining himself, observing his own ability to see and to record what he sees.

WRITING STYLE

Steinbeck's writing style in storing his experiences in *Travels with Charley* is for the most part plain as far as the language goes, often informal and colloquial—especially in dialogues—and commonplace as far as the subject matter goes, dealing with everyday concerns. But these characteristics do not obscure the sophistication of his sentence style and the sincerity and acuity of his philosophical observations. Like Thoreau, he blends the commonplace with eternal verities. For discussion purposes the sentences in the following illustrative passage are numbered:

> [1] Even while I protest the assembly-line production of our food, our songs, our language, and eventually our souls, I know that it was a rare home that baked good bread in the old

days (107). . . . [2] It is the nature of man as he grows older, a small bridge in time, to protest against change, particularly change for the better. [3] But it is true that we have exchanged corpulence for starvation, and either one will kill us. [4] The lines of change are down. [5] We, or at least I, can have no conception of human life and human thought in a hundred years or fifty years. [6] Perhaps my greatest wisdom is the knowledge that I do not know. (107-08)

This passage typifies Steinbeck's style and serves to show its variety and sophistication. Sentence one is a periodic sentence, a complex sentence with the main clause last, in which he uses parallelisms: "our food," "our songs," "our language," "our souls." Notice the progression from the concrete and tangible—"food," "songs," and "language"—to the abstract and metaphysical "souls," a typical philosophical move for Steinbeck who is always concerned with the inner human being as well as with the outward world of human beings.

Sentence two is cumulative, adding a qualifying phrase at the end to emphasize the kind of change human beings protest against as they grow older, that is, "particularly change for the better." This sentence also illustrates Steinbeck's typically fresh use of metaphor: the older human being is "a small bridge in time." Sentence three is compound, with two joined main clauses. It begins with the coordinate conjunction "but," which provides cohesion with the previous sentence and offers an opposing view. The last three sentences are all simple, illustrating, however, the variety which Steinbeck achieves within this form. Sentence four is simple and quite short. Sentence five is simple but has a compound subject and ends with a prepositional phrase. And sentence six is simple, but it ends with an adjective clause, "that I do not know," which tells what kind of knowledge of the future fifty or a hundred years ahead which Steinbeck claims to have.

Variety, sophistication, sincerity, and acuity of vision Steinbeck thus offers in plain, seemingly effortless prose. Typical elements of his style also are his skillful use of analogy, epigrammatic statements, catalogs, literary, geographical, and historical allusions, and rhetorical questions.

Steinbeck's use of analogy gives his writing an affinity to poetry. Consider the freshness of these four numbered examples: (1) The New England patrons of a roadside restaurant he describes as being "folded over their coffee cups like ferns"—a stance showing their "taciturnity" which "reaches its glorious perfection at breakfast" (34). (2) Revealing his own confused emotions when he calls home "three times a week" to re-establish his "identity in time and space" are a series of analogies: "For three or four minutes I had a name, and the duties and joys and frustrations a man carries with him like a comet's tail. It was like dodging back and forth from one dimension to another, a silent explosion of breaking through a sound barrier, a curious experience, like a quick dip into a known but alien water" (114). (3) Getting ready to leave California, Steinbeck realizes that his "impressionable gelatin plate was getting muddled," that it is not possible to see everything, and describes his experience thus far in an extended analogy: "This journey had been like a full dinner of many courses, set before a starving man. At first he tries to eat all of everything, but as the meal progresses he finds he must forgo some things to keep his appetite and his taste buds functioning" (210-11). (4) Discussing current racial animosities with a man in New Orleans, he observes that "the subject skims the joy off a pan of conversation" (263). This image which compares conversation to a pan of milk rich with cream shows at the same time the joy of human communication and companionship and the niggardliness of spirit of which human beings are capable—they can skim off "the joy." Note that these analogies are organic, not merely ornamental excrescences. Each serves to portray and to highlight a peculiar characteristic, a confused emotional state, a typically human frailty, the intractableness of problems like prejudice.

Like Thoreau, Steinbeck is a master of the epigrammatic statement, those gems of thought that can stand alone, apart from the body of the work in which they appear. For instance, wondering how a "down-Easter" from New England can long endure the perpetual summer of Florida, Steinbeck muses: "For how can one know color in perpetual green, and what good is warmth without cold to give it sweetness?" (36). Doubts for Steinbeck bring thoughts of critics: "In literary criticism the critic has no choice but to make over the victim of his attention into something the size and shape of himself" (76-77). Commenting on human subjectivity, he writes: "So much there is to see, but our morning eyes describe a different world than do our afternoon eyes, and surely our wearier evening eyes can report only a weary evening world" (77). All of these pithy, epigrammatic statements can stand alone. Their wisdom and accuracy of vision need no interpretation.

Occasionally Steinbeck utilizes the catalog, or listing. He provides one, for example, to satisfy "the passions of the mapifiers": "I can report that I moved north in Maine roughly parallel to U.S. Highway 1 through Houlton, Mars Hill, Presque Isle, Caribou, Van Buren, turned westward, still on U.S. 1, past Madawaska, Upper Frenchville, and Fort Kent, then went due south on State Highway 11 past Eagle Lake, Winterville, Portage, Squa Pan, Masardis, Knowles Corner, Patten, Sherman, Grindstone, and so to Millinocket" (71). The effect of this listing, however, goes beyond satisfying "the passions of the mapifiers." Steinbeck loves words, and these place names roll off the tongue or through the mind like music, a peculiarly American music. For surely such place names do not exist anywhere else in the world—they have an American flavor.

Another example of Steinbeck's use of the catalog occurs in his description of "a touching reunion in Johnny Garcia's bar in Monterey" (199-200). Here, in a dialogue with Johnny, Steinbeck catalogs the dead:

> "Where are the great ones? Tell me, where's Willie Trip?"
> "Dead," Johnny said hollowly.
> "Where is Pilon, Johnny, Pom Pom, Miz Gragg, Stevie Field?"
> "Dead, dead, dead," he echoed.
> "Ed Ricketts, Whitey's Number One and Two, where's Sonny Boy, Ankle Varney, Jesús María Corcoran, Joe Portagee, Shorty Lee, Flora Wood, and that girl who kept spiders in her hat?"
> "Dead—all dead," Johnny moaned. (203)

Like the analogies, these catalogs add a poetic quality to the book, serving also an organic purpose—the catalog of place names providing a sense of movement and the flavor of

America and the catalog of the dead enumerating one name after another like a hammer pounding in Steinbeck's point that "the great ones" are dead.

By giving a greater depth of perception, the literary, geographical, and historical allusions provide another dimension alongside the immediate one of the journey, America, Steinbeck, and Charley. The most obvious literary allusion, of course, is the truck named Rocinante after Don Quixote's horse. All kinds of connotations stem from this association—that the journey is eccentric, like Don Quixote's quest; that it is visionary, a mystical quest; or simply that middle-aged men sometimes do things that appear crazy to those looking on. Setting up housekeeping for the evening beside a stream in New Hampshire, this modern Don Quixote finds in Rocinante "a well-remembered cover" which he brings "out to the sunlight—a golden hand holding at once a serpent and a mirror with wings, and below in scriptlike letters '*The Spectator,* edited by Henry Morley' " (37). Joseph Addison, Steinbeck observes, "plays the instrument of language as Casals plays a cello" (38). And for the next two pages, he playfully molds his own observations into long, coruscating sentences modeled after the style of Addison. For example, consider his explanation for growing a beard:

> I cultivate this beard not for the usual given reasons of skin trouble or pain of shaving, nor for the secret purpose of covering a weak chin, but as pure, unblushing decoration, much as a peacock finds pleasure in his tail. And finally, in our time a beard is the one thing a woman cannot do better than a man, or if she can her success is assured only in a circus. (39-40)

Like this one, the literary allusions to Lewis Carroll, Sinclair Lewis, the "lost generation in Paris," and Thomas Wolfe serve to show Steinbeck himself at ease as a writer among writers.

The occasional reference to geographical names and places other than the American serve to place Steinbeck in a more cosmopolitan, sophisticated perspective: Prague, Pamplona, "the Ufizzi in Florence," "the Louvre in Paris," and "the Prado in Madrid" place him against a larger backdrop than the roadside stands and restaurants of America (77, 108-09). Allusions to Roosevelt, Martin Luther King, Jr., Gandhi, Khrushchev, and the United Nations function similarly, giving the work's general sense of immediacy a depth and perspective it would not otherwise have.

Steinbeck's use of the rhetorical question serves sometimes as a transitional device, questions about what people think of when they drive and about the areas of their regrets, to illustrate, leading to discussions of these topics based on observations of his own experiences. On other occasions the rhetorical question serves to remind him of the purpose of this journey: "Am I learning anything?" (139). At other times it serves as a means of questioning what he has learned: "Can I then say that the America I saw has put cleanliness first, at the expense of taste?" (141). And he seeks for answers to hard questions: "If this people has so atrophied its taste buds as to find tasteless food not only acceptable but desirable, what of the emotional life of the nation?" (142). Note once more that the emphasis is on what he himself is learning, on his own ability to see clearly, not on instructing anyone else. The rhetorical questions, therefore, lend the work a tentative, searching tone. He does not claim to have final answers or solutions for himself or for anyone else.

ORGANIZATION

The organization of *Travels with Charley* is primarily based on the central persona Steinbeck and his companion Charley who get ready for a journey, go on a journey, and return home. In this sense the movement is essentially circular, unified by the journey motif and the main characters. But this is not just a physical journey. It is a psychic, metaphysical journey in which an artist seeks to inform himself and to see clearly. As such, it is essentially private discourse, a private search. Readers could justifiably, therefore, approach it in the same way they read Thoreau's journals—for the joy of what they say rather than what they make. There is, however, more artistic balance here than that. As a record of an artist's regaining the ability to see and understand, a motif running throughout the work, it has organic unity.

Tammaro is troubled because Steinbeck returns home "a lost man."[20] Astro finds ironic his returning home with a "profound feeling of loss."[21] Literally, Steinbeck is lost but only in the sense that caught in the press of traffic in New York City, he does not know where he is. (Steinbeck's propensity for getting lost in heavy traffic recurs throughout the book. Evidently, like some of the rest of us, Steinbeck did not have a very good sense of direction and despised traffic. These instances are recorded here as elsewhere—as humorous self-revelations.) The tone of the ending, however, does not lend credence to the interpretation that he is lost in a psychic sense, a lost self. Rather, he is elated both at being home (paradoxically, even though he is for the moment lost) and at having regained the ability "to see."

Like an Odysseus, thoughts of home have consumed Steinbeck during the latter part of his journey, and the closer he gets, the more centered his goal becomes, a longing which Charley evidently shares because he "carried out his functions like a sleepwalker, ignored whole rows of garbage cans" (276). In the last two pages, Steinbeck uses the word "home" six times, the phrases "my own town" and "where I live" one time each. This home, however, is in lower New York, where "every evening is Pamplona" because of the crush of commuter traffic and where even a policeman can get lost on occasion. "Boxed in the middle of a crossing by a swirling rapids of turning people," he pulls "to the curb in a no-parking area" (277). In a paroxysm of laughter over the irony of getting lost in his "own town," Steinbeck explains his situation to a policeman who grins "happily," telling his own story of getting "lost in Brooklyn only Saturday" (277). Paradoxically, even a native can get lost in New York, and getting lost in New York for Steinbeck is a part of the flavor of this place, a part of returning home. The warm humor of this ending belies any notion that he is "a lost man." He is at home, and he has found himself.

Tammaro's essay on *Travels with Charley* ends on a thought-provocative note: "I think of prophets and prophecy."[22] Steinbeck's determination to inform himself and to see clearly on occasion goes beyond the immediate and places him among seers, bards, prophets—a tendency more evident in *America and Americans* than in this predecessor of that work. On the tendency of "the new Americans" to find challenge and love in "traffic-choked streets," he comments, "And I am sure that, as all pendulums reverse their swing, so eventually will the swollen cities rupture like dehiscent wombs and disperse their children back to the countryside" (72). Of the growth of Salinas from four thousand, to eighty thousand, to "perhaps two hundred thousand in ten" years, he worries, "Even those people who joy in numbers and are impressed with bigness are beginning to worry, gradually becoming aware that there must be a saturation point and the progress may be a progression toward strangulation" (196). Facing the twentieth century fear which we all share but which very few of us voice—that human beings now have the power to "eliminate" not only ourselves but "all other life" as well—Steinbeck muses:

> Even our own misguided species might re-emerge from the desert. The lone man and his sun-toughened wife who cling to the shade in an unfruitful and uncoveted place might, with their brothers in arms—the coyote, the jackrabbit, the horned toad, the rattlesnake, together with a host of armored insects—these trained and tested fragments of life might well be the last hope of life against non-life. The desert has mothered magic before this. (218)

Thus looking into the bleakest future any of us can imagine, Steinbeck typically sees light and hope and magic. The Romantic, the mystic, the seer, the prophet—Steinbeck is not lost. He sees clearly, and at the end of his journey, he has a lot to think about and to mull over, the results of which will appear in *America and Americans,* in which he has had time to meditate on these experiences and to tell "the small diagnostic truths."

NOTES

1. John Steinbeck, *Steinbeck: A Life in Letters,* eds. Elaine Steinbeck and Robert Wallsten (New York: Viking Press, 1975), p. 665. To be identified as *SLL* hereafter.

2. *Ibid.*, pp. 666-67.
3. *Ibid.*
4. Jackson J. Benson, *The True Adventures of John Steinbeck, Writer* (New York: Viking Press, 1984), p. 865.
5. *SLL*, p. 669.
6. *Ibid.*, p. 670.
7. *Ibid.*, p. 672.
8. *Ibid.*, p. 683.
9. *Ibid.*, pp. 683-84.
10. *Ibid.*, p. 687.
11. *Ibid.*, pp. 687-89.
12. *Ibid.*, p. 690.
13. *Ibid.*, p. 699.
14. *Ibid.*, pp. 702-03.
15. *Ibid.*, p. 703.
16. John Steinbeck, *Travels with Charley in Search of America* (New York: Penguin Books, 1962), p. 4—hereafter cited parenthetically in the body of the text.
17. Richard Astro, "Travels with Steinbeck: The Laws of Thought and the Laws of Things," in *Steinbeck's Travel Literature*, ed. Tetsumaro Hayashi (*Steinbeck Monograph Series*, No. 10) (Muncie, Indiana: Steinbeck Society of America, Ball State University, 1980), p. 8.
18. John Ditsky, "Steinbeck's *Travels with Charley:* The Quest That Failed," in *Steinbeck's Travel Literature*, ed. Hayashi, pp. 56-61.
19. Thom Tammaro, "Lost in America: Steinbeck's *Travels with Charley* and William Least Heat Moon's *Blue Highways*," in *Rediscovering Steinbeck: Revisionist Views of His Art, Politics, and Intellect*, edited by Cliff Lewis and Carroll Britch (*Studies in American Literature*, Vol. 3) (Lewiston, New York: Edwin Mellen Press, 1989), pp. 268-69.
20. Tammaro, p. 273.
21. Astro, p. 10.
22. Tammaro, p. 275.

IV. TOPICS FOR RESEARCH AND DISCUSSION

(1) After examining Odell Shepard's *The Heart of Thoreau's Journals,* discuss similar concerns that Steinbeck and Thoreau share. Both, for example, write about inequality and discrimination. Steinbeck is concerned with racial tensions during the 1960s, and Thoreau helps a fugitive slave named Henry Williams on his escape to Canada.

(2)   Compare and contrast Steinbeck's journey with Charley and
       Thoreau's trip with his brother John which he writes about in
       A Week on the Concord and Merrimack Rivers.
(3)   Using library sources, such as a good handbook to literature
       and *Preminger's Encyclopedia of Poetry and Poetics,* study the
       attributes of Romanticism. To what extent is Steinbeck a
       Romantic? Consider, for example, his "faith in the essential
       saintliness of humans," his determination to take back roads
       and avoid cities, and his concern for nature and the environ-
       ment.
(4)   *Travels with Charley in Search of America* and *America and
       Americans* are both highly autobiographical, revealing much
       about Steinbeck as a person. Using these works and Elaine
       Steinbeck and Robert Wallsten's edition of *Steinbeck: A Life in
       Letters,* Jackson J. Benson's *The True Adventures of John
       Steinbeck, Writer,* and Robert DeMott's *Steinbeck's Reading,*
       discuss the ethos, or character and personality, of Steinbeck
       himself as it is revealed in *Travels.*
(5)   Compare and contrast *Travels with Charley* with *America and
       Americans.* In what sense does *America and Americans* fulfill
       his desire to tell "the small, diagnostic truths" that he discovers
       on the journey, truths that he only discovers in retrospective
       meditation?

V. SELECTED BIBLIOGRAPHY

1.   Jackson J. Benson, *The True Adventures of John Steinbeck, Writer*
      (New York: Viking Press, 1984). As the definitive biography
      of Steinbeck, Benson's work gives a backdrop for the writing of
      Travels and serves to place it in perspective, providing a full
      discussion of events before, during, and after its writing and
      publication.
2.   John Ditsky, *"Steinbeck's Travels with Charley,"* in *Steinbeck's
      Travel Literature,* ed. Tetsumaro Hayashi (*Steinbeck Monograph
      Series,* No. 10) (Muncie, Indiana: Steinbeck Society of America,
      Ball State University, 1980), pp. 56-61.
3.   Tetsumaro Hayashi, "Steinbeck's America in *Travels with
      Charley,*" *Steinbeck Quarterly,* 23 (Summer-Fall), 88-96.
4.   Cliff Lewis and Carroll Britch, eds., *Rediscovering Steinbeck:
      Revisionist Views of His Art, Politics, and Intellect* (*Studies in
      American Literature,* Vol. 3) (Lewiston, New York: Edwin
      Mellen Press, 1989). Thom Tammaro's essay "Lost in America:

Steinbeck's *Travels with Charley* and William Least Heat Moon's *Blue Highways*," provide a thoughtful and insightful comparison and contrast between the two writers' records of their journeys.

5. Roy S. Simmonds, *"Travels with Charley,"* in *A Study Guide to Steinbeck (Part II),* ed. Tetsumaro Hayashi (Metuchen, New Jersey: Scarecrow Press, 1979), pp. 165-90. This chapter in an earlier study guide provides an excellent background, synopsis, and critical explication.

6. John Steinbeck, *Steinbeck: A Life in Letters,* eds. Elaine Steinbeck and Robert Wallsten (New York: Viking Press, 1975). Steinbeck's own letters, together with the editors' commentary, provide the best source for the book's background and writing. Some of these letters stand alongside events recorded in *Travels,* furnishing further—and sometimes fuller—insights.

10. STEINBECK'S *THE WINTER OF OUR DISCONTENT* (1961)

MICHAEL J. MEYER

I. BACKGROUND

Steinbeck's *The Winter of Our Discontent* grew out of two aborted attempts at transforming and modernizing older texts. Begun in 1958, the first work, *Don Keehan,* was a modern Western and was evidently a takeoff on Cervantes' *Don Quixote;* it was also interrelated with a second work, an adaptation of Malory's *Morte D'Arthur,* since both legends and quests were direct descendants of each other and were, Steinbeck felt, in some way intermingled with the American Dream. In each, Steinbeck was experimenting with present-day idiomatic American speech as a literary language.

The work on *Arthur* which he had set up for himself required an iron discipline; it was to be several volumes, a translation complete with introduction and running commentary. Steinbeck's biographer Jackson J. Benson relates that "he dared not think about finishing it or else the despair would be too great even to start."[1] The loneliness of such a large task created a great deal of stress and eventually caused Steinbeck to return to a "less well defined position," hoping that the diversion would ultimately remove the roadblocks that made the *Arthur* text seem unattainable.

Letters also stress Steinbeck's insight into the interrelatedness of the works and their eventual transformation into *Winter.* He notes in an August 26, 1958 letter to Joseph Fontenrose that the questor myth always seems present, citing years of reoccurrence and that "the sleeping anlage

seems to be brought to life by need arising from circumstances, usually external ones." Thus the heroes, no matter
what the time period, are the same figures, giving aid "when
the skeins of existence get bollixed up."[2]

For a while Steinbeck bounced back and forth between
the two texts, but the work on *Don Keehan* was frustrating
since Steinbeck realized it was helping him put off the
translation of Malory. By December of 1958, he had rejected
the former as a hack book and avowed that the latter would be
his final work. The year 1959 found him on site in England,
trying to recreate "the intimate feeling of today's man who in
his daily thought may change tomorrow, but who in his
deeper perception, I am convinced, does not change at all"
(5/13/59).[3]

But inspiration for the author was somehow missing
despite his visiting of the sites. It was as though Steinbeck,
like Joseph Wayne in *To a God Unknown,* was searching for
some belief, ritual, or mystic procedure which would solve his
dilemma: the belief that a writer must aim at perfection even
while realizing that it doesn't exist (8/27/59).[4]

Benson states that in a sense the difficult *Arthur* was a
type of first draft for *Winter,* an association Steinbeck makes
himself in a letter to Elizabeth Otis on September 18, 1959,
even prefiguring the title of this last novel.[5] Steinbeck
eventually had decided to use the translation of *Arthur* to say
what he wanted to say about his own time: condemning its
immorality and decrying the decay of such values as loyalty,
courtesy, courage, and honor. This decision to emphasize
current relevance may have been prompted after Steinbeck
suffered what may have been a small stroke shortly after
Thanksgiving 1959 and was hospitalized for a week to ten
days. In a later letter Steinbeck reveals his own preoccupation
with morals and the fact that Arthur must fight an enemy
without as well as an enemy within. He identifies the inner
demon as "the failure of men toward men, the selfishness that
puts making a buck more important than the commonwealth"
(9/28/59).[6]

In addition to these related works, critic Warren French
has also drawn attention to another source, the Steinbeck
short story "How Mr. Hogan Robbed a Bank," which was

first published in the *Atlantic Monthly,* March 1956. In fact, some of the story's details have direct parallels in *Winter.* Hogan is a grocery clerk like Ethan, and he schemes to rob the bank next to his grocery on the Saturday night before Labor Day. Unlike Ethan, however, he goes through with the robbery, obtaining $8,320.

Other repetitions from the story that are evident in *Winter* are the use of the Knight's Templar uniform which again serves as a symbol of purity and good deeds, and a repetition of William Randolph Hearst's "I Love America" essay contest. Nevertheless, in the Hogan story neither repetition is exact. In *Winter,* the Knight's Templar uniform appears several times with several meanings while in "Hogan" its only function is as a uniform case that serves as a hiding place for the stolen money. Similarly, the "I Love America" contest is also modified. In *Winter* it serves as more evidence of the corruption of America, while in "Hogan" no mention is made of plagiarism, and the corruption is seen in Hogan who uses $10 from the proceeds of the robbery to reward his son and daughter for participating in the contest. The son receives $5 for winning an honorable mention and the daughter a similar amount for being a good sport about not winning. According to French, the purpose of "Hogan" seems to be an attempt to show that an alert consciousness unbothered by scruples can easily exploit those whose thought patterns have become stereotyped.

Although Ethan possesses this trait in *Winter,* it is questionable whether the novel is all that related to "Hogan." French seems to feel that the short story is more successful, since its satire does not disintegrate into sentimentality and the conclusion is naturalistic rather than soggy. Nevertheless, other parallel stories/novels which exist in the Steinbeck canon have been significantly changed during revision. For example, Steinbeck's short stories "Breakfast" and "The Raid," which have been suggested as sources for later novels, were significantly altered when placed in the context of a larger work. Similarly, the Hogan story is transformed into a different tale as it is utilized in *Winter.* The expansion not only adds depth, but its complexity indicates that Steinbeck's thoughts had matured rather than disintegrated.[7]

Yet another factor in the composition of *Winter* was the fact that Steinbeck had discovered that the new generation, including his own sons, was being raised by example to believe that success was more important than honesty and that greed and lack of principles had become an accepted norm. It seems evident that Steinbeck's concern for his two boys took up a great deal of his energy during this time. He tried to redirect their lives and to remove the influence of their mother, Gwyn, from the shaping of their moral characters. Consequently, he took in both Thom and Catbird, traveled with them, and tried to expose them to some of the greatest works and thoughts of Western man. He hoped they would somehow see the lessons of history as well as discover their own potential. This interest in history, both past and present, may account for the incorporation of real historic events into the text.

Specifically, the television quiz show scandals and the election of 1960 influenced the production of *Winter*. Steinbeck felt the scandal over *The $64,000 Question,* especially scholar Charles van Doren's involvement in the fraud, asserted America's superficiality and greed. What was worse, however, was that the public reaction seemed to indicate that the cheating wasn't so bad, since no one was hurt and everyone did it. The crime was being found out. In the political arena, it also seemed as though right and wrong were of little concern and that the ends justified the means. "Whatever works must be good" was the politicians' motto. By March of 1960, Steinbeck had begun work in earnest on the new novel, rejoicing that it was the first to grow out of his immediate experience, his present-day situation. His usual warmups—letters, journals, etc.—were eliminated as Steinbeck worked full tilt at a book that "had a life of its own and vitality and newness" (3/30/60).[8]

Most research indicates the novel was probably begun around March 1 of 1960 and finished in July of the same year. It is the only novel in the Steinbeck canon in which the time scheme of the text parallels the author's actual work schedule. Steinbeck struggled to make the idea immediate in every respect, incorporating his own eccentric ways of thought and speech into the text. He also set free tender, somewhat melodramatic emotions which most critics felt should either have been understated, severely controlled, or suppressed entirely. Steinbeck obviously disagreed. In a letter to Elia Kazan, Steinbeck notes that values have been crossed up and that "courtesy is confused with weakness and emotion with sentimentality. Cleverness has taken the place of feeling and cleverness is nearly always an aversion."[9]

In assessing the work as a whole, it is evident that Steinbeck saw the conflict around which the novel centers (Ethan Hawley's betrayal of himself and his brother, Danny Taylor) in larger terms. He related the event not only to the flow of history and the tradition of literature, but he found that significant connections also were evident in his reading and his journalistic endeavors. Thus the *Bible,* Shakespeare's sonnets and plays, especially *Richard III,* Malory's *Morte D'Arthur,* Eliot's "The Waste Land," documents from American history, and the short stories of Kafka are all alluded to in important ways by the text.

Steinbeck's letter of November 5, 1959 to Adlai E. Stevenson seems to relate his own dismay at America's continuing course toward decay. "A strange species we are," he says. "We can stand anything that God and Nature can throw at us save only plenty. If I wanted to destroy a nation, I would give it too much, and I would have it on its knees, miserable, greedy, and sick."[10]

The Republican candidate for president, Richard Nixon, became for Steinbeck a symbol for such degradation in the political scene. His given name of Richard fit well into America's Revolutionary past (Ben Franklin's *Poor Richard's Almanack*) and also provided an association with the villainous Richard III who betrayed both his brothers for a kingdom and for an increase in his estate. The biblical characters of Judas were also natural associations with tricky Dick, suggesting still another betrayal of a friend/brother to his ultimate death.

As Steinbeck told a reporter in England, the theme of *Winter* was about immorality, about taking out more than one is willing to put in. The novel condemns the American nation as soft, comfortable, and content. Steinbeck views the people as no longer versatile except at craftiness and deception, and their weaknesses keep him fearful about the eventual extinction of the human race.

The following July (1961) marked Steinbeck's reception of reviews on his experimental novel. Largely negative comments concentrated on its dissimilarity to *The Grapes of Wrath* and offered little or no appreciation of the risks Steinbeck had taken or the enormous changes and technical innovations he had attempted in the text. Few critics recognized its greatness or its success at putting its finger on the present malaise of the American soul. Instead, it was perceived as a potboiler written for monetary gain and to please a public insatiable for more Steinbeck, no matter how weak the quality.

Steinbeck defended the work by claiming that, although it was not a novel like any he had seen or read or heard of, it did have direction and rhythm as well as intent. A novel, Steinbeck stated, "at worst should amuse, at half-staff move to emotion and at best illuminate."[11] His intention was, of course, the third. Now, thirty years later, recent Steinbeck criticism seems to assert that *The Winter of Our Discontent*'s complexity of structure went unappreciated by early readers who failed to see it as a successful portrait and call to action against an ever-increasing American decadence which had invaded the very soul of the times.

II. PLOT SYNOPSIS

The Winter of Our Discontent begins as the protagonist, Ethan Allen Hawley, and his wife Mary awaken on Good Friday morning in New Baytown, Long Island, New York. Their ensuing discussion reveals Ethan's past heritage (his Puritan ancestors and his lost wealth) and his present state (a grocery clerk in a store he used to own). Though despairing, he nevertheless jokes playfully with his wife, making mock-serious comments about their situation. Through mismanagement Ethan has lost the family business to a Sicilian immigrant, Alfio Marullo, and he feels intense pressure from within and from without (his friends and family) to regain his ancestors' lost fortune and standing.

After discussing plans for Easter with his wife, Ethan sets off for his job, engaging in joking conversation with both the banker's dog and sparrows before he encounters his friend, Joey Morphy, a bank teller, also on his way to work. The conversation again turns to Ethan's heritage and whether it is Puritan or pirate. While discussing the latter, the subject of a bank robbery surfaces, and, as Ethan listens, Joey relates four basic rules to be a successful thief.

The story intrigues Ethan, but at the moment he is too ethical to pursue its possibilities. However, when he arrives at work, he recognizes the store as a new American Cathedral. In a sermon to the canned goods, he repeats the Gospel message of Good Friday and contemplates the agony and death of Christ on the cross. Ethan then opens the store, and he encounters the town's bank president, Mr. Baker. Baker encourages Ethan to invest his wife's inheritance in "new opportunities" which may help Ethan regain social prestige and prominence. Baker also advocates using different business ethics for changing times and reminds Ethan of a previous business association between their families when their forefathers owned the whaling vessel, the *Belle-Adair*. In this past endeavor, questionable ethics were used in order to save the family fortunes, and now there is no exception. Later the town whore and descendant of witches, Margie Young-Hunt, enters the store and offers Ethan a second, bodily temptation. When Ethan resists by quoting scripture, Margie predicts a successful but demanding future, a Midas touch. After Margie's departure, Ethan's boss, Marullo, arrives and also lectures him on ways to make more money through deceptive practices and encourages him to look after himself. Again Ethan is outraged by unethical behavior and rejects the idea that "business is money and money is not nice."[12] A final temptation comes from a wholesaler, Mr. Biggers of B.B.D. & D., who offers Ethan a 5% bribe to steer business toward him. He gives Ethan a billfold and asks him to think about a deal, and, as he leaves, reminds Hawley that such collusion is practiced by "everybody in modern society. Everybody" (30).

When Morphy arrives for his noon sandwich, he suggests Ethan might be wise to take the offer—in the interest of his wife and children, of course. Ethan again repeats the words of

Christ, *"lama sabachthani,"* suggesting his own forsaken character, and he waits despairingly to close the store and return home.

When he arrives, his children, Allen (Ethan, Jr.) and Ellen, tell him of their plans to enter the National "I Love America Contest" and beg for help. Ethan suggests the great books, now out of use and stored in the attic. A short time later his wife, Mary, relates her excitement at the tarot card reading given by Margie Young-Hunt. She reveals Margie's conclusion from the cards that Ethan will be rich, perhaps even the biggest man in town. Ethan again questions the value of money, but Mary sees his reluctance to conform as evidence of his holier-than-thou attitude and upbraids him for wallowing in his losses and retaining an old-fashioned attitude.

Later that evening Ethan spends time reflecting on the temptations in his secret place in the old harbor, a $4 \times 4 \times 5$ cavelike retreat. Here he can contemplate his present and sort out his past, his ancestral history, his father's losses, and his commitment to Mary. Ethan also recalls his long-time brotherly relationship to Danny Taylor and Danny's present persistent alcoholic state. As Ethan attempts to sort out his reaction to fortune and business, he draws a parallel to Danny, who owns a significant amount of property but who is unwilling to sell it for a monetary profit. Nevertheless, when Ethan returns home, he has decided to ignore Danny's example and to pursue the destiny of fortune, regardless of the ethical cost.

The following morning Ethan reflects on Christ's death and his own Puritan heritage, but he remains determined to pursue wealth even if it involves robbing the bank. Although he expresses concern for Danny to the town constable, Stoney Smith, Ethan appears callous in his determination to gain fortune and success at the expense of others. In another soliloquy to the canned goods and produce in the store, Ethan now asserts the accuracy of Biggers's statement that corruption is everywhere. It was true in the Hawley past, and it was true for the early settlers and the following immigrants as well. Ethan considers whether indeed he is a naive kid as far as money goes. When Margie returns, Ethan now finds her appealing and recognizes the deep-down underwater change that is going on within him. Several characters also tell him that he is acting differently and that he is a new man. When Marullo arrives, Ethan craftily suggests a return to his native Sicily and tries to confirm his suspicions that Marullo is an illegal alien. Then he confronts Biggers with a counteroffer, hoping the salesman will up the ante and increase the proffered bribe. His initiation into evil has begun.

After Ethan returns home, the evening is punctuated by a conversation with his son about the family's past glories and by his own remembrance of the great literature stored in the attic. As they search for material for Allen's essay, Ethan somewhat sadly recognizes that the corruption of wealth without effort has infected his own offspring as well as himself. Later Margie Young-Hunt comes over for dinner, and Ethan must once more face the dangers of his new-found unethical stance. Again the tarot cards are read, and once more Ethan's good fortune is stressed. Though the last card is the hanged man, Margie stresses it could mean salvation rather than destruction; she also recalls her vision of a snake changing its skin as another resurrection image for Ethan. Despite his own negative premonitions, Ethan appears strangely unmoved and adamant about his new choice. However, after the reading, Mary expresses her fear of the impending prophecy.

Ethan later proclaims that his future is predestined by a Congress of the Dark and that he is fated to succumb to evil. He then proceeds to find examples of other New Baytown citizens who have compromised their values. In his night thoughts he reflects on Danny Taylor, his old friend, and he wonders what price he will have to pay for his setting aside of morality. Will he, too, like the Bakers, betray a best friend and profit from it?

Easter Sunday brings a visit from Marullo, who has heard of Biggers's offer and is pleased that Ethan has refused the bribe. For a brief moment Ethan's tarnished soul does not seem so bleak as he attends church and is inspired by the resurrection message. Back home, however, the corruption returns as he dreams of Danny Taylor who appears to melt despite Ethan's attempts to save him.

Later in the afternoon at the Bakers', Ethan learns Baker's role in his father's financial demise and is surprised by the banker's new-found interest in rehabilitating the Hawley fortune. Baker's plan is to buy up property and facilities in the town. After the acquisition, the banker and his associates would turn out the present town council and manager and run New Baytown as they wish. Ethan's participation will be to acquire Taylor's Meadow from his friend Danny as a potential site for a new airport, essential for growth and financial stability. A potential betrayal is suggested as Mary and Ethan argue on the way home over their personal need for money. Later, however, the betrayal becomes certain as Ethan decides he has the killer instinct and goes to visit Danny, offering to pay for a cure for his alcoholism. They speak of Baker, and Danny reveals the banker has been his source for liquor, hoping to get him to sell his property while he's drunk. Ethan sympathetically reveals Baker's plan for an airport and warns Danny that he could be institutionalized as an incompetent alcoholic and that his property could be confiscated.

Though Ethan appears to have Danny's welfare at heart, he knows that when his friend is offered a $1,000 loan, he will misuse the cash for alcohol and that perhaps Ethan himself can get the deed to Taylor's Meadow as collateral for the loan. Trying to sleep after his deceptive acts, Ethan recognizes how his conscience has died. At that point, however, he finds his daughter, Ellen, sleepwalking and clasping the family talisman—a mound of translucent stone. The stone leaves Ellen with an ethereal glow and momentarily renews Ethan's spiritual nature.

Monday morning Ethan meets with Morphy, who helps confirm Ethan's suspicions about Marullo's citizenship problems. Morphy also reveals more details about the bank, and the potential for a real bank robbery grows in Ethan's mind. He does a practice run to prepare for the theft but is interrupted by Constable Smith who reveals that Danny has had two official papers witnessed in his presence.

Marullo's reappearance at the store leads Ethan to further question his boss about his past. From the resulting conversation, Ethan discovers that Marullo trusts him implicitly and wants him to buy back into the business. Since all events seem to favor further deception, Ethan proceeds with his plan. To the dismay of Baker, he withdraws $1,000 from

Mary's account and leaves it at Danny's lean-to. When he comes home, still other ethical decisions await. His children bring up the essay contest, and Ellen questions her father about what constitutes plagiarism. Dinner with Margie closes the evening, but not before Ethan regrets his betrayal of Danny; he knows the money will cause Danny's death, but he rationalizes that this sacrifice is necessary in order for Ethan to regain his position as King of the Mountain. Hearing the jets pass overhead in the morning, Ethan remembers the price he has paid for the airport—Danny's life. Ironically, he also finds a copy of Danny's will at his doorstep along with a promissory note pledging his property if he does not repay the $1,000 loan.

Part II of the novel begins with a shift in time to the end of June and the approaching national holiday, the Fourth of July, and an examination of New Baytown political ethics and the decaying morality of the town fathers. When Ethan and Joey discuss Marullo and how Ethan may be able to grab back the business, Ethan decides another betrayal is in order. Shortly afterward, he calls the FBI and the Immigration and Naturalization Service to report his suspicion about his boss. A discussion with Allen follows about the importance of money and the value of dishonesty in attaining it. Next Steinbeck examines Margie Young-Hunt's route to money: marriage and relationships with New Baytown men.

Ethan, corrupted by his decisions to betray his brother and his boss, is now somewhat attracted to her, but still he resists the temptation. Margie, surprised by Ethan's fortitude, then proclaims her fear of his new selfish and egocentric image. Mr. Baker's arrival at the store brings the revelation that Danny Taylor is missing and that the state is investigating New Baytown's corrupt politicians. All of Ethan's plans seem to be working. To strengthen his resolve, Ethan remembers his years in the armed services and an officer/role model who taught him that love inhibited the killing instinct. Ethan must stop "feeling" if he is to continue to exploit people. Ethan then makes plans with Mr. Baker to take over the grocery store if Marullo is deported.

By July 1st the disintegration of Ethan's ethical and moral nature seems almost complete, yet fortunately he still holds on to his talisman, an indication of potential redemption. When Constable Smith reveals a grand jury indictment of the town fathers, Ethan decides his fortune will soon be made. He now rejects the overt crime of bank robbery, knowing that the easy way of manipulation and betrayal holds fewer risks. Marullo's arrest is subsequently announced by a Department of Justice official, and Ethan is surprised that his old boss gives him the store because he admires his honesty and straightforwardness. Ironically, the government official says that such honesty and morality are worth preserving—like a light in the darkness. Ethan, of course, realizes his light is not only flickering but, in fact, is in danger of going out. Not surprisingly, his good luck talisman remains with him again as an indicator of hope.

While Ethan and Mary escape to Montauk for a holiday weekend, Allen is announced as one of the winners of the "I Love America Contest." His fortune too has changed; he has become a celebrity. Later that evening Ethan retreats to his secret place to contemplate the events which have occurred. In a dream he enters the past and sees his own grandfather's dishonesty. Then he dreams of the future and recalls his betrayal of Danny. When he wakes at dawn, he goes to the store where Mr. Baker confirms the indictment of the town fathers, and Ethan finalizes the bribe with Mr. Biggers. Danny's suicide is confirmed by Constable Smith, and Ethan now has all he has worked for: social prestige, money, and power. Of course, he uses his new-found position to pressure Mr. Baker into a partnership which he will control. He also refuses the opportunity to be town manager, saying it would be a conflict of interest. Baker, stunned at Ethan's competence in deception and craftiness, concedes to his demand.

Thus Ethan's return on the eve of the Fourth of July seems totally successful, but ultimately his good feelings are tempered by his disapproval of Allen, who is always looking for the easy way to success and who revels in his new reputation. Depressed by his son's weakness, Ethan heads for the cave to contemplate his changed existence. On his way to the Old Harbor, he meets Margie in the darkness and is tempted sexually once more. Distressed that she knows him so well, Ethan tries to revive his moral sense, but instead, Margie offers to be Ethan's confidante and to help him to continue with his deception and trickery. Ethan returns home only to find out Allen has been guilty of plagiarism and that his cheating has been reported to contest officials by an anonymous postcard which Ethan recognizes has been sent by his still ethical daughter.

Realizing that he has failed to provide a role model for the next generation by his succumbing to unethical acts himself, Ethan contemplates suicide and returns to the cave with razor blades, hoping to redeem his many betrayals through his own death. As he considers all the moral lights that have been dimmed and put out, he reaches into his pocket and discovers that the talisman has been placed there by Ellen. Buoyed by her potential as a new light-bearer, Ethan forgoes self-destruction, fights the rising tides, and returns home to nurture the moral and ethical potential of his daughter, whose moral character still holds hope for the world.

III. CRITICAL EXPLICATION

The Winter of Our Discontent, like many other Steinbeck titles, is rich in the complexity of its meaning. An exploration of the different thematic levels requires a sophisticated background in religion, history, and literature. Steinbeck alludes to each area as he tells the story of the Hawleys of New Baytown, widening the narrative and creating archetypes of human existence, characters whose actions mirror the duality of mankind over the centuries and who also predict problems of the future.

Steinbeck's manipulation of religious images is perhaps the most obvious technique used in *The Winter of Our Discontent.* The Temptation, Betrayal, Crucifixion, and the Burial of Christ provide a time pattern for the first half of the novel and shape its characters as well. However, the interrelationships between Ethan's story and the Passion of Jesus are neither simplistic nor easily understood. This is because Steinbeck utilizes a syncretic approach to the imagery, combining associations and ideas so that there are many possible interpretations of his intent. Religious images thus appear and disappear, and some merge into paradoxical opposites that suggest the characters' good and evil natures simultaneously.

The first section of the book begins on Good Friday and ends on Easter Tuesday. During this brief time period, Steinbeck brings his protagonist Ethan Allen Hawley (suggesting a New England pronunciation of "holy") to a confrontation of his two natures—sinful and godly. Like Christ before him, Ethan must decide if he can bear the temptations of the world and conquer them. The other option is, of course, to capitulate, worshiping power, prestige, and money as the new American gods and ignoring the moral beliefs on which this country was founded.

Steinbeck cleverly uses these Christological parallels, but he presents them in an inverted manner. Therefore, *Winter* depicts Ethan's pure self dying on Good Friday. He has reached a turning point, a crisis which motivates him to deny his primitive Puritanism and to convert to the materialistic world's values. The effect of this symbolic "death" to faith is the reverse of Christ's literal death on the cross. Christ's sacrifice is efficacious; Ethan's is selfishly motivated. Christ dies to sin, while Ethan's sinless life dies. Here Steinbeck combines life and death for Ethan. For his "life" in the world to occur, Ethan's moral nature must die and his tendency to sin must be reborn. Ironically, Ethan has resurrected his old self—the "old man" of the scriptures who is evil and depraved—and has buried the new man, the resurrected image of Christ, in deliberate opposition to the advice of Scripture (II Corinthians 4:16 and 5:17). Consequently, Ethan is both bound and free, having an inclination toward sin through his human heritage and yet a will to choose otherwise if through God's Spirit he is moved to believe.

However, Steinbeck makes clear that the hour of Ethan's death—the sixth hour—has not yet arrived. Three more temptations remain before Ethan capitulates to "death." His dilemma is like that of Christ in the wilderness being tempted three times by Satan (Matthew 4:1-11). The first temptation occurs as Ethan is sweeping the walk and the bank president, Mr. Baker, stops for conversation. Baker urges Ethan to invest his wife's legacy from her brother in order to gain more money and renew his pride. However, Ethan's reaction to the suggestion reveals his moral heritage. Despite this religious influence of his past, Ethan has eventually reached bankruptcy in less than two years as a result of his ethical actions. It is no wonder that his anger bridles at his failure and his slow descent into insolvency, while foreigners with less moral sense than he are successful. However, despite Baker's convincing argument, Ethan recognizes that at this point he is unwilling to risk his wife's legacy to gain more wealth. He must endure two more temptations before closing up the store on Good Friday. The second temptation, Margie Young-Hunt, the town whore, is sexually promiscuous and animal-like. For her, the virtuous Ethan is a challenge, a god she might be able to seduce from his pedestal. Yet despite her suggestive words and her attempts at seduction, Ethan is able to resist the temptation of the flesh by quoting the Gospel for Good Friday. This use of scripture indicates he still believes that using God's word will help him overcome the power of Satan.

At this point Ethan seems willing to bear his own cross, purchased at the price of a high moral code, but Margie's parting prophecy touches another side of his psyche, offering the prediction that he will be a Savior, a leader of men, a potential Midas. Ethan's job, however, prevents him from contemplating this fascinating prophecy until noon. Following the Holy Day procedure, Ethan closes up shop early, only to realize that the darkness of the store reflects the darkness of the heart which has fallen on the world and on himself. Critic Joseph Fontenrose even notes that Ethan stays in the darkened store with shades down from 12 o'clock to 3 o'clock, paralleling Christ's time in darkness on the cross.[13] In the sixth hour—the hour of Christ's death—Ethan is experiencing the torment of his imminent demise as a moral individual.

Shortly thereafter, Ethan is confronted in the dark store by Mr. Biggers, an agent for B.B.D. & D. Wholesalers. Biggers provides yet a third and final enticement by flaunting the sins of greed and aggressive behavior. Ethan is invited to take the risk of deceiving his boss Marullo and buying from

Biggers, an action which will gain him 5% of the store's orders as a kickback. Biggers jests at Ethan's honesty and his suggestion that he will turn the 5% over to Marullo. To Biggers, no sin is involved, and he offers a richly constructed wallet as a bribe.

When Ethan shares the dilemma with his friend Joey Morphy, he realizes that his ethical concerns are not shared by others. Instead, Morphy advocates money and prosperity as appropriate American gods; ethical actions are foolish if they result in monetary loss. Morphy's capitulation is the last straw for Ethan, who more than ever identifies with Christ of the Cross who also lamented that God had forsaken him. Isolation marks the last hours of Ethan's work day, and, as he carries home his cross of heavy grocery bags and guilt, he contemplates his capitulation to evil once more. Ethan, as the potential Christ of the novel, will soon reject his "Hawley" heritage and his initial revulsion at worldliness and sin and will become the Judas of the novel, betraying his boss, his friends, and his "brother," Danny Taylor, for "thirty pieces of silver." The latter betrayal is especially significant because Danny, a ruined man both physically and mentally, illustrates how moral corruption affects "good" individuals and prefigures Ethan's own fate.

The Judas role is seen as beneficial since Ethan recognizes that a betrayal of Marullo will win him the grocery store, a betrayal of Baker will bring him power and prestige, and a betrayal of Danny will restore riches as well as an increased social status (he can sell Danny's property for a planned airport). Later in the novel, the reader will see even more Judas-like actions as Ethan's daughter betrays her brother, as Baker betrays the town fathers, and as Margie Young-Hunt betrays Ethan's wife, Mary. As the novel's central metaphor, betrayal symbolizes that selling one's soul has become the norm of society. It also allows Steinbeck the opportunity to examine the thirty pieces of silver: America's new god, Mammon. The store becomes the new American congregation and its crafty owner Marullo the symbol of the corruption brought about by the almighty dollar. According to Ethan's pal Joey Morphy, the bank has become the new holy of holies complete with mystic numbers for the safe, and its customers stand in awe outside the rail, like humble communicants waiting for the sacrament (221). "Then the time lock springs and Father Baker genuflects and opens the safe, and we all bow down to the Great God currency" (136). The obvious parallel to the open tomb and the rolling away of the stone of Easter morning are no doubt additional intentional implications about America's new God.

Ethan's subsequent visit to his "Place," a cave about four feet wide and five feet deep carved into the harbor, also prefigures his eventual death and burial. He will ignore "God-given" rules and succumb to the way of the world. Ironically, unlike Christ, whose entry into the tomb on Good Friday signified a conquering of sin, death, and Satan, Ethan's entry into the cave begins a subsequent moral decline and a loss to this unholy Trinity. At this point, instead of examining his soul, Ethan takes stock of his earthly situation, his family, and his desire for money.

After contemplating his Judas-like actions, Ethan re-enacts the role of Pontius Pilate by questioning "What is truth" and by acting as judge, condemning Marullo, Baker, and Danny to various forms of death. Like Pilate he also rationalizes that hurting others will be beneficial for him, and he acknowledges that a "me-first" attitude now dominates his society. Ethan's descent into hell begins approximately on Holy Saturday, "the only day in the world's days when Jesus is dead" (60). Ethan's eyes are now open to the world around him, and he appears to others as a changed man. Ironically, he also receives more respect for his Judas traits than for his Christian ones.

The expected resurrection becomes a prolonged fall as Ethan gains the whole world but loses his own soul (Matthew 16:26). Sadly, Easter in the novel is depicted as a pagan ceremony complete with bunnies and chocolate rather than as a Christian victory. The holiday is also portrayed as the moral center from which man has strayed as salvation by trickery has replaced salvation by propitiation. Ethan's ethical absolutes fade as he dies to Christ (rejects him) in order to provide new directions for his growth in a temporal world. His ironic metamorphosis away from good and toward increased evil is evident as he facetiously jokes about the thorn-crowned Christ and as he preaches to his canned goods. Similarly, he rejects his Christian upbringing and refuses to acknowledge that his childhood has resulted in his body being in the shape of a cross. Instead, he confesses his own depravity and denies his willingness to choose the good even if he could.

Not surprisingly, very few residents of New Baytown are shocked by Ethan's changes since he maintains the facade of respectability and makes his motives appear pure rather than tainted. Easter Tuesday reveals an Ethan who has been thoroughly "converted" to evil but who maintains a paradoxical revulsion for moral betrayal on higher levels. Although Ethan maintains he has changed goals and is no longer influenced by morality, he still exhibits a double standard by expecting his children to reject his self-centered role modeling. Unfortunately, he fails to see his own duplicity and continues his "descent into hell," though at times he inexplicably calls out to Mary, his wife, to serve as his intercessor (cf. Virgin Mary) and to guard him from evil within and without.

Other biblical symbols used by Steinbeck involve Margie Young-Hunt's visions—seeing Ethan as *"la pendu,"* the hanged man in the tarot pack, and as a snake shedding its skin. The first image envisions an inverted Christ hung upside down while the snake image could relate to Ethan's crafty Satan-like actions toward Danny Taylor. Another possibility is the renewal image or change suggested by the shedding. Thus the serpent recalls an image of resurrection related to the serpent raised by Moses in the wilderness to save the exiles from death.

This snake image also brings to mind Steinbeck's preoccupation with the book of Genesis and the first stories of mankind. Thus Ethan's association with the serpent not only reminds the reader of the first temptation in Eden but is complicated by the fact that Ethan also functions as the innocent Adam who is tempted by Margie's sensual Eve. Further examination of the Genesis imagery reveals that Steinbeck also repeats his fascination with the Cain/Abel story. Like the Judas parallel mentioned earlier, this biblical tale reiterates betrayal and questions whether man needs to be his brother's keeper. Ethan is both Cain (persecutor) and Abel (sufferer), and he perceives a similar dual heritage in his own son when he calls him "Charles" and "Allen" (82-83).

Although the complexity of the religious references continues the second half of the novel, the time frame changes to July 4th, and the imagery shifts to more historical parallels as Steinbeck attempts to interweave America's heritage into his thematic threads. Steinbeck first examines specific early forefathers including the protagonist's given name, Ethan Allen. The name recalls a revolutionary war figure who can be historically identified as "a rambunctious 'green mountaineer' patriot of mixed motives who risked everything for principles," and "who captured [Fort] Ticonderoga from the British." The original Ethan Allen subsequently "worked for independent status for Vermont, playing off the British against his own countrymen."[14] In addition, Hawley's historical namesake is appropriately associated with a takeover of land and with secret attacks on a neighboring country. Moreover, some of Allen's unethical acts were approved by the United States Congress, giving him respectability and prestige despite his tendency to play both ends against the middle for his own benefit. The strong parallels to the present-day Ethan are obvious.

The book also examines the original American stock from which Ethan has descended and suggests that it is not nearly as pure as he might claim. First of all, Ethan acknowledges that he is descended from both Puritans and pirates. This duality of American heritage has been rationalized from the beginning of Ethan's ancestry. According to Mary, the evil perpetrated by the pirates has been condoned since it was done in the name of the government with letters of "what you call it from the Continental Congress" (1). Ethan agrees by stating that Puritanism and piracy aren't so unalike when you come right down to it. He asserts that "both had a strong dislike for opposition, and both had a roving eye for other people's property. Where they merged they produced a hard bitten, surviving bunch of monkeys" (44).

Steinbeck here contends that the New Baytown of the past has unwisely been identified as the promising new world or Eden, a world of perfection like that envisioned by the

Dutch sailors in *The Great Gatsby*. Unfortunately, this clean, new, unused, and undirtied world has methodically been devoured by the fierce and crafty element of society which had already begun to grow in America as soon as the first settlers arrived. Ethan recalls his great-grandfather's account of how his own ship was burned at anchor and begins to think that the crime was intentional rather than accidental. Thus, he argues that, even in the ideal past, the desire for money (insurance) had caused individuals to sell out their moral values. Yankee shrewdness overcame the religious precepts brought over from the European mainland. Since morality is entrusted to single men only (55), the example of his forefathers leads Ethan to proclaim the futility of ethics and the value of selling out.

Yet the Puritan faith of his Aunt Deborah seems to temporarily counteract Ethan's initial despair at the past, and he recognizes that his great-aunt has planted something religious in him and that it counteracts his tendency to worship success and money. Unfortunately, Ethan's reaction at the moment is to refuse to listen, to get away from Deborah's influence. During a one-sided conversation, Ethan continues to stress the historic negatives and to reject his supposedly pure ancestors. He further notes that although his forefathers had commissions to raid commerce and were very patriotic and virtuous in their own eyes, they were pirates in the eyes of others. The Hawley family fortune has thus been developed by sin and greed rather than admirable action. Given the illegal means used to attain his family's stature, Ethan acknowledges that his money has grown respectable only because he has kept it for a while. Steinbeck suggests that this is true of other family dynasties as well. Historically, most American fortunes had been acquired by betrayal and deception, for "Where money is concerned, the ordinary rules of conduct take a holiday" (66).

The text thus suggests what Ethan is about to do has a historical precedent. The genteel piracy of the early Hawleys has only been refined. Even though piracy is out, the impulse lingers: people want something for nothing, wealth without effort. Steinbeck asserts that a new generation of greedy Americans, some of the biggest people in the country, have defected from honor, ethics, and morality and have chosen evil methods to attain such desired success.

Steinbeck also incorporates the witchcraft associated with New England into the historical background revealed in *Winter*. For example, Margie Young-Hunt reveals that her great-grandmother was sentenced to exile in Alaska for witchcraft. In addition, the cat in Ethan's store is symbolic of the evil that must be chased away before it preys on Ethan and his family. Finally, Ethan believes that his American heritage includes a Congress of the Dark which has already decided his fate for him. As he observes the past, he recognizes that all of New Baytown is involved in a similar sellout of morality. Granted, they were small violations, but still the founding fathers had

> abolished part of the Decalogue and kept the rest. And when one of the successful men had what he needed or wanted, he reassumed his virtue as easily as changing a shift and for all one could see, he took no hurt from his derelictions, always assuming he didn't get caught. (104-05)

Consequently, the value of the historical past has become relative since Ethan's present tarnished reputation is revealed to be an inherited trait from the patriarchs who first settled America. Even the admirable words of famous men like Henry Clay, Daniel Webster, Thomas Jefferson, and Abraham Lincoln cannot resuscitate the dying morals and values which were once so important. Similarly, writers like Whitman, Emerson, Thoreau, and Twain have also lost their appeal.

The reputation of the past is seen to be hypocritical, and yet men persist in believing otherwise. When there is honesty about the hypocrisy that existed in America's history, there is automatically disbelief. Ethan, however, realizes that the hard fact of society is that in business and politics "man must carve and maul his way through men to get to be King of the Mountain. Once there, he can be great and kind—but he must get there first" (173).

Morally asleep, the present residents of New Baytown are as numb as their fathers before them; they do not remember the differences between legal and illegal, right and wrong. The seed of evil, so long in germination, has begun to produce fruit in the present. Morals are simply words. Considering the lessons of the past, it is no wonder that the upright citizen can also be corrupt beneath the surface. Success through trickery is not "crooked but clever." Historically, the positive reactions to Hitler, Mussolini, and Stalin serve as examples of man's approval and participation in evil. It is not surprising then that the outlines of Ethan's American ancestors are "vague and wavery where they should have been sharp as photographs" (216). Hate, mistrust, and destruction surely accompany the love, care, and giving usually attributed to the America past.

Yet Ethan's so-called honesty is still impressive to Marullo who wants to make a monument to what America once was (255), a down payment so the light of morality will not flicker and die out. To Marullo, the Statue of Liberty, the Declaration of Independence, and the Bill of Rights are still praiseworthy. The positive side of America still is alive. In fact, Steinbeck symbolizes Marullo's hope for America's future in the July 4th setting of a land of justice, love, and equality. A revitalization of an American heritage is possible for

> The year of 1960 was a year of change, a year when secret fears come into the open, when discontent stops being dormant and changes gradually to anger. And it wasn't only the nation. The whole world stirred with restlessness as discontent moved to anger tried to find an outlet in action, any action, so long as it was violent. (280-81)

The future offers a possibility for redemption, a second metamorphosis, a return to ethics, and an emphasis of light over darkness. Ethan, as the American Everyman, must falter and fail in order to be reborn. The inversion of traditional patriotism (where the dispossessed is evicted rather than welcomed and where words of trust in the nation are no longer current but plagiarized borrowings from a lost past) can be transformed to a previous normality. Steinbeck's historical references are designed to reform American society: to motivate the removal of ethnic prejudices, kickbacks, political manipulation, sexual blackmail, and phony real estate promotion. Ethan's remorse about his history, his simultaneous action, and regret of action indicate that perhaps his integrity will return and his morality and America's will be renewed.

One final element that deserves exploration in this novel of moral accusation is Steinbeck's use of literary allusion. Again the complexity is significant as Steinbeck taps ancient manuscripts and Renaissance plays as well as contemporary writers for effect.

The earliest manuscripts utilized by Steinbeck are the Anglo-Saxon quotes that form the wonder words of Ethan's Aunt Deborah. The first is Eve's account of how she was tempted by the serpent in Caedmon's *Genesis*. The second, though spliced to the first, is from Boethius's *De Consolatione de Philosophiae*. In the first passage, Eve protests her inculpability for her action; the snake is her scapegoat. Yet the second passage suggests that man, like the lion, contains something of the wild and, given the proper opportunity, will revert back to his original animalistic and wild state. Critic Richard Bedford suggests that both texts are related to free will and depravity—man's choice and opportunity to exercise his innate and purely human characteristic.[15] Man is only innately *man* since neither good, nor innate bad, is totally clear. All acts are essentially morally ambiguous and the blend of good and evil is merely a given that Ethan must accept. Consequently, man's choices are hopelessly inadequate and always based on the individual's biased evaluation of the situation. These quotes are significant because Ethan feels he is intrinsically bad, doomed by the Congress of the Dark to evil.

Steinbeck's next literary allusion is to Shakespeare. Although the references to *Richard III* are most significant given the title of the novel, there are brief allusions to Ethan's dilemma as similar to Hamlet's (an act stalemated by moral scruple) and to Macbeth's (an act motivated by witches involving the murder of close friends and an attempt to appear blameless despite one's personal evil). The exploration of the parallels to Richard, however, reveals most of Steinbeck's effort.

The title is taken from the opening soliloquy of Shakespeare's *Richard III* and is spoken by the title character himself. Richard says:

> Now is the winter of our discontent / Made glorious summer by this sun of York; / And all the clouds that loured upon our house / In the deep bosom of the ocean buried. / And therefore, to entertain these fair well-spoken days, / I am determined to prove a villain / And hate the idle pleasure of these days. / Plots have I laid, inductions dangerous, / By drunken prophecies, libels, and dreams, / To set my brother Clarence and the King / In deadly hate the one against the other. . . .[16]

This soliloquy effectively sets up the theme of opposites, for in Shakespeare's play, the winter of discontent has been miraculously transformed into summer by the ascension of the Yorkist monarch and the abdication of Henry VI, the Lancastrian holder of the throne. Furthermore, Richard himself is revealed as a paradox. Outwardly he appears to be the helpful servant of his brothers, King Edward IV and the Duke of Clarence, but inwardly he is plotting their deaths and his own ascension to power. Reloy Garcia points out that

> [j]ust as Shakespeare's hero-villain, Richard, degenerates in the conflict with his brother, from a cold Machiavellian plotter to an emotional sinner who derives pleasure from pain and evil, so too does Ethan degenerate in conflict with his "brother," Danny Taylor, over the "kingdom" of Taylor's Meadow.[17]

Richard is the epitome of duplicity, and the parallelism to Ethan is significant. Liquor is a factor in both plot lines as well. In a reversal of *Richard III,* where the drunk Clarence in no way suspects his brother, Richard, of plotting his death, Danny sees through Ethan's righteous offer. He recognizes that Ethan is betting that a thousand dollars' worth of booze will kill him, and Ethan will inherit Taylor's Meadow which has been put up as collateral for the loan. Ironically, another parallel in the two works is that drink causes the death of both Clarence and Danny. Clarence is drowned in a vat of malmsey, and Danny's demise results from alcoholism toward the end of Part I. Eventually, the literary allusion of the title is repeated by Ethan to show that, like Richard, he has caused his own fortunes to change from bad to good through his own duplicity.

However, most readers realize that the discontent is not Ethan's only but is rampant in his society. For example, the uneasiness of Ethan's family with poverty, the unfulfilled greed of Mr. Baker, and the unsatisfied lust of Margie Young-Hunt all relate to the title. Such discontent leads to betrayal, a tie-in with the religious imagery, and to a rejection of the past in order to attain a brighter future. The latter, of course, relates to Steinbeck's historical emphases. The repetition of the allusion to the Yorkist dynasty reoccurs a third time in Chapter XXI as Ethan again quotes the words of Richard III's soliloquy as a recognition of Allen's accomplishment (295). In this new picture the role of Richard has been assumed by Allen rather than Ethan, and now Ethan functions as the ancestor, the Duke of York, whose greed for the throne taught all his sons so well. The role model of avarice has been copied by the next generation. However, Steinbeck questions whether the "summer" of capitulation will be followed by a "fall" from "grace" and a recognition of the duplicity of the Ethan/Richard character. The mock heroic parallel of the two protagonists suggests values have again been turned topsy-turvy, and that greed, duplicity, and aggression have replaced virtue as the absolute values of present-day society.

Yet a third important literary referent is to the Arthurian legend and the Grail Quest. As was noted in the background section, Steinbeck had begun research for an updated version of Malory's *Morte D'Arthur* so this material was heavy on his mind. Steinbeck also stated in letters to Elizabeth Otis that the "Arthur" was perhaps the most important influence on his childhood and that he felt the legend was timeless.[18] In *Winter* the allusion to Arthurian legend occurs mainly in regard to Ethan's membership in The Knight Templars. When his son Allen asks to use his Knight Templar sword, Ethan is ironically associated with Lancelot, who betrays a human rather than an almighty king. The knight's hat, complete with plume, has yellowed, indicating the moral decay of its owner.

Yet another related element to the medieval legend is the Hawley talisman—a translucent stone four inches in diameter. Somehow, it provides sustenance to the Hawleys and changes its "color and convolutions and texture as their needs changed." As Ellen removes the stone from the holy relics of the Hawleys, the importance of the Arthurian Grail is recalled. The talisman, like the Grail, has the power to renew and at times transforms Ellen with luminescent power. Steinbeck here seems to be alluding to Ellen as Elaine/the Grail Mistress and protector of the holy relic.

The stone, as defined by Aunt Deborah, becomes an amulet to avert evil or to bring fortune to the bearer. Accordingly, the talisman has as much power as its owner endows it with. This is also similar to the Grail, which according to Arthurian legend, gains its power through faith. The talisman picks up the symbolism of light (good) versus dark (evil) that was introduced earlier in the novel by Marullo as he endeavors to recreate the ideal America he sought as an immigrant.

As Ethan contemplates suicide and returns to the cave to slit his wrists, he is paralleled to Arthur, who despairs over the decline of the Round Table and the rise of his evil nephew/son Mordred. Fortunately, Ethan comes to the realization that everyone carries his own light—his own sense of morals and virtuous thoughts. However, since he has himself extinguished and blackened his virtues, he now desires to die to reach the other side of home where the lights are given. But as Arthur is revived by the Grail and recovers sufficiently to defeat the evil Mordred and Morgana la Fey, it appears that Ethan will eventually persevere as well. Though Arthur/Ethan may die, the lightbearer of the future, Ellen, is ready to reassume the moral task. Thus as Ethan reaches for the razor blades to slit his wrists, he discovers the talisman instead. Its discovery motivates his leaving of the cave and dismissing suicide. Indeed the talisman becomes his salvation. As Ethan puts it, "no matter that his light was out and blacker than a wick." The talisman is necessary to its new owner, "else another light might go out" (311).

Although a metamorphosis occurs a second time as Ethan dismisses suicide, the reader is still unsure of both Ethan's future and that of his family. The heritage of truth, justice, and honesty is hanging in the balance and its continuance is questionable. It is still threatened by materialism, greed, and selfishness. The reader, as in the Arthur myth, must wait for the return of the king (Jesus/religious morality) before a restored Camelot (Paradise) can be attained. This renewal takes on historical meaning as well when associated with the Kennedy presidency and the descriptions of a return to Camelot, where knightly actions would right wrongs by means of potent deeds and legislation.

The final literary allusions move Steinbeck into a more contemporary period and affect his style as well as his theme. First of all, Steinbeck utilizes T. S. Eliot's "The Waste Land" as a comparison to present-day America. In the poem, Eliot decries the aridity of his America and its moral decay. Hawley becomes Eliot's questor, the Knight Templar, searching for answers to insoluble questions. In addition, the details used by Steinbeck provide significant evidence of his dependence on the poem to provide analogies and to illumine his thematic emphasis. The presence of the tarot pack, a Madame Sosostris (Margie Young-Hunt), a Teiresias (Joey Morphy), and a Mr. Eugenides (Mr. Biggers) all suggest Steinbeck's reliance on Eliot, but critic Donna Gerstenberger suggests the similarities go even deeper.[19] She cites the substitution of secular rituals in the absence of more meaningful sacred ones, the protests to the empty secularized world in nonsense phrases, and the questioning of "Four Quartets" in an attempt to find magic answers which will unlock the prison of self. She also draws attention to the lines from the poem about "the corpse in the garden," relating it to the destruction of both Marullo and Danny Taylor in the novel. Finally, Gerstenberger cites the setting of "The Waste Land"—the arid climate, the lack of winds, and the inability of Ethan, the questor, to find a sea change, a life-giving water.

Gerstenberger's conclusion states

Hawley's experience of evil is complete; his quest has led him into the heart of corruption, but the way out is not as clear as the way in. The novel ends as does the poem, with the arid plain much in evidence, the quest having altered little except the individual's own knowledge of the meaning of experience—past and present. The solutions are no easier, it would seem, in 1961 than they were in 1922.[20]

Despite the general negative tone of "The Waste Land," Eliot does hold out hope for man's recognition of his plight. The solution is in symbolic water. In *Winter* this epiphany occurs for Ethan when he goes to his cave to commit suicide. Located on Whitsun Reef (suggesting the descent of the Holy Spirit on the Apostles), the cave is accessible only at low tide. Thus in the depths of despair, Ethan experiences the sea change, the life-giving water which restores his hopes.

Undoubtedly, the richness of imagery indicates the complexity of Steinbeck's final novel. One final allusion is suggested by critic Lawrence William Jones, who contends that Steinbeck, always an experimenter in genre as well as form, finished his career as a fabulist. Citing the larger meanings of such works as *The Pearl* and *East of Eden*, Jones argues that the form which Steinbeck uses in *Winter* is very close to fable. Consequently, he argues that although limitations in the text result due to this choice, critics are unfair to the work if they judge it with the expectations placed on realistic fiction.[21.]

As a fabulist, Steinbeck must be considered as similar to such contemporaries as Kurt Vonnegut, Joseph Heller, and John Updike. Consequently, his use of hyperbole and black humor must be seen not as a flaw but rather as an experiment with a new form of writing, perhaps even related to the absurdist playwrights Beckett and Ionesco. Thus the characters who are not fully or carefully developed suggest the shallowness of society. Similarly the childlike language and silly terms reflect the emptiness of conversation in a world of confusion. This "cuteness" also betrays the lack of meaning in communication. Finally the shifting point of view purposefully demonstrates the isolation of Ethan. The reader is exposed to both an objective and subjective viewpoint, providing a record of the country's malaise, of its unfulfilled dreams and unmet obligations, and of what happens to principles, to dreams, and to ideals in the case of money lenders.

Although at first glance Ethan's euphemistic nicknames for Mary and his preaching to the canned goods may seem stupid and far-fetched, these elements are merely experiments in technique and in fact foreshadow the absurdist black comedy of writers like Donald Barthelme and John Irving while echoing Vonnegut and Barth. Ethan's conversational tone may seem unrealistic but then Yossarian in Heller's *Catch-22* and Garp in Irving's *The World According to Garp* also suffer from the same problem. Their way of dealing with an absurd world is similar to Ethan's. They create a clever laughing mask of unconcern and apathy. The only way they can face reality is by "clowning" and pretending that the "real" is fantastic and incomprehensible. If the comic mask falls, so too does the ability of the character to cope with a sin-sick world.

The Winter of Our Discontent, though greeted with disdain and heavy criticism at its publication, appears to have weathered the years well. Steinbeck's interweaving of biblical, historical, and literary texts in this story of America's declining morals indicates the complexity of the work. What appeared to the early critics as weakness now seems an insightful and innovative technique utilized by a determined experimenter. Steinbeck's final novel is an excellent example of the well-crafted tale. His interweaving of opposites, his merging of symbols, and his experimentation with style and humor make the novel a worthy successor to *The Grapes of Wrath* as a social document calling on all of America to account for its ambivalent reaction and commitment to moral uprightness. Such self-knowledge and deep introspection were surely what Steinbeck wished for his readers: an appreciation and understanding of *The Winter of Our Discontent* on all of its levels of meanings.

NOTES

1. Jackson J. Benson, *The True Adventures of John Steinbeck, Writer* (New York: Viking Press, 1984), p. 836.
2. *Ibid.,* p. 839.

3. *Ibid.*, p. 850.
4. *Ibid.*, p. 857.
5. *Ibid.*
6. *Ibid.*, p. 858.
7. Warren French, *John Steinbeck*, 2nd revised ed. (Boston: Twayne Publishers, 1975), p. 159.
8. Benson, p. 871.
9. *Ibid.*, p. 874.
10. John Steinbeck, *Steinbeck: A Life in Letters*, eds. Elaine Steinbeck and Robert Wallsten (New York: Viking Press, 1975), pp. 651-53.
11. *Ibid.*, pp. 676-77.
12. John Steinbeck, *The Winter of Our Discontent* (New York: Penguin Books, 1982), p. 27. Hereafter references to the novel will be incorporated parenthetically into the text.
13. Joseph Fontenrose, *John Steinbeck: An Introduction and Interpretation* (New York: Holt, Rinehart and Winston, 1963), p. 134.
14. Reloy Garcia, "*The Winter of Our Discontent*," in *A Study Guide to Steinbeck*, ed. Tetsumaro Hayashi (Metuchen, New Jersey: Scarecrow Press, 1974), p. 245.
15. Richard C. Bedford, "The Genesis and Consolation of Our Discontent," *Criticism*, 14 (Summer 1972), 277-94.
16. William Shakespeare, *Richard III*, Signet Classic ed. (New York: New American Library, 1964), pp. 33-34.
17. Garcia, p. 244.
18. See "Appendix" to John Steinbeck, *The Acts of King Arthur and His Noble Knights* (New York: Ballantine Books, 1976), pp. 351 ff.
19. Donna Gerstenberger, "Steinbeck's American Waste Land," *Modern Fiction Studies*, 11 (Spring 1965), 59-65.
20. *Ibid.*, p. 65.
21. See Lawrence William Jones, *John Steinbeck as Fabulist*, ed. by Marston LaFrance (*Steinbeck Monograph Series*, No. 3) (Muncie, Indiana: Steinbeck Society of America, Ball State University, 1973).

IV. TOPICS FOR RESEARCH AND DISCUSSION

(1) Discuss how Steinbeck inverts the normal Holy Week/Easter images in the novel.

(2) Discuss how Steinbeck utilizes past political heritage as a contrast to present goals and morality in America.

(3) Examine how Steinbeck presents two types of women in the novel—the whore and the virgin—and examine the appeal of each.

(4) Point out the parallels Steinbeck saw in Ethan to the character of Richard III in Shakespeare's play of the same name.

(5) Determine what is the significance of Ethan's Puritan forebears (his grandfather, aunt) and discuss what Puritan beliefs have been handed down over the years.

(6) Show the way Steinbeck incorporates the ideal of knighthood and the King Arthur myth into his text.

(7) Prove that archetypal light/dark imagery is utilized in this novel.

(8) Demonstrate that the language used by Steinbeck is satirical and mocking rather than an attempt to parallel actual speech patterns.

(9) Point out the fablelike structure of the story and how symbolic names underpin the allegory.

(10) Demonstrate Steinbeck's debt to Eliot in his portrayal of a literal American wasteland and one man's attempt to redeem it.

V. SELECTED BIBLIOGRAPHY

1. Richard Bedford, "The Genesis and Consolation of Our Discontent," *Criticism*, 14 (Summer 1972), 277-94. Bedford's discussion emphasizes the ambiguity of man's moral choices centering specifically on interpreting the wonder words of Aunt Deborah (*Winter of Our Discontent*, 262) and on placing the novel in its proper perspective to religious faith as a story of "man's tragic-comical futile attempt to distinguish good and evil."

2. Joseph Fontenrose, *John Steinbeck: An Introduction and Interpretation*. New York: Barnes & Noble, 1963. One of the first critical commentaries on *Winter*, this analysis celebrates Steinbeck's command of myth inversion and his exploration of both Christian and patriotic ethics. Fontenrose's explanation of the inversion of Christian images stresses that today's religions are business houses and banks and that in this tradition Judas is the Savior and Richard III is a hero (p. 136). However, he concludes that Ethan Hawley is improbable and so is his story since Steinbeck seems to try too hard, creating

tastelessness instead of profundity, a tiresome repetition instead of beauty.

3. Warren French, *John Steinbeck,* revised edition. Boston: Twayne Publishers, 1975. Chapter 11, "The Drama of Consciousness," deals very briefly with *Winter* suggesting it is little more than a fleshed out short story that doesn't work. French contends that sentimentality replaced satire, and he compares *Winter* to Steinbeck's first novel *Cup of Gold* and to Willa Cather's *The Professor's House.* "Moral decay," French insists, is everybody's crime, and he suggests that for Steinbeck an equal development of conscience must accompany all consciousness.

4. Warren French, "Steinbeck's Winter Tale," *Modern Fiction Studies,* 11 (Spring, 1965), 66-74. French's essay discusses the relationship between *The Winter of Our Discontent* and the short story "How Mr. Hogan Robbed a Bank," first published in *The Atlantic Monthly* in March 1956. The contention is that a delightful comic and satiric fantasy has been turned into a contrived melodrama. The remainder of the article concentrates on the resemblance between *Winter*'s protagonist, Ethan Allen Hawley, and Holden Caulfield, the central character of Salinger's *Catcher in the Rye.* The major parallels, according to French, are that both disillusioned heroes are reconciled to their adulterated world by a recognition of these responsibilities and that both authors envision a world where corruption by materialism affects both innocent youth (Holden) and innocent elders (Ethan). The busy, indifferent, and materialistic successful characters (Holden's father and Ethan's son) are evidence that the evil of mammon worship is not confined to one generation.

5. Donna Gerstenberger, "Steinbeck's American Waste Land," *Modern Fiction Studies,* 11 (Spring 1965), 59-65. Gerstenberger's essay, seminal to a re-evaluation of *Winter*'s complexity, contends that T. S. Eliot's poem "The Waste Land" extends the range of the novel's meaning and provides a source of tension and depth for the "surface" meanings of the novel. The spiritual sterility of Eliot's poem is incorporated in the thematic skein of the text, and Gerstenberger suggests several specific borrowings from "The Waste Land" text. These include the characters of Mr. Eugenides and Madam Sosostris (Biggers and Margie Young-Hunt) and the section "Death by Water." Some action, even if corrupt, is seen as necessary as a possible penultimate step to salvation. Aridity

and spiritual dryness are as unrelieved in Steinbeck as in Eliot, and the quest for renewal ends ambiguously, with little achieved except an individual's own knowledge of self.

6. Lawrence William Jones, *John Steinbeck as Fabulist,* ed. Marston LaFrance (*Steinbeck Monograph Series,* No. 3). Muncie, Indiana: Steinbeck Society of America, Ball State University, 1973. This monograph contends that Steinbeck's later novels were misunderstood because his critics expected realistic fiction, and Steinbeck had matured and begun to write fables and parables. Jones also defends Steinbeck's moralistic attitude in his work by defining fable as an analogical tale designed to reveal human truth and to translate ethical ideas into prose. Thus the sermonlike passages of *Winter* are justified by the genre Steinbeck is using, and Jones's explication of the religious analogues emphasizes the complexity of the novel's use of myth and biblical allusions.

7. Howard Levant, *The Novels of John Steinbeck: A Critical Study.* Columbia: University of Missouri Press, 1974. Chapter 12, "The End of the Road," draws similarities between *Winter* and *The Grapes of Wrath* as stories of the decayed times. However, Levant sees the excellence as marred by sermonic, essayish, and mechanical language and flawed elucidation of character. Levant also points out Ethan's paradoxical actions: desire and disgust, acquiescence and self-loathing, and his resulting ambiguity for readers who must decide whether to pity or to despise him. Structure is identified as the major flaw, although Levant finds much to praise about Steinbeck's innovations and complex thematic structure.

8. Todd Lieber, "Talismanic Patterns in the Novels of John Steinbeck," *American Literature,* 44 (May 1972), 262-75. This essay discusses the significance of the stone which symbolizes the Hawleys' good fortune and ultimately serves as Ethan's salvation. Other talismans evident in the Steinbeck canon and their effect on his characters are also explored.

9. Peter Lisca, *John Steinbeck: Nature and Myth.* New York: Thomas Y. Crowell, 1978. Chapter 7, "Essays in Christianity," discusses Steinbeck's experimentations with new forms and freedom in *Winter.* Lisca accuses Steinbeck of self-indulgence and of confusing himself with his main character and calls it one of his weaker serious novels. If there is richness in the novel, it lies in the plethora of allusions contained in the text amplifying the meanings. Lisca's analyses of allusions to Christian myths are especially thorough as is his

insight into the new American god, money. Ethan is shown trying to balance the mystic or religious view of life with scientific non-teleological thinking.

10. Paul McCarthy, *John Steinbeck*. New York: Frederick Ungar Publishing Company, 1980. Chapter 7, "Searches in the Last Years," praises Steinbeck for the detailed setting of *The Winter of Our Discontent* and for his incorporation of past American history into his plot. Inversions of mythical, biblical, and national symbols are analyzed as positive additions by the author, but McCarthy suggests the time frame of four months is difficult to accept and that Ethan's actions are ultimately cowardly rather than tragic.

11. Louis Owens, *John Steinbeck's Re-Vision of America*. Athens: University of Georgia Press, 1985. "The Conclusion: *The Winter of Our Discontent* and the American Conscience" analyzes the American myth of Eden and suggests the influence of Steinbeck's Arthur translation on the content of the novel. The Grail quest, complete with references to Fraser's *The Golden Bough* and Eliot's "The Waste Land," is also thoroughly examined. Owens also draws attention to the Christian imagery, incorporating the biblical allusions with the Arthurian legend. Owens ultimately describes the novel as a "jeremiad" (a warning) or as a final exploration of America's idea of self.

12. John H. Timmerman, *John Steinbeck's Fiction: The Aesthetics of the Road Taken*. Norman: University of Oklahoma Press, 1986. Chapter 9, "The Voice from Heaven," describes the background of the work. the moral darkening of an age. Structurally, Timmerman criticizes the artificiality of language and triteness of imagery while like Owens noting the link between *Winter* and the translation of Malory's *Morte D'Arthur*. Timmerman concludes that Steinbeck was attempting to recapture a bygone age, and he thoroughly explores the religious as well as the patriotic imagery utilized by the author. However, he ends by questioning the reasonableness of Steinbeck's artistry and by suggesting that the character of Ethan lacks interest and fails to raise a moral pathos in readers.

11. JOHN STEINBECK: THE ART AND CRAFT OF WRITING

TETSUMARO HAYASHI

As Jackson J. Benson, Robert DeMott, John Ditsky, and other critics have already pointed out, John Steinbeck was an artist sensitively conscious of his own creative process.[1] It is true that he sometimes detested his friends' asking him about the book he was writing, as he told Pascal Covici in *Journal of a Novel:*

> I want to ask and even beg one thing of you—that we do not discuss the book any more when you come over. No matter how delicately we go about it, it confuses me and throws me off the story. So from now on, let's do the weather or fleas or something else, but let's leave the book alone.[2]

Yet Steinbeck, in his own terms and by his own initiatives, loved to discuss his books and the art and craft of writing in his essays and diaries and often in his letters to his friends and associates. This is an important dimension of Steinbeck's work which needs to be emphasized—that he was a "total" writer in love with his craft and that he was absorbed by the nature of writing. Thus he talked candidly about the agony and ecstasy of his creative process, his emotional, psychological, and intellectual upheavals while writing, his unique strategy, emphasis, focus, and goal in writing, and his advice on how to solve writer's block and how to overcome a series of dilemmas and frustrations common to the creative writer. In doing so, he revealed his fanatic dedication to the art and craft of writing and the nature, extent, and intensity of that commitment.

274

His remarks on the art and craft of writing reveal something unique, insightful, and exhilarating. Steinbeck was willing to share his expertise as an experienced writer with his aspiring writer-friends, especially when they faced a series of difficulties and crises in their writing careers. Steinbeck advised Dennis Murphy, for instance, "to defend yourself against success":

> You've done well against failure. Now let's see how you defend yourself against success. Your only weapon is your work. Take everything you can but keep your work pure and innocent and fierce. . . . While you are doing it, for God's sake, keep your holy loneliness.[3]

By the same token, Steinbeck told Elizabeth R. Otis and Chase Horton that he could write better under pressure of all kinds including "poverty, death, emotional confusion, and divorces."[4] The Nobel Prize laureate early declared and maintained that "A man's best work is done when he is fighting to make himself heard, not when swooning audiences wait for his autographs," and that "If you don't want to fight them, you shouldn't be writing. One can force attention by making one's work superb. Only practice can do that" (*SLL,* p. 34). Here Steinbeck seems to enforce this philosophy as he explained in *The Log from the Sea of Cortez:* "The protected human soon loses his power of defense and attack," "Where there is little danger, there seems to be little stimulation" (p. 227), and "the removal of obstacles automatically atrophies a survival drive. With warm water and abundant food, the animals may retire into a sterile sluggish happiness. This has certainly seemed true in man. Force and cleverness and versatility have surely been the children of obstacles," and finally, "Little enough is known about the function of individual pain and suffering, although from its profound organization it is suspected of being necessary as a survival mechanism" (p. 264).[5]

Another piece of advice he gave his friends touched on thematic focus and its supreme importance in writing. Steinbeck always demanded not a searchlight but a spotlight: "Make your point and make it angrily" (*SLL,* pp. 527-28), he commanded. "Until you can put your theme in one sentence, you haven't it in hand well enough to write a novel" (*SLL*, p. 74). This advice reminds us also of what Ernest Hemingway said in 1933: "I am trying to make, before I get through, a picture of the whole world—or as much of it as I have seen. Boiling it down always, rather than spreading it out thin."[6] Steinbeck urged Pascal Covici, Jr. to "write it [a novel] *to* someone, like me. Write it as a letter aimed at one person. This removes the vague terror of addressing the large and faceless audience and it [writing to one person] also, you will find, will give a sense of freedom and a lack of self-consciousness" (*SLL*, p. 528). Thus he advocated the imperative requirement of "spotlight"—selectivity and focus in his aesthetic pursuit in writing.

Steinbeck made even more specific, pertinent suggestions to his friends on how to overcome writer's block. For instance, he gave Robert Wallsten, his writer-friend, the following advice:

(1) Abandon the idea that you are ever going to finish. Lose track of the 400 pages and write just one page for each day, it helps. Then when it gets finished, you are always surprised.

(2) Write freely and as rapidly as possible and throw the whole thing on paper. Never correct or rewrite until the whole thing is down. Rewriting in process is usually found to be an excuse for not going on. It also interferes with the flow and rhythm which can only come from a kind of unconscious association with the material.

(3) Forget your generalized audience. In the first place, the nameless, faceless audience will scare you to death and in the second place, unlike the theatre, it doesn't exist. In writing, your audience is one single reader. I have found that sometimes it helps to pick out one person—a real person you know, or an imagined person and write to that one.

(4) If a scene or a section gets the better of you and you still want it—bypass it and go on. When you have finished the whole, you can come back to it and then you may find that the reason it gave you trouble is because it didn't belong there.

(5) Beware of a scene that becomes too dear to you, dearer

> than the rest. It will usually be found that it is out of
> drawing.
> (6) If you are using dialogue—say it aloud as you write it.
> Only then will it have the sound of speech. (*SLL,* pp.
> 736-37)

Most of these tips are still pertinent to any aspiring writer who needs to overcome writer's block, as well as related obstacles and crises. Further, these specific suggestions disclose Steinbeck's concern for his fellow artists and his desire to teach younger writers such practical lessons.

In *East of Eden* Steinbeck defined his philosophy as a writer. What he believed in was "the free, exploring mind of the individual"; what he would fight for was "the freedom of the mind to take any direction it wishes, undirected"; and what he would fight against was "any idea, religion, or government which limits or destroys the individual." Thus he revealed himself as an artist living in a democratic society, proudly exercising his freedom for "lonely, creative, searching"[7] endeavors. Furthermore, Steinbeck described the writer's duty in his Nobel Prize acceptance speech in 1962:

> He is charged with exposing our many grievous faults and failures, with dredging up to the light our dark and dangerous dreams for the purpose of improvement.

He continues to discuss the writer's mission:

> The writer is delegated to declare and to celebrate man's proven capacity for greatness of heart and spirit—for gallantry in defeat, for courage, compassion, and love.[8]

Steinbeck also declared, "I hold that a writer who does not passionately believe in the perfectibility of man has no dedication nor any membership in literature."[9] He continues his fervent assertions: "It is the duty of the writer to lift up, to extend, and to encourage,"[10] and "Great writing has been a staff to lean on, a mother to consult, a wisdom to pick up stumbling folly, a strength in weakness and a courage to support sick cowardice."[11] These remarks account for Steinbeck's strong moral tone, theme, and commitment in general, but especially in his moral trilogy: *The Winter of Our Discontent* (1961), *Travels with Charley in Search of America* (1962), and *America and Americans* (1966). They further reveal Steinbeck's public position and responsibility—like those of William Faulkner—as a Nobel Prize laureate and as a grand old teacher lecturing to the world with a sense of mission—a moral crusader.

Steinbeck, as a conscious artist sensitively aware of the process of creative writing, extensively and frequently discussed the concept of writing. He defined "the craft or art of writing" as "the clumsy attempt to find symbols for the wordlessness. In utter loneliness a writer tries to explain the inexplainable" and "a good writer always works at the impossible."[12] These definitions remind us of Louis Untermeyer's and Carter Davidson's definition of poetry, "Poetry is the power to define the undefinable in terms of the unforgettable,"[13] as well as what Kino says in *The Pearl*, "I am a man," and how Steinbeck's narrator interprets it, "that meant that he was half insane and half god."[14]

Steinbeck once explained the ecstasy of having the creative impulse: "I am overwhelmed with joy because something in me has let go and [because] the clear blue flame of my creativeness is released. I am uplifted but not humbled because I have paid for this with the currency of confusion and little sufferings and it is mine sealed and registered." He continued, "It makes me want to scream with a kind of orgiastic triumph" (*SLL,* pp. 627-28). Such was Steinbeck's pride, dedication, and commitment as a writer, luxuriating and suffering the agony and ecstasy of creative endeavors, acutely conscious of his own overflowing creative energy.

Steinbeck reported to his friends about his own creative impulse and energy, saying, that "The dams are burst. Work is pouring out of me" (*SLL,* p. 349) and "I throw myself into work" (*SLL,* p. 50). He also revealed his serious attitude toward writing, as he said, "I want to write this [*East of Eden*] as though it were my last book. Maybe I believe that every book should be written this way."[15] In his discussion of writing, Steinbeck often disclosed his philosophy of writing, which affirms his proud, total commitment to art: "I work because I know it gives me pleasure to work. . . . I have a book to write. I think about it for a while and then I write it. There is nothing more" (*SLL,* p. 87). As a writer he glorified his work, saying that "The work has been the means of making me feel that I am living richly, diversely, and, in a few cases and for a few moments, even heroically. All of these things are not for me, for I am none of these things. But sometimes in my own mind at least I can create something which is larger and richer than I am. . . . Not being brave I am glad when I can make a braver person whom I believe in" (*SLL,* p. 119). He seems to suggest that a writer can create the "brave new world" with Prospero's faith in the future.

As a novelist Steinbeck always regarded himself as "a minstrel" who stressed the importance of "sound, sight, and sense" (*SLL,* p. 19). He shaped a full orchestra and created a melody, a specially delicious rhythm and appropriate tone to present a theme designed to delight and to teach the reader. With musically gifted ears, Steinbeck was able to recreate the speech of working men and women and their vibrant vernacular language "as a highly developed speech form," as in *In Dubious Battle* (1936), *Of Mice and Men* (1937), and *The Grapes of Wrath* (1939). Such a vernacular language indeed became the dynamic means of communication in most of his major works (*SLL,* p. 105). Steinbeck, as a poetic fictionist, strove to create in his novels "smoothness, coordination, and rhythm all together,"[16] putting specific emphasis on "pause symbols" that "contain the meat of the speech."[17] He practices Hemingway's secret: "Nobody really knows or understands and nobody has ever said the secret. The secret is that it is poetry written in prose and it is the hardest of all things to do."[18] In his perceptive study of Steinbeck's *East of Eden* manuscripts, Mark W. Govoni maintains that the "strong confidence in his [Steinbeck's] ear for the spoken word is most clearly evidenced by Steinbeck's retention of almost all of his original dialogue *verbatim.*"[19]

As a craftsman, Steinbeck the novelist went "over it [his speech] word by word to see whether each word has the value and meaning I want it to have" (*SLL,* pp. 756-57). Sometimes he confessed, "[I am] feeling very literary these days with words crowding up to come tumbling out and the time between putting them down crowding with them like the forming eggs in a chicken or the spare fangs of a rattlesnake" (*SLL,* p. 163). Like a composer, he thus identified himself to be a word-magician, manipulating the "intricate music" of the language for dramatic effect, suspense, metaphor, and imagery. Steinbeck, as a prose-musician, infused his writing with "a rhythm as honest and unshaken as a heartbeat" and said that "the sound of them [his words] is sweet in my ears so that they seem to me to have the strength and sureness of untroubled children or fulfilled old men" (*SLL,* p. 622). Steinbeck never lost the sense of wonder when he used the magic of words, as Hemingway reminded us of it: "All my life I've looked at words as though I were seeing them for the first time."[20]

Further, Steinbeck regarded a writer as a storyteller, by saying, "What I proposed to do is to tell story, setting, character, and mood using absolutely nothing except dialogue."[21] In his storytelling he always made sure of its musical, poetic, and dramatic quality to entertain and teach the audience as Horace once said in his *Ars Poetica: "Omne tulit punctum, qui miscuit utile dulce / lectorem delectando, pariterque monendo"* ("He gains universal applause who mingles the useful with the agreeable, at once delighting and instructing the reader").[22]

With his own fanatic interest in writing, Steinbeck told his friends a great deal about his work habit as "monomania"; he could not help talking exclusively, incessantly, and extensively about writing and more writing. In the process he revealed how intense his commitment to writing was and how creatively his mind functioned as a writer who took his art and craft dead seriously. As a Stanford freshman, he had the audacity to declare to his friends, among them his roommate, Carlton A. Sheffield, "I want to be the best writer in the world." However, he later modified the statement and told Carlton, "I want to *try* to be the best writer in the world" (*SLL,* p. 753). Unmistakably, he had a lofty goal and a ruthless drive to get there. In his letter to Amasa Miller, Steinbeck observed, "To be anything pure [to become a writer] requires an arrogance he [his father] did not have, and a selfishness he could not bring himself to assume."[23] Steinbeck confessed "the complete ruthlessness of my design to be a writer in spite of mother and hell."[24]

Steinbeck further admitted that "the process of writing a book is the process of outgrowing it," and that he was still "writing scared," just as he was twenty-five years ago (*SLL,* p. 462). Mark W. Govoni testifies to the fact that "He [Steinbeck] defines *East of Eden* as his attempt to restore the spirit of inventor and courage to American writing. It is a curious cutting loose from the Hemingway school. His desire is to write a portrait of the artist, to impart a strong sense of self through philosophical commentary and stories about his heritage."[25] His literary canon proves that he always remained a dynamic, experimental writer capable of constant growth and daring exploration into a variety of genres, themes, and narrative techniques, regardless of his age and fame. After all, he published not only novels, short stories, and plays, but also filmscripts, reportage, and moral, political, and scientific essays, among other genres of writing, including some of Lyndon B. Johnson's political speeches in the 1950s and 1960s.

As a demanding self-critic, Steinbeck was a very slow writer. He often admitted, "I do not write easily. Three hours of writing require twenty hours of preparation" (*SLL,* p. 64) and "I think it will take me two years to write a full-length novel, counting the periods when I walk the streets and try to come up with enough courage to blow out my brains" (*SLL,* p. 11). Believing in the value of meticulous, frequent revisions in search of the finest music, rhythm, and flow in prose, he once confessed, "I cut 90,000 words out of my most recent book [*East of Eden*] but I think it's a pretty good book. It was a hard one. But they're all hard" (*SLL,* p. 456). This reminds us of Hemingway, another slow writer—a disciplined perfectionist who said: "I . . . threw away about 100,000 words which was better than most of what was left in. It [*To Have and Have Not*] is the most cut book in the world."[26] Hemingway further displayed this kind of vigorous discipline as he said: "Since I have started to break down all my writing and get rid of all facility and try to make instead of describe, writing has been wonderful to do. But it was very difficult, and I do not know how I would ever write anything as long as a novel. It often took me a full morning of work to write a paragraph."[27] As for his slow writing habit, Steinbeck revealed that he often read his manuscript aloud and taped it to insure the desirable rhythms when he wrote a novel (*SLL,* pp. 756-57; 737; 44); certainly it was indeed a time-consuming but indispensable method of writing a novel as "minstrel."

Always adamant about revisions, he told his editor, Pascal Covici, "You will not ask me to make one single change for the sake of sales except in terms of clarity."[28] He always chose integrity over marketability. He also held the same attitude toward literary criticism: "I will not let it [criticism] change one single thing about the story or the method"[29] because "the critic can tell a writer what *not* to do." Steinbeck further stated, "If he [a critic] could tell him what to do, he'd be a writer himself. What *to do* is the soul and heart of the book" (*SLL,* p. 458). As a result, he instinctively distrusted critics and defied their negative approaches to his literature, the purpose of which was indeed "to lift up, to extend, and to encourage."[30]

To conclude, attention to Steinbeck's candid remarks on writing as well as to his novels and other writings proves not only exhilarating and enlightening but also reveals, as Govoni reminds us, a great deal about him "as a sharper formulator of ideas and structures" and as "a patient, diligent, and self-conscious craftsman who was attempting to give form to an exhaustive range of thought and feeling."[31] The very fact that he wrote so many letters about writing as well as *Journal of a Novel, The Log from the Sea of Cortez, Working Days: The Journal of "The Grapes of Wrath,"* and other essays on writing also testifies to Steinbeck's fierce dedication and commitment to the art and craft of writing. Steinbeck was a writer and to him writing had to be, as he once confessed to Jack Valenti, "my trade, my profession, and my obsession."[32]

NOTES

1. Jackson J. Benson, *The True Adventures of John Steinbeck, Writer* (New York: Viking Press, 1984); Robert DeMott, *Steinbeck's Reading: A Catalogue of Books Owned and Borrowed* (New York: Garland Publishing, 1984); and John Ditsky,

Essays on "East of Eden" (*Steinbeck Monograph Series,* No. 7) (Muncie, Indiana: Steinbeck Society of America, Ball State University, 1977).

2. John Steinbeck, *Journal of a Novel: The "East of Eden" Letters* (New York: Viking Press, 1969), p. 58.

3. JS/Dennis Murphy, February 1957 in Steinbeck, *"Your Only Weapon Is Your Work": A Letter by John Steinbeck to Dennis Murphy,* ed. Robert DeMott (San Jose, California: Steinbeck Research Center, San Jose State University, 1985), [n.p.].

4. JS/Elizabeth Otis and Chase Horton, 3/14/1958 in *Steinbeck: A Life in Letters,* eds. Elaine Steinbeck and Robert Wallsten (New York: Viking Press, 1975), pp. 575-76. The quotations from this book will hereafter be identified in the text as *SLL* with page numbers.

5. John Steinbeck, *The Log from the Sea of Cortez* (New York: Viking Press, 1951), pp. 227 and 264.

6. Ernest Hemingway, *Ernest Hemingway on Writing,* ed. Larry W. Phillips (New York: Scribner's, 1984), p. 3.

7. John Steinbeck, *East of Eden* (New York: Viking Press, 1952), p. 132.

8. John Steinbeck, "The Nobel Prize Acceptance Speech" in *The Portable Steinbeck,* ed. Pascal Covici, Jr. (New York: Viking Press, 1971), p. 691.

9. Steinbeck, *Journal of a Novel,* p. 115.

10. *Ibid.,* pp. 115-16.

11. *Ibid.*

12. *Ibid.,* p. 4.

13. Quoted in Laurence Perrine, *Poetry: Theory and Practice* (New York: Harcourt, Brace and World, 1962), p. 180.

14. John Steinbeck, *"The Pearl"* and *"The Red Pony"* (New York: Penguin, 1975), p. 56.

15. Steinbeck, *Journal of a Novel,* p. 8.

16. *Ibid.,* p. 38.

17. JS/Elizabeth R. Otis, 9/24/1955 in *Letters to Elizabeth: A Selection of Letters of John Steinbeck to Elizabeth R. Otis,* eds. Florian J. Shasky and Susan F. Riggs (San Francisco: Book Club of California, 1978), p. 54.

18. Hemingway, p. 4.

19. Mark W. Govoni, " 'Symbols for the Wordlessness': The Original Manuscript of *East of Eden,*" *Steinbeck Quarterly,* 14 (Winter-Spring 1981), 17.

20. Hemingway, p. 7.

21. JS/Elizabeth R. Otis, 9/24/1955 in *Letters to Elizabeth*, eds.
     Shasky and Riggs, p. 52.
22. Horace, *Ars Poetica*, quoted in *Robert Greene, James IV*, ed. J.
     A. Lavin (London: Ernest Benn, 1967), p. 2.
23. Steinbeck, *Journal of a Novel*, p. 103.
24. *Ibid.*
25. Govoni, p. 18.
26. Hemingway, p. 78.
27. *Ibid.*, p. 33.
28. Steinbeck, *Journal of a Novel*, p. 55.
29. *Ibid.*, p. 65.
30. *Ibid.*, p. 115.
31. Govoni, p. 14.
32. JS/Jack Valenti, 6/15/1965 (Lyndon Johnson Library, Austin,
     Texas).

Note: This is a revised version of my article, published in *John Steinbeck on Writing*, ed. Tetsumaro Hayashi (*Steinbeck Essay Series*, No. 2) (Muncie, Indiana: Steinbeck Research Institute, Ball State University, 1988), pp. 34-42.

BIBLIOGRAPHY: A CHECKLIST OF WORKS CITED, CONSULTED, AND RECOMMENDED

Alexander, Stanley G.
"*Cannery Row:* Steinbeck's Pastoral Poem," in *Steinbeck: A Collection of Critical Essays,* ed. Robert Murray Davis, pp. 135-48.

Astro, Richard and Tetsumaro Hayashi (eds.)
Steinbeck: The Man and His Work. Corvallis: Oregon State University Press, 1971.

Autrey, Max L.
"Men, Mice, and Moths: Gradation in Steinbeck's 'The Leader of the People,' " *Western American Literature,* 10 (November 1975), 195-204.

Barbour, James and Tom Quirk (eds.)
Writing the American Classics. Chapel Hill, North Carolina: University of North Carolina Press, 1990.

Bedford, Richard
"The Genesis and Consolation of Our Discontent," *Criticism,* 14 (Summer 1972), 277-94.

Benson, Jackson J. (ed.)
The Short Novels of John Steinbeck: Critical Essays with a Checklist to Steinbeck Criticism. Durham, North Carolina: Duke University Press, 1990.

Benson, Jackson J.
The True Adventures of John Steinbeck, Writer. New York: Viking Press, 1984.

Britch, Carroll (ed.)
See Lewis, Cliff (ed.)

Buerger, Daniel
" 'History' and Fiction in *East of Eden* Criticism," *Steinbeck Quarterly,* 14 (Winter-Spring 1981), 6-14.

Davis, Robert Con (ed.)
Twentieth Century Interpretations of "The Grapes of Wrath": A Collection of Critical Essays. Englewood Cliffs, New Jersey: Prentice-Hall, 1982.

Davis, Robert Murray (ed.)
Steinbeck: A Collection of Critical Essays. Englewood Cliffs, New Jersey: Prentice-Hall, 1972.
Degnan, James P.
"In Definite Battle: Steinbeck and California's Land Monopolists," in *Steinbeck: The Man and His Work*, eds. Astro and Hayashi, pp. 65-74.
DeMott, Robert
"Creative Reading/Creative Writing: The Presence of Dr. Gunn's *New Family Physician* in Steinbeck's *East of Eden*," in *Rediscovering Steinbeck: Revisionist Views of His Art, Politics, and Intellect*, eds. Lewis and Britch, pp. 35-57.
DeMott, Robert
"The Interior Distances of John Steinbeck," *Steinbeck Quarterly*, 12 (Summer-Fall 1979), 86-99.
Ditsky, John
Essays on "East of Eden" (*Steinbeck Monograph Series*, No. 7). Muncie, Indiana: Steinbeck Society of America, Ball State University, 1977.
Ditsky, John
"Steinbeck's *Travels with Charley*," in *Steinbeck's Travel Literature*, ed. Hayashi, pp. 56-61.
Donohue, Agnes McNeill (ed.)
A Casebook on "The Grapes of Wrath." New York: Crowell, 1968.
Fensch, Thomas (ed.)
Conversations with John Steinbeck. Jackson: University Press of Mississippi, 1988.
Ferrel, Keith
John Steinbeck: The Voice of the Land. New York: M. Evans & Co., 1986.
Fontenrose, Joseph
John Steinbeck: An Introduction and Interpretation. New York: Barnes and Noble, 1963.
French, Warren (ed.)
A Companion to "The Grapes of Wrath." New York: Viking Press, 1963.
French, Warren
A Filmguide to "The Grapes of Wrath." Bloomington: Indiana University Press, 1966.
French, Warren
John Steinbeck. New Haven, Connecticut: College and University Press, 1961.
French, Warren
John Steinbeck, 2nd ed. Boston: Twayne, 1975.

French, Warren
   "*The Red Pony* as Story Cycle and Film," in *The Short Novels of John Steinbeck,* ed. Benson, pp. 71-84.
French, Warren
   "Steinbeck's Winter Tale," *Modern Fiction Studies,* 11 (Spring 1965), 66-74.
Frohock, W. M.
   "John Steinbeck: The Utility of Wrath," in his *The Novel of Violence in America,* pp. 124-43.
Frohock, W. M.
   The Novel of Violence in America. Dallas, Texas: Southern Methodist University Press, 1958.
Geismar, Maxwell
   "John Steinbeck: Of Wrath and Joy," in his *Writers in Crisis: The American Novel Between Two Wars,* pp. 260-63.
Geismar, Maxwell
   Writers in Crisis: The American Novel Between Two Wars. Boston: Houghton Mifflin, 1942.
Gerstenberger, Donna
   "Steinbeck's American Waste Land," *Modern Fiction Studies,* 11 (Spring 1965), 59-65.
Gladstein, Mimi R.
   " 'The Leader of the People': A Boy Becomes a 'Mensch,' " in *Steinbeck's "The Red Pony": Essays in Criticism,* eds. Hayashi and Moore, pp. 27-37.
Gladstein, Mimi R.
   "Steinbeck's Juana: A Woman of Worth," in *Steinbeck's Women: Essays in Criticism,* ed. Hayashi, pp. 49-52.
Goldhurst, William
   "*Of Mice and Men:* John Steinbeck's Parable of the Curse of Cain," *Western American Literature,* 6 (Summer 1971), 123-35; reprint, in *The Short Novels of John Steinbeck,* ed. Benson, pp. 48-59.
Hashiguchi, Yasuo (ed.)
   See Hayashi, Tetsumaro (ed.)
Hayashi, Tetsumaro (ed.)
   See Astro, Richard (ed.)
Hayashi, Tetsumaro
   "*The Pearl* as the Novel of Disengagement," *Steinbeck Quarterly,* 7 (Summer-Fall 1974), 84-88.
Hayashi, Tetsumaro
   "Steinbeck's America in *Travels with Charley,*" *Steinbeck Quarterly,* 23 (Summer-Fall 1990), 88-96.

Hayashi, Tetsumaro (ed.)
Steinbeck's Travel Literature (*Steinbeck Monograph Series*, No. 10). Muncie, Indiana: Steinbeck Society of America, Ball State University, 1980.

Hayashi, Tetsumaro (ed.)
Steinbeck's Women (*Steinbeck Monograph Series*, No. 9). Muncie, Indiana: Steinbeck Society of America, Ball State University, 1979.

Hayashi, Tetsumaro (ed.)
A Study Guide to Steinbeck (Part II). Metuchen, New Jersey: Scarecrow Press, 1979.

Hayashi, Tetsumaro, Yasuo Hashiguchi, and Richard F. Peterson (eds.)
John Steinbeck: East and West (*Steinbeck Monograph Series*, No. 8). Muncie, Indiana: Steinbeck Society of America, Ball State University, 1978.

Hayashi, Tetsumaro and Thomas J. Moore (eds.)
Steinbeck's "The Red Pony": Essays in Criticism (*Steinbeck Monograph Series*, No. 13). Muncie, Indiana: Steinbeck Research Institute, Ball State University, 1988.

Hirose, Hidekazu
"From Doc Burton to Jim Casy: Steinbeck in the Latter Half of the 1930s," *John Steinbeck: East and West*, eds. Hayashi, Hashiguchi, and Peterson, pp. 6-11.

Hughes, Robert S., Jr.
Beyond "The Red Pony": A Reader's Companion to Steinbeck's Complete Short Stories. Metuchen, New Jersey: Scarecrow Press, 1987, pp. 90-103.

Hughes, Robert S., Jr.
"The Black Cypress and the Green Tub: Death and Procreation in Steinbeck's 'The Promise,' " in *Steinbeck's "The Red Pony": Essays in Criticism*, eds. Hayashi and Moore, pp. 9-16.

Hughes, Robert S., Jr.
"Steinbeck's *Travels with Charley* and *America and Americans*," *Steinbeck Quarterly*, 20 (Summer-Fall 1987), 76-88.

Jones, Lawrence William
John Steinbeck as Fabulist, ed. Marston LaFrance (*Steinbeck Monograph Series*, No. 3). Muncie, Indiana: Steinbeck Society of America, Ball State University, 1973.

Knox, Maxine and Mary Rodriguez
Steinbeck's Street: "Cannery Row." San Rafael, California: Presidio Press, 1980.

Levant, Howard
"The Natural Parable," in his *The Novels of John Steinbeck: A Critical Study,* pp. 185-206.

Levant, Howard
The Novels of John Steinbeck: A Critical Study. Columbia, Missouri: University of Missouri Press, 1974.

Lewis, Cliff and Carroll Britch (eds.)
Rediscovering Steinbeck: Revisionist Views of His Art, Politics, and Intellect. Lewiston, New York: Edwin Mellen Press, 1989.

Lieber, Todd
"Talismanic Patterns in the Novels of John Steinbeck," *American Literature,* 44 (May 1972), 262-75.

Lisca, Peter
John Steinbeck: Nature and Myth. New York: Thomas Y. Crowell, 1978.

Lisca, Peter (ed.)
John Steinbeck, "The Grapes of Wrath": Text and Criticism. New York: Viking Press, 1972.

Lisca, Peter
The Wide World of John Steinbeck. New Brunswick, New Jersey: Rutgers University Press, 1958; reprint, New York: Gordian Press, 1981.

Loftis, Anne
"A Historical Introduction to *Of Mice and Men,*" in *The Short Novels of John Steinbeck,* ed. Benson, pp. 39-47.

Martin, Stoddard
California Writers. New York: St. Martin's Press, 1983.

McCarthy, Paul
John Steinbeck. New York: Frederick Ungar, 1980.

Meyer, Michael J.
"Precious Bane: Mining the Fool's Gold of *The Pearl,*" in *The Short Novels of John Steinbeck,* ed. Benson, pp. 161-72.

Moore, Thomas J. (ed.)
See Hayashi, Tetsumaro (ed.)

Morsberger, Robert E.
"Steinbeck's Zapata: Rebel Versus Revolutionary," in *Steinbeck: The Man and His Work,* eds. Astro and Hayashi, pp. 51-54.

Owens, Louis
"The Grapes of Wrath": Trouble in the Promised Land. Boston: Twayne Publishers, 1989.

Owens, Louis
    John Steinbeck's Re-Vision of America. Athens: University of
    Georgia Press, 1985.
Owens, Louis
    "The Mirror and the Vamp: Invention, Reflection, and Bad,
    Bad, Cathy Trask in *East of Eden,*" in *Writing the American
    Classics,* eds. Barbour and Quirk, pp. 235-57.
Owens, Louis
    "The Story of a Writing: Narrative Structure in *East of Eden,*"
    in *Rediscovering Steinbeck,* eds. Lewis and Britch, pp. 60-76.
Peterson, Richard F. (ed.)
    See Hayashi, Tetsumaro (ed.)
Quirk, Tom (ed.)
    See Barbour, James (ed.)
Rodriguez, Mary
    See Knox, Maxine.
Simmonds, Roy S.
    "The Place and Importance of 'The Great Mountains' in *The
    Red Pony,*" in *Steinbeck's "The Red Pony": Essays in Criticism,* ed.
    Hayashi and Moore, pp. 17-26.
Simmonds, Roy S.
    "Steinbeck's *The Pearl:* Legend, Film, Novel," in *The Short
    Novels of John Steinbeck,* ed. Benson, pp. 173-84.
Simmonds, Roy S.
    "*Travels with Charley,*" in *A Study Guide to Steinbeck (Part II),*
    ed. Hayashi, pp. 165-90.
Spilka, Mark
    "Of George and Lennie and Curley's Wife: Sweet Violence in
    Steinbeck's Eden," *Modern Fiction Studies,* 20 (Summer 1974),
    169-79; reprint, in *The Short Novels of John Steinbeck,* ed.
    Benson, pp. 59-70.
Tammaro, Thomas M.
    "Erik Erikson Meets John Steinbeck: Psychosocial Develop-
    ment in 'The Gift,' " in *Steinbeck's "The Red Pony": Essays in
    Criticism,* eds. Hayashi and Moore, pp. 1-9.
Timmerman, John H.
    John Steinbeck's Fiction: The Aesthetics of the Road Taken.
    Norman: University of Oklahoma Press, 1986.
Timmerman, John H.
    "*The Pearl,*" in his *John Steinbeck's Fiction: The Aesthetics of the
    Road Taken,* pp. 194-209.
Waldron, Edward E.
    "*The Pearl* and *The Old Man and the Sea:* A Comparative
    Analysis," *Steinbeck Quarterly,* 13 (Summer-Fall 1980), 98-106.

INDEX

NOTES ON CONTRIBUTORS

GARCIA, RELOY. Professor of English at Creighton University, Omaha, Nebraska; author of *John Steinbeck and D. H. Lawrence: Fictive Voices and the Ethical Imperative* (1972) and several other works on Steinbeck and D. H. Lawrence; twice chairman of the Editorial Board of the *Steinbeck Quarterly;* senior vice president of the International John Steinbeck Society; Ph.D. (Kent State University).

HADELLA, CHARLOTTE COOK. Assistant professor of English at Southern Oregon State College, Ashland, Oregon; member of the Editorial Board of the *Steinbeck Quarterly;* director of the MLA Steinbeck Society Meeting for 1991-92; has presented scholarly papers and published articles on teaching composition and 19th-20th century American writers, particularly John Steinbeck; Ph.D. (University of New Mexico).

HEAVILIN, BARBARA. Assistant professor of English at Taylor University, Upland, Indiana; published reviews and articles on Steinbeck in *Kyushu American Literature,* the *South Dakota Review,* and the *Steinbeck Quarterly;* Ph.D. (Ball State University).

LOJEK, HELEN. Professor of English at Boise State University, Boise, Idaho; published in *Western American Literature, Canadian Journal of Irish Studies,* and *Eire/Ireland;* editor of *The Rectangle* (a national journal of student writing); Ph.D. (University of Denver).

MEYER, MICHAEL J. Lecturer, University of Wisconsin at Milwaukee; contributor to Jackson J. Benson's *Short Novels of John Steinbeck* (1990); published articles on Steinbeck in the *Steinbeck Monograph Series, Literature and Myth,* and *Literature and Religion;* a new member of the Editorial Board of the *Steinbeck Quarterly;* Ph.D. (Loyola University of Chicago).

OWENS, LOUIS. Professor of literature at the University of California at Santa Cruz; author of *John Steinbeck's Re-Vision of America* (1985), *"The Grapes of Wrath": Trouble in the Promised Land* (1989), and numerous essays on American literature and native-American literature; Fulbright lecturer in American literature at the University of Pisa, Italy, in 1980-81; NEH fellowship recipient in 1987 and NEA fellowship recipient in 1989; co-editor of *American Literary Scholarship: An Annual;* Ph.D. (University of California at Davis).

SHAW, PATRICK W. Professor of English at Texas Tech University, Lubbock, Texas; author of *Literature: A College Anthology* and *Willa Cather and the Art of Conflict;* has published numerous articles on Willa Cather, Ernest Hemingway, William Faulkner, Saul Bellow, and other American writers in *American Imago, American Literature, Genre,* the *Steinbeck Quarterly, Studies in Short Fiction,* and other journals; Ph.D. (Louisiana State University).

ABOUT THE EDITOR

TETSUMARO HAYASHI, PH.D., is a native of Japan and president of the International John Steinbeck Society. Dr. Hayashi has published twenty-eight books and twenty monographs on British and American literature as author/editor in the U.S. and England; he has also had more than 100 scholarly articles on English and American literature published here, in Europe, and in Asia. A professor of English at Ball State University, he also served as the editor-in-chief of the *Steinbeck Quarterly* and the *Steinbeck Monograph Series* and as director of the Steinbeck Research Institute.

Dr. Hayashi has lectured widely in the U.S., Britain, Canada, and Japan and received fellowships and grants from the Folger Shakespeare Library, the American Council of Learned Societies, the American Philosophical Society, the Lyndon B. Johnson Foundation, and other foundations. He received the Outstanding Research Award in 1981-82 at Ball State University, the Outstanding Educator Recognition in 1971-72, and the Outstanding Service Awards from the John Steinbeck Foundation in California in 1984 and 1992, the Steinbeck Society of Japan in 1988, the Tokoha Gakuin University, Japan, in 1990, and the Outstanding Lifelong Achievement Award from the Steinbeck Society of Japan in 1991.